MAI GONZÁLEZ

BUSES AND BACKPACKS

ALSO BY MAI GONZÁLEZ

UnSettled

Routes and Roots

Between Stations

BUSES AND BACKPACKS

A MEMOIR: SIX MONTHS IN SOUTH AMERICA

By Mai González

ISBN (Paperback): 978-1-0696821-4-7

ISBN (eBook): 978-1-0696821-5-4

Published by Mai Gonzalez

Abbotsford, British Columbia, Canada

First Edition

Legal deposit – Library and Archives Canada, 2026

Cover design by Mai Gonzalez

This is a memoir based on true events and personal experiences. While every effort has been made to accurately portray the events and individuals described some names and identifying details have been changed to protect the privacy of those involved.

"Travel isn't always pretty. It isn't always comfortable. Sometimes it hurts, it even breaks your heart. But that's okay. The journey changes you; it should change you"

- Anthony Bourdain

Acknowledgements

I am endlessly grateful to my mum and my nanny for instilling in me a love of books from as early as I can remember. Stories have always shaped my world, and they're what inspired me to turn my own wild escapes into writing. Mum, thank you for guiding me through the technical maze of formatting and self-publishing. I truly couldn't have done this without you.

To my mother-in-law, Rosemarie. Thank you for the countless hours you spent caring for the children so I could write and edit. This book exists because of you. You also shared with me a part of the continent I never would have experienced otherwise. It was an intimate privilege to witness it by your side.

And to my husband, Carlos. We still laugh at how wildly impractical it was to set off on this adventure together after only months of knowing each other. Now here we are, living in Canada with a mortgage, two kids, and a cat. Life has a funny way of unfolding, and there's no one I'd rather adventure with than you.

Table of Contents

PERU
BOLIVIA
CHILE
URUGUAY
ARGENTINA

PART I

Making the Time

People love to talk about someday.

Someday when work calms down. Someday when there's more money, more certainty, fewer loose ends. Someday when the kids are older, the relationship is steadier, the world a little less chaotic. Someday, when it's the right time.

Standing in an airport departure hall with an oversized backpack, I couldn't help but think that for many, *someday* easily becomes a synonym for never.

"This is the kind of thing people dream of doing," I said, bouncing on the balls of my feet and grinning like a lunatic, "but never actually do because it's never the right time."

"That's because you have to make the time," Carlos, my boyfriend of barely a year replied, far too calmly for someone about to board an eleven-hour flight to the other side of the world with someone he was still getting to know.

But that was it. The sentence. *Make the time*. The one that followed me across a continent.

We were queued up at Auckland Airport, surrounded by the usual chaos of international travel. Crying babies, frantic families redistributing luggage, couples already mildly irritated with each other. A mixture of different languages drifted through the air from somewhere behind us, mingling with the hum of announcements and the clatter of rolling suitcases.

I've always loved international airports. They're one of the few places where everyone is suspended between lives. Everyone is either arriving from something that mattered or leaving toward something that might. They're thresholds. Liminal spaces. Places where excitement and fear coexist. And that morning, I was feeling both.

We were leaving New Zealand for six months to backpack through South America. No fixed itinerary. No rigid plan. Just a vague route, and a mutual agreement that we'd figure it out as we went. We had jobs waiting back home, families who were mostly supportive but gently concerned, and friends who oscillated between envy and disbelief.

Some people called us brave. Some called us crazy. How could we leave our pay cheques, our shiny apartment, our community? But I didn't necessarily feel that way. I felt restless. Like staying would cost me more than leaving ever could. Because this trip wasn't about escape. It was about new experiences and figuring out who I was. It was about learning how to be uncomfortable on purpose. About seeing how I moved through the world when stripped of familiarity, fluency, and routine. About understanding people whose lives were shaped by systems wildly different from my own, not through news headlines or statistics, but through shared spaces and everyday interactions.

We boarded the plane with a mix of adrenaline and exhaustion, the cabin already buzzing with anticipation. I'd clocked more than two hundred flights in my lifetime, so I had my own little flying ritual down to a pat. I changed the time on my watch as soon as I sat down, claimed an aisle seat, wiped everything down with baby wipes, brushed my teeth, wrapped a scarf over my eyes to help me sleep. Tiny hacks that made all the difference.

The airline we were flying with had a sketchy reputation, but the flight was blissfully uneventful. Nothing fancy. Nothing dramatic. No lost baggage. The food was surprisingly decent. Spinach, beans, pumpkin, extra fruit. I slept, read, wrote, and let the low hum of the plane lull me into that strange airborne limbo where you kind of sleep but not peacefully.

As we began our descent into Santiago, I looked out the window and caught my first glimpse of the Andes. Vast, snow-capped, impossibly grand. It felt like a threshold moment. A window into the new life we were flying into.

We had *made the time.*

And that mattered more than anything.

I didn't know then what South America would give me. I couldn't have predicted the heat, the storms, the language frustration, the friendships, the moments of wonder, or the days of sheer fatigue. I didn't know how deeply certain places would get under my skin, or how much I'd learn from missed buses and awkward conversations. I didn't yet understand how profoundly this trip would change the way I listen, the way I wait, the way I interpret silence.

All I knew was that this was necessary. Not because my life was lacking, but because I wanted to know what it looked like when pushed to its limit. When exposed to friction in all kinds of situations. When removed from the familiar day-to-day interactions that told me who I was.

We were finally doing the thing people always talk about.

Not someday.

Now.

Learning to be Foreign

- SANTIAGO, CHILE -

I fell in love with Santiago almost immediately, which was a shock, because everyone I knew who had been here described it as… boring. A stepping stone to the "real" adventures of South America—the Mars-like landscapes of the Atacama Desert, the magic of Machu Picchu, Patagonia's wild roads. I had expected a dry, dull, forgettable city. Instead, we stepped out of the airport, and the Andes truly challenged all my preconceptions.

Seven million people live under these mountains; their peaks dusted with snow. For someone who's called New Zealand home for nearly a decade, I can confidently say these were the most dramatic mountains I'd ever seen. Carlos and I stumbled a bit trying to find the mysterious family friend who was going to pick us up, eventually using the free Wi-Fi at a local café to message him. We had no idea what he looked like, but somehow, we found each other.

Santiago itself was a delightful mix of contradictions. Some areas showed their age, worn and tired, but scattered among the streets were stunning European-style buildings, curious statues hinting at its complicated history, and vibrant street art spilling from walls. After a short drive, we reached our Airbnb on the 25th floor of a city-centre building. We dumped our tiny amount of luggage and went hunting for lunch. I mistakenly thought it was a "late" lunch but quickly learnt that South Americans generally eat later in the day compared to what I'm used to in England and New Zealand.

The restaurant of choice, Fuente Alemana, delivered what might have been the largest sandwich of my life. Half a bottle of mayo, a mountain of bread, tomatoes, cheese, mushrooms, and lettuce. The vegetarian option, of course. As we walked it off, we wandered through a plaza filled with the strangest music. Cowbells clicked, horse jawbones clacked, drums banged. The sun was lowering behind the snow-capped mountains, purple light spilling across the city. I was jet-lagged but euphoric. I collapsed into bed around 7:30 p.m., reading a book about Santiago, letting the last couple of days soak in, before drifting into a deep, happy sleep.

By the next morning, we had adjusted to the new time zone beautifully. Sunlight poured through the condensation-soaked windows, and the city felt alive in a way I hadn't expected. We layered up and headed straight for *empanadas*—cheese-filled, warm, and belly-filling. The streets were bustling with commuters, and the corner shop-style *empanada* stand felt like a hidden gem.

With breakfast in hand, we hunted down the Plaza de Armas, Santiago's main square, surrounded by historic architecture, including the Catedral Metropolitana. From there, we joined a free walking tour, led by Franco, a Chilean who had spent a year living on Cuba Street in Wellington, just metres away from where Carlos and I had been living. What were the chances? Franco's energy was infectious, and I soaked up the history like a sponge. Mapuche and Inca empires, bloody battles, military dictatorships, and the origins of Chile's flag. Red for blood shed, white for snow, blue for the ocean, and the star for unity. For a while, we stood outside the palace where tanks once rolled in, with bullet holes still marking statues. For a history nerd like myself, it was a powerful moment to see where the past met the present.

We learned local quirks, too. For example, Café Blumenau is basically the Chilean Hooters. *Pica* is the Chilean word for a "cheap, nice, good" restaurant. And if you want a Chilean drink, skip the *Pisco* Sour. Instead, try a *Piscola* or, for the brave, a *Terremoto*, which is a cheap white wine, pineapple ice cream, and fernet. It's so boozy that the ground literally shakes when you finish one.

We spent the afternoon simply walking. We climbed Cerro San Cristóbal, Santiago's second-highest hill, taking a wild route that had us navigating loose rocks and makeshift homes. Not entirely safe, but the view—snow-capped mountains against the sprawling city below—was worth every precarious step. Next, we explored Bellavista's streets, alive with salsa music, colourful buildings, and the smell of street food. We stopped for gelato, then late lunch at El Rápido, a fast-food spot unchanged since the 1940s, demolishing *empanadas* with *pebre* while watching the Chilean news.

Even after just a day and a half, I noticed my Spanish improving. I could follow snippets of conversations, pick up context clues, and even start thinking about setting language goals, like ordering meals confidently within a week.

Next, a stop at a supermarket for apples and muesli bars, which brought another kind of excitement… The thrill of recognizing and deciphering everyday items in a foreign country.

Later, we met Alex, a friend I had studied with in Poland years ago, who had settled in Santiago. Over cheap, hearty food, we swapped tips, asked questions, and soaked in the local perspective.

By the end of the day, I was buzzing. History, culture, food, language, mountains, chaos, charm. It all collided into this intoxicating first taste of Santiago. I had no idea what lay ahead, but I was already completely in love with this city.

The Luxury of Being Looked After

- ARAUCO & CONCEPCIÓN, CHILE -

After a couple of whirlwind days in Santiago, we were ready to trade the city buzz for a bus ride to a small town called Arauco to meet Carlos' cousin. We woke around nine, grabbed more *empanadas* and fresh orange juice from a street stall, and were soon met by the friend who had greeted us at the airport. He handed us a transport card, navigated the public transit system with us, and helped secure our bus tickets. With his guidance, a journey that could have been stressful felt completely manageable, giving us the confidence to do it ourselves next time.

The bus itself was a revelation. A double-decker with semi-reclining seats on top, beds below, footrests, movie screens, headphones, and even stats on the driver's hours and speed. It was absurdly luxurious for public transport. I'd eventually learn that this was called a *semi-cama* bus. The movies were in Spanish, perfect for sneaking in some language practice, and I picked up casual phrases like "What is your problem?"

Outside the window, Santiago's outskirts unfolded. Worn-down neighbourhoods, occasional shacks, and thickening smog. Mountains that had taken my breath away the day before were nowhere in sight, replaced by three distinct landscapes. Dry cactus-stung land, rolling green fields that reminded me of New Zealand, and finally dense pine forests clinging to steep roads along the black-sand Pacific coastline. The sun dipped over the ocean as we rolled into Arauco, and the thought that thousands of kilometres away, New Zealand was just a speck across the ocean, felt surreal.

As we stepped off the bus, we were immediately greeted by Carlos' cousin, Maribel. The first meeting between cousins was immediately warm and welcoming, and I was relieved that our journey into the unknown had such a reassuring welcome.

Maribel's home was cozy and inviting, with a little fire warming the room. Finally, no more cold nights. For the first time since arriving in Chile, I felt toasty and completely safe. Despite the cultural differences, I wasn't overwhelmed by the country at all. The streets felt manageable, the bus ride harmless, the city navigable. Part of this comfort came from having Carlos by my side, his Spanish skills shielding both of us. My Spanish, though rudimentary, was already improving.

Listening, repeating, picking up words. Everything I had done with Duolingo and listening to Spanish podcasts, plus years of studying another Latin-rooted language (French), clicked into context here.

The night passed in a perfect, quiet rhythm. Homemade pizza for dinner, late by my standards but totally normal in Chile, and hours of conversation around the table. Mostly I listened, nodded, and asked Carlos to translate, frustrated but aware that this was how learning happens. By the time I went to bed, I was already imagining the trip back to Arauco in a few months, hoping my Spanish would be sharper, my sentences more coherent.

The next day, we headed to Concepción, a city of three hundred thousand people and Chile's "rock capital." The city had been devastated by an 8.8-magnitude earthquake in 2010, but now it was rebuilt, bustling, and vibrant. As we drove, I noticed the steep, chaotic roads, supersized log trucks ruling the lanes, and the curious system of tolls and emergency stops, and a few dead dogs. The city itself was impressive. A massive Stonehenge-like monument commemorated earthquake victims, and the university campus, with its Greek-style architecture and wide green spaces, made me nostalgic for student life—lectures, parties, budget meals. All the magic of young independence.

Back in the commercial centre, we navigated malls cautiously, keeping pockets zipped and scarves close. A pop-up show caught our attention. A performer in a puppet costume pulled Carlos into the centre of a crowd. Dancing aggressively, shouting Spanish lyrics about jealousy. I had no idea what was happening, but the chaos had me laughing uncontrollably, playing along with the spectacle. The crowd applauded, and we walked away with one of those stories you'll retell for years.

As we headed back to Arauco, the sun set over black-sand beaches and copper hills. The small-town economy revolved almost entirely around a single plastic plant, which carried the looming fragility of relying on one employer for the livelihoods of thousands. Travel is full of these kinds of lessons and experiences. Seeing the fragility of communities first hand, realizing how interconnected politics, economics, and human lives are, and appreciating how each place is unique and has its own story.

The following day was calm. A warm bedroom, a long sleep, and breakfast at the table. Fresh bread, honey from nearby bees, and homemade blackberry marmalade. Meals together became a ritual I cherished. Learning Spanish passively, soaking in family conversations, slowly untangling tricky words like *espina* versus *piña*, or *abogado* versus *palta.* We spent the day cooking—soups, salads, cheese and spinach pies—and when we couldn't fit any more food in our bellies, we walked along a black-sand beach. Maribel's son and his friend collected shells, fossils lay scattered in the sand, and a stray dog followed us loyally, growling at other dogs, as if protecting us. Along the way, we discovered street stalls selling *sopaipillas*, a local delicacy I had dreamt about for months.

By the end of the week, days were already starting to blur together. When I first jotted notes in my small, pink journal, I labelled one entry 26th July instead of the 27th. Honestly, it barely mattered. Sunrise and sunset seemed to roll one into the other anyway. The small victory was that I could finally ask what day it was in Spanish, even if I still mixed up the answer half the time.

The next day started with a quick trip into the centre of Arauco, a tidy little spot with a central plaza, bakeries, butcheries, and ice cream stores. At noon, a siren wailed so fiercely it felt like a tsunami warning; my stomach dropped until I learned it was just the town clock striking twelve. Crisis averted.

We went to the school where Maribel teaches and where her son attends. It was the sort of visit only possible when you know someone, and I loved every second of it. The halls were colourful, alive with children's laughter. We snapped photos of educational posters—numbers, emotions, the works—and I marvelled that even a small-town school could be so well equipped. Computers, sports gear, classroom resources. All funded by the state. The only gap? Heating. But hey, a cold classroom was nothing a hot water bottle couldn't fix. I'd learnt that the hard way after two years of high school back in New Zealand.

Next came the coast. We wound through steep, curving roads to Punta Lavapie, a tiny seaside hamlet with rugged forests on one side and a cold, rough ocean on the other. The 2010 tsunami had left its mark here. Maribel told us that debris and fish had been trapped on all the barbed wire around us. Yet Punta Lavapie itself was charming in its own rough way, fragrant with the smell of fresh fish, littered with crab shells, and patrolled by dark, gliding vultures—ominous birds that made me wonder whether humans ever fell prey to their keen eyes.

Along the way, we stopped at a tiny restaurant where Carlos experimented with local cuisine. A blended concoction of white wine, egg, and starfish. I stuck with Chilean salad, cheese *empanadas*, and tea, letting him describe the drink. "Eggnog," he said.

Later, we visited Tulbul, a fishing town with visible poverty despite the obvious income from the sea. Maribel explained that drinking and drugs consumed the wealth the fishermen earned. It was a reality check for me. Poverty is complicated.

The day ended perfectly at a friend's house just five minutes away. The family was Brazilian-Uruguayan, with a two-year-old who, after hearing that New Zealanders call themselves "Kiwis," scampered to the kitchen to offer us a kiwifruit. We laughed, ate *empanadas*, and drank Chilean red wine. We asked them how they ended up in place like Arauco. A small town in the middle of nowhere. The husband laughed and said he was mesmerized by his wife's eyes, and now here he was, married with two children, "in CHEEEEE-LAY", with an eye roll for the full effect. Years later, Carlos and I would make the same joke about the little town we'd eventually move to in Canada and have children ourselves.

The following day started late, around midday, as we slid further into the "Latin" rhythm of life. Late rises, late lunches, very late dinners. Breakfast at the table continued being one of my favourite activities: bread, honey, *dulce de leche,* coffee. Then we explored the local weekend market, a cacophony of sights and smells dominated by fresh fish. I was offered a *"Mote con huesillo,"* a sweet, filling Chilean summer drink made of grains and peaches in syrup. It was delicious, and I could already imagine myself returning on a warm summer day in a few months' time to savour it properly.

We ventured to Lota; a small town of colourful shacks stacked like *favelas.* Once a coal-mining hub, the town's industry collapsed in the 1990s under economic pressure from cheaper, imported Colombian coal. The city was a real-life illustration of what happens when a town fails to diversify. Lota's mine, Chiflón del Diablo, now a tourist attraction, gave us a raw glimpse into the harsh lives miners endured—low tunnels, damp sludge, dust in every breath, coal embedded in skin and hair. Birds perched above tunnels served as gas detectors; children sometimes assisted their fathers underground. I left with a small piece of coal, a black souvenir inscribed with "Lota, Chile," and a new respect for those who laboured in such conditions.

We finished the day watching the sun set over the Pacific from a lighthouse above the town, munching fresh *sopaipillas*, and navigating home with the help of a kind taxi driver. A quick supermarket stop for *vino tinto*, salsa music playing overhead. Only in Latin America.

At Home Away from Home

- ARAUCO, CHILE -

The next day was quieter. It was one of those days where the joy of travel comes from doing very little. By now, I had fully settled into the household. Maribel's home, small but warm, smelled of burning wood from the stacked logs in the yard. Staying in her son's room, lined with books in Spanish and English, reminded me of my childhood. It made me think of my nanny reading to me, my mother's love of books, and the comfort they bring.

Daily routines had become rituals. Breakfast at the table, the little boy calling for his bread and juice from upstairs. Afternoons spent wandering or cooking. Dinners pulled late, around 9 p.m. Meals were light but lovingly prepared. Bread, cheese, ham, salads, fruit. Always accompanied by conversation, laughter, and, in my case, tea.

Nights stretched into movies, games, and reading, sometimes until 2 a.m.

There was something special about simply being at home away from home, immersed in daily life, and slowly learning not only the language, but the rhythm of Chile. It was the quiet beauty of travel. The kind that seeps into you while you think you're doing nothing at all.

Midnight struck, and so did my birthday. Technically it was July 30th, though it still felt like part of the previous day. I had just popped upstairs for a quick shower, part of my nightly ritual. Little did I know, a small chaos was brewing downstairs.

Carlos appeared around the corner, wide-eyed. "God damn, that was quick! Go back upstairs!" he whispered. Excitement prickled through me. I knew exactly what was happening. I lay on the bed, straining to hear the rummaging, the Spanish murmurs I couldn't understand. Soon came the gentle strumming of a guitar.

I was summoned downstairs with my eyes covered. Step by cautious step, I descended, feeling corners and furniture with my toes, until finally, the sight of everyone gathered, singing "*Feliz Cumpleaños*" in Spanish and English, greeted me. A homemade cake, *torta chilena*, crafted over two days, sat on the table with "*Feliz Cumpleaños*" inscribed in *dulce de leche*. I was ceremoniously shoved into the cake, face down, and the room erupted in laughter as cream and cake decorated my face.

My last birthday had been spent with close friends in a cottage among New Zealand's mountains, when I'd only known Carlos for a few days. Now I was turning twenty-six in rural Chile with his cousins, surrounded by laughter, homemade cake, and the strum of a guitar, and it felt magical.

The rest of the day was slower, reflective. Carlos and I wandered the streets of Arauco, sun shining, the town quiet as schools and workplaces emptied. We meandered to the beach, posed by the town signs, munched fried *empanadas*, and sipped peach juice in the plaza.

I thought about my first impressions of Arauco. The nervous uncertainty of arriving by bus, the fear of poverty or danger, now replaced by a profound sense of belonging. I cherished the warmth of the house, the smell of burning wood, the rugged coastline, and the feeling that a home could exist far from home.

Maribel had some guests over later on, and they brought chocolates and hugs. The kitchen came alive again as we prepared *sopaipillas*, this time with *pebre* spiced with capsicum. I listened and learned as instructions flew at me in Spanish, "*mas, mas, mas!*" The night ended with homemade cake, *mate*, Chilean red wine, and laughter.

The next day was our final one in Arauco. For the time being, at least. Once again, we slept it until late morning. Followed by the chaos of trying to fit everything back into our backpacks. My remarkable talent for ranger rolling coats and belongings was already testing me.

Lunch was lentil stew with beetroot salad, courtesy of Maribel and her paid helper. Full and satisfied, we drove fifteen minutes to Laraquete, another coastal town. We wandered along the river, spotting several Chiastolite stones with their distinctive cross patterns. The beach walk was brief, interrupted by the pleading eyes of stray dogs that followed us along the shore.

We detoured down an alley to find a house with a low-fenced garden, where crates of crabs steamed and steamed. Fresh, ready to take home. From there, we visited Maribel's friend in Concepción, a tiny home bursting with family photos and warmth, her laughter infectious despite loss.

In the evening, we went back to the school to meet the Maribel's son at 7 p.m., waiting in the cold as the sun set and the air turned sharp. The gates finally opened, and families poured in. Nearby, a cart frying *sopaipillas* completed the scene, a quintessential Chilean sight.

Dinner was a feast of *completos*—hot dogs loaded with diced tomato, sauerkraut, smashed avocado, and sauces—preparing us for the 11 p.m. bus back to Santiago. We didn't know it yet, but eating *completos* would become a tradition every time we left Arauco during our six months in South America. Strapped in, full bellies, and a little tipsy on wine, we settled into the journey ahead. Eight hours of road stretching before us. It was time to go north.

Asleep Across Borders

- SANTIAGO, CHILE -

The last time I had taken a gravol pill was back in Wellington, hungover and desperate for relief from nausea and motion sickness. It had knocked me out cold for hours. I wondered if it would help knock me out for an overnight bus ride—and it turned out to be the best decision of the trip.

I barely remembered a thing. Backpack with essentials strapped to my belly, scarf over my eyes, *semi-cama* seat fully reclined, I drifted into oblivion. The front seats on the bus's second level gave me a perfect vantage point to doze undisturbed until staff nudged us awake at the Santiago terminal.

Arriving at 7:30 a.m., we had hours to kill before checking into our Airbnb. Coffee in hand, we scouted a café near the station, sipping and slowly waking from our gravol-induced comas. The plan had been to take the metro seven stops, but we opted to walk, despite our backpacks weighing in at thirteen kilograms each, taking our time to explore streets we hadn't yet seen. Two hours later, another café break—*empanadas*, coffee, and an hour and a half of reading—passed the time perfectly.

Once settled in our rooms, we hit the streets again for museum day. The Plaza de Armas buzzed with people of all nationalities; fountains gurgled, performers juggled, and the sun shone down on the historic square. A map from the tourist office led us first to the National History Museum, where a quick stroll left us wanting something different.

Earlier, while reading, I had come across a story about a girl sent to a place called Londres 38 during a coup, where torture was commonplace. I spotted a museum of the same name on our map, and insisted we go. The twenty-minute walk took us along narrow, cobbled streets named Londres and Paris, until we found number 38. Graffiti on the wall declared, "my son was tortured here." Bleak. We wandered, resting briefly in a church, trying and failing to enter the Colonial Museum, finally realizing lunch closures meant we had to wait.

By 3 p.m., Londres 38 was finally open. Forty minutes inside and my heart ached. This wasn't a sanitized, polished museum. It was raw..The air itself seemed heavy with the past. I felt the presence of those who had suffered, the weight of lives cut short. Visiting such a place on vacation may seem morbid, but it's necessary. To remember. To reflect. To honour. To vow, silently, that history should not repeat itself. In the same way that people travel to visit places such as Auschwitz in Poland or the Killing Fields in Cambodia.

After leaving, we walked the streets for fresh air and to lighten our spirits. Twice we were mistaken for Brazilians. Carlos and I also invented a new verb: "Sparrowing." It describes our method of keeping watch while one of us takes care of a task—money, photos, or otherwise—just like sparrows, half feasting while the other half stands guard.

In the evening, we went on a quest to find the famous Chilean *Terremoto* and *Piscola.* In Bellavista, Santiago's nightlife hub, we sat outside a rowdy bar. One *Terremoto*, one Piscola. Too much for us both. The *Terremoto*, a syrupy concoction of *fernet*, white wine, and pineapple ice cream, was overwhelmingly sweet. The *Piscola*, cola with *pisco*, was a lighter, more refreshing companion. Tipsy and laughing, we wandered home, the cool night air sobering us gently.

Finally, alone in our Airbnb, a space all our own for the first time in over a week, we relished the simple pleasures.... Healthy food, family calls over Skype, and YouTube videos teaching us more about Chilean history.

Santiago Part Two ended quietly and perfectly. The kind of day that balances heavy reflection with the joy of discovery.

The Airbnb in Santiago wasn't quite what we had hoped for. It had a smart TV, a big kitchen, and even a bathtub, but as the night drew on, the cold crept in. There was no heating. No plug-in heater, nothing. Worse, the sheets were covered in hair. The host was unresponsive. It was disappointing, especially since the place had good reviews, and felt both safe and comfortable. But without warmth and clean bedding, it fell short of the bare minimum.

Still, we packed and were whisked away to the airport by the same friend who had met us there a few weeks before. Smog hung thick over Santiago, hiding the Andes we had been lucky to see on arrival. I remembered warnings that photos of the city from Google didn't reflect reality; now I understood.

At the airport, a uniformed man approached Carlos and I, badge in hand, asking for our driver's name and our own. We complied, uneasily. Soon after, Carlos' phone rang. He left abruptly, returning fifteen minutes later with the news that giving cash to cover fuel to our friend outside the airport technically broke the law. Had we done it discreetly inside a car or elsewhere, it would've gone unnoticed. But the police, tasked with preventing smuggling and trafficking, had rules about transferring money in an airport. After apologies and explanations, we were let go without consequence. Just another story to add to the collection.

Learning Lima

- LIMA, PERU -

The flight into Peru felt like an omen of contrasts to come. Santiago disappeared beneath a thick blanket of smog, and then suddenly, like a curtain lifting, we were above the Andes, endless and dramatic, the kind of scenery that makes you forget how cramped your seat is. Hours later, the mountains gave way to the Pacific, a flat grey sheet hidden under clouds until Lima finally emerged. It revealed itself in sharp opposites. A dark, restless ocean dotted with fishing boats, and a dry, sandy desert pressed right up against the coast.

We opted for one of the official airport taxis, the slightly pricier option that buys you peace of mind. The driver chatted easily, answered our questions, and handed over his number for future rides. Within minutes, I understood why that extra couple of dollars mattered. Lima's roads were pure chaos. Horns blared constantly, cars swerved with confidence that bordered on faith, and Carlos and I found ourselves gripping the seats like we were on a rollercoaster. Somehow, miraculously, it all worked.

Our Airbnb was a private room in a penthouse apartment in a neighbourhood called Magdalena. It was owned by an elderly woman who managed to be both sweet and slightly terrifying at the same time. She wore heavy makeup, shuffled fiercely around the apartment, and lived there while renting out two rooms that her son managed remotely from Madrid. The apartment itself was beautiful, perched high above the city with a huge balcony overlooking rooftops that blurred into sea mist. We wandered out to a nearby shopping strip, grabbed sandwiches, and then did nothing at all—one of the underrated joys of travel: simply arriving and letting your nervous system catch up.

Magdalena felt lived-in and local, and that became more obvious the next day when we decided to walk all the way into the historic centre. Seven kilometres didn't seem unreasonable—Machu Picchu training, right?—but Lima attacked my senses through smell and sound. The car fumes were so thick they felt almost intoxicating, and the noise was relentless. Horns used constantly. Every driver seemed to be communicating an entire emotional range through short, sharp honks. It wasn't until we stumbled into a brief pocket of quiet that I realised my ears actually hurt. Still, amid the chaos, there was a strange order to it all. Everyone seemed to know the rules, even if we didn't.

We paused at a Greek café for coffee and croissants before continuing, arriving slightly late to the walking tour and briefly attaching ourselves to the wrong one. The wrong guide tried to convince us that free walking tours weren't official and therefore not worth our time. He said we should pay for his instead, which made me laugh internally. I've trusted free walking tours all over the world, with only one truly terrible exception in Austria. Eventually, we spotted the familiar sky-blue vests of the tour we were looking for and joined in.

I realised quickly how little I knew about Peru. Beyond Machu Picchu, vague bus etiquette *("Baja, baja!"),* and a rainbow mountain, my knowledge was embarrassingly thin. The tour filled in the gaps. Lima's historic buildings glowed in a dark, mustard-yellow hue, a legacy of Spanish colonial influence. Cusco had once been the capital, until Lima's strategic coastline and reliable weather shifted power to the coast. In the main square, there was a black fountain dating back to the 1600s—ancient by New Zealand standards—and our guide told us about the time it was filled with *pisco.* Locals arrived en masse with plastic cups, morale soared, terrorism briefly declined, and the Catholic Church and police were… less impressed.

Vultures circled overhead, drawn by the low-running Rimac River. Nearby, colourful shacks clung to hillsides, stacked atop one another like precarious building blocks. Many of these communities had formed during years of terrorism, when people fled the countryside for safety. They now lived in poverty, but alive. The railway system never recovered from being a frequent target, which explained why buses were the backbone of travel here.

The tour wandered through politics and public health too. Mandatory voting enforced with fines, bars closed during election weekends to ensure sobriety, churches banned from using real flowers to combat mosquito breeding (especially during Zika outbreaks), candles outlawed after devastating fires. It was a lot to take in, but it made the city feel layered and real, not just something to pass through on the way to more famous destinations like Cusco.

We ended, as all good tours should, with free shots of *pisco* in a souvenir market. We tipped generously, found a nearby restaurant where prices dropped dramatically just a few streets away from the square, and I tried Inca Cola for the first time. It tasted exactly like a cheap, yellow, fizzy drink from home, which felt strangely comforting.

The next day, we ate sandwiches and local fruit on our balcony, wrapped in Lima's persistent haze. I'd initially assumed it was pollution but learned it was something more meteorological. A collision of cold air from the south, desert dryness, and jungle humidity.

We kept the day intentionally slow, walking back toward the city centre again and observing the rhythms of daily life. Long bank queues, roundabouts so jammed they looked frozen in time, pedestrians playing real-life Frogger at every crossing. Driving here seemed less like a convenience and more like a dare. We high-fived after surviving several intersections.

I also learned the hard truths of Peruvian plumbing. Toilet paper rarely lived where you expected it, flushing it was often forbidden, and trash cans sat beside toilets with firm instructions. On the upside, supermarkets had dedicated checkouts for elderly people and pregnant women. We accidentally used one, were swiftly reprimanded, and sent back to the "everyone else" line. Lesson learned. I tried *chicha* that day too, thick and purple and sweet, tasting like a corn-based cousin of the blackcurrant-based drink called Ribena in England.

When we eventually moved to an Airbnb in Miraflores, it felt like stepping into another country entirely. The drive was short, but the shift was dramatic. Magdalena had felt nice and authentically Peruvian. Miraflores felt curated. Flower-filled streets, fewer horns, clear signage discouraging honking altogether. For the first time in weeks, I heard English everywhere. I felt guilty for how quickly my shoulders relaxed.

I loved backpacking for its challenges. The constant problem-solving, the language barriers, the way simple tasks could drain you. But Miraflores was intoxicatingly easy. You could take out your phone without fear. Restaurant staff spoke fluent English and knew exactly how to lure you in with charm and free *pisco.* My ears no longer hurt from the sound of cars honking. It was so much more relaxed.

The highlight for me was the central park, home to dozens of well-fed cats lounging under trees with bowls of food placed deliberately at their bases. There was even an adoption stall. The beach below the city was rocky and cold, accessed via steep stairways carved into black cliffs. Surfers dotted the water, and locals called out offers of lessons. It wasn't beautiful in a postcard sense, but it was alive.

Even the supermarket was a different experience. Compared to the hectic local store in Magdalena, the Miraflores version felt like a spa. Classical music, neatly stacked shelves, free samples, imported cheeses and wine priced like home. It was more expensive, yes, but convenient, and by the end of the night we were full and content. I was grateful we'd seen both sides of Lima. The polished and the raw.

Our final deep dive took us to Barranco and Chorrillos on another walking tour. The bus cost almost nothing, and the streets changed again. This time bursting with street art. Murals climbed walls and stairs, surreal and vibrant, framed by cacti and cobblestones. Our guide, half Peruvian, half Cuban, looked like a younger Will Smith and narrated everything through hilarious, slightly unhinged personal stories involving cactus juice and questionable culinary experiments.

We learned about inequality. How a tiny fraction of the population lived extravagantly, with exclusive beachside clubs costing more to join than most people earned in years, sitting right next to fishing shacks where poverty was unavoidable. In Chorrillos, we visited an area that brought us uncomfortably close to *favela* life. Roosters crowed constantly, bred for fighting, knives sometimes strapped to their legs. It was disturbing, especially knowing our presence as tourists was part of the economy that allowed it to continue. And yet, it was legal, cultural, and deeply embedded.

We met a man who built boats by hand, forty-five days per boat, hundreds over his lifetime, selling them cheaply while larger companies profited. The neighbourhood was a patchwork of scrap wood and corrugated metal, but people welcomed us in. We ate cake, drank juice, danced a little, and climbed to a hilltop cross overlooking coastal Lima as the city stretched endlessly below.

I didn't know what to think about Lima after all this. It was exhausting and comforting, confronting and indulgent, chaotic and strangely ordered. I was surprised by how easily my guilt and relief could coexist, and I quickly learnt how important it was to see more than one version of a place.

To The Oasis

- ICA, PERU -

Leaving Lima meant starting the day far earlier than either of us wanted to acknowledge. We'd learned enough about traffic to know that optimism was dangerous, so we ordered a Cabify while it was still barely morning. The app told us exactly what we'd pay, we could choose cash, and once again it worked flawlessly. Something that still felt mildly miraculous on this continent. The drive to the bus terminal was a white-knuckle exercise in faith as our car slid confidently between buses that looked big enough to end us with a shrug, but somehow, we arrived intact.

The terminal itself was surprisingly civilised. Plush seats, free tea and coffee, filtered water. Honestly better than some airports I've been to. We stocked up on snacks like coffee, an *alfajor*, and Pringles. When the bus pulled in, my expectations were immediately exceeded. It was fancy.

Front-row seats, personal TV screens loaded with movies and games, large, shared screens above, professional staff who checked passports like we were boarding a flight. Then came snack boxes. Actual snack boxes. Muffins, crackers, candy, fizzy drink. South American buses were officially showing off.

The landscape unfurled in dramatic shifts as we drove. Harsh black coastline, endless beige desert, then sudden green fields that looked like someone had dropped them there by mistake. After hours of grey haze in Lima, the sky finally turned blue and the sun made an appearance, like it had been waiting for us to leave the city. Along the highway, poverty sat openly in view. Farmers bent over crops, chicken farms where birds were packed so tightly their heads poked through cages. It wasn't hidden or softened. It what was it was.

When we arrived in Ica mid-afternoon, something in me instantly relaxed. I hadn't realised how much Lima had stressed me out until that moment. I didn't know if it was culture shock, hormones, or just a mismatch, but stepping off that bus into the dry, punishing desert heat weirdly made me feel lighter. Energised. Even dodging leaking sewage and the unmistakable smell that came with it couldn't dent my mood. I could see the sky properly again. I walked differently. With a bounce.

We were staying in a backpackers' hostel this time. A private room, but it had the right adventurous energy. The rooftop terrace offered mountains on one side and towering sand dunes on the other. As the sun dipped, we drank *chicha* and watched the sky fade through pinks and purples, the desert glowing softly. It felt like a reset. Peru: Part Two.

Ica itself was dusty and strange and deeply charming. Tourism clearly kept it ticking—Huacachina nearby, Paracas within reach, Nazca tempting from a distance—and yet it didn't feel overwhelmed by it. The town buzzed without shouting. People swept sand away constantly, like an ongoing, losing battle they refused to give up on. Even our hostel gleamed despite the desert trying its best to reclaim it daily.

It was Carlos' birthday, which meant I finally got to reveal the surprise I'd been hoarding for weeks. A video stitched together from messages sent by his friends and family scattered across the world. He talked about it all day, which made me pat myself on the back. Breakfast came next. A simple hostel fare eaten on the terrace with coco leaf tea and coffee. I crossed my fingers that the clouds would clear. We had plans.

A quick wander through town confirmed what we already sensed. Ica wasn't about grand sights. There was a square, a church, honking cars, shops. Nothing remarkable. But it felt safe. Comfortable. After twenty minutes we'd seen enough and found lunch instead—an entirely vegetarian restaurant, which felt like discovering a unicorn in South America. For ten soles I was served an enormous meal, followed by a jug of fresh juice the size of my head. I was so full that I basically had to be rolled out.

Getting to Huacachina happened faster than I could think about it. Carlos flagged down a mototaxi (like a tuk-tuk) with confidence that startled me. The thing rattled violently, every bolt apparently reconsidering its necessity, and I held on like my life depended on it, which it actually might have. Once we hit the desert, though, everything else faded. The dunes rose around us like mountains made of silk. I'd been to deserts before, including in Dubai and Australia. But these were different. Grander in scale, even.

Huacachina itself was exactly what you'd expect from a place that boasts its status as an oasis. A lagoon cradled by palm trees, ringed with hostels, bars, and tour operators who descended immediately with offers of dune buggies and sandboarding. We'd already booked, so we spent the afternoon climbing a nearby dune. It nearly killed me. I tried not to think too hard about the Salkantay Trek looming in my future and whether I'd be physically fit in time. Clouds spared us from sunstroke but also dulled our photos. Still, I scored a neck scarf for a fraction of what it would've cost at home.

The dune buggy experience began in a spot that looked like it doubled as a scrapyard. Then suddenly we were flying. Up dunes, down dunes, over edges that made my stomach flip. I loved it. It was terrifying and exhilarating and exactly why I travel. The sandboarding that came next was intense. Far more intense than I'd anticipated. And after one particularly fast run I lay at the bottom convinced I'd broken something. I hadn't. Just bruises and grazes.

We finished at sunset on a high dune overlooking Huacachina, people scattered around drinking beer and soaking it all in. We promised ourselves we'd come back. Carlos' birthday ended with a rooftop dinner, cocktails, and the most indulgent drink I could justify ordering: a Bailey's Banana Colada. Getting home involved another mototaxi. This one marginally more legitimate, with ropes holding the doors shut. Our standards were slipping, clearly. The driver joked with us the whole way, proud to now have friends from New Zealand. We tipped him extra for the banter and crawled into bed buzzing.

The next morning hurt. A 6 a.m. start was rough. We were herded into a shuttle with other half-asleep humans and driven to Paracas for a boat tour of the Ballestas Islands. The so-called "poor man's Galapagos." I slept until we reached the boat. The cruise, however, was worth waking up for. Pelicans everywhere. Hundreds of them. Penguins, sea lions, birds slicing through the sky in long, dramatic lines. The water shifted from calm to aggressive in minutes, and I was impressed by how close the captain dared to take us to the rocks.

There was also frustration. Construction had destroyed much of the birds' natural habitat, leaving them cramped into narrow stretches of coastline. Our guide talked about protesting, about being ignored. Tourism, ironically one of the region's biggest industries, wasn't enough to protect the very thing it relied on.

What surprised me most was how familiar it all felt. After years in New Zealand, I'd seen much of this before. It made me oddly grateful. To realise that people travelled across the world to witness what had once been my everyday. I slept almost the entire way back to Ica. When I wasn't asleep, the bus ride gave me a chance to self-reflect. Travel was incredible, yes. But I was already realising that there was luxury in routine. Stability. Hanging clothes instead of rolling them. Knowing where your spices live. Not constantly planning the next move. It felt strange to admit, because I wanted to be seen as adventurous. I guess two things can be true at once.

We did a vineyard tour that afternoon, and it was chaos in the best way. The company forgot to pick us up, so we ended up with a private driver and zero idea where we were going. When we arrived at Tacama winery, complete with armed guards and passport checks, it felt surreal. The vineyard was modern, industrial, impressive. Nothing like what I'd imagined Peruvian wine to be. The second stop, El Catador, was the opposite. Dusty, hands-on, welcoming. Grapes squished underfoot, generous tastings poured freely, and suddenly we were tipsy with bags full of bottles we definitely didn't need but absolutely wanted.

Dinner was at a Chifa restaurant—Chinese-Peruvian fusion—and once again I marvelled at how easy vegetarian life became there. Huge meals. Tiny prices. Happy bellies. I officially ticked "*pisco* vineyard tour in Peru" off my mental list.

Our final day in Ica was quieter, softer. I loved that we'd chosen to stay there instead of Huacachina, dipping into the touristy spots when we wanted and retreating when we didn't. The hostel felt like home. Every return involved ringing the bell and hearing one of the brothers who owned it shout "*Chicos*!" from somewhere above before letting us in. They remembered Carlos' birthday. They hugged him. They cleaned relentlessly, fighting the desert grain by grain.

When people asked where I was from and I said New Zealand, they often brought up Māori culture. It surprised me every time. Somehow, this small country at the bottom of the world had made an impression here. Maybe because of how New Zealand beams pride in the Indigenous culture. Maybe because Kiwis travel loudly and often. Either way, it made me proud.

I loved Ica. It revitalised me. It reminded me why I love this kind of adventurous life. Why discomfort can be a good thing, why moving around matters, why kindness from strangers lingers longer than grand landmarks that look good in a photo. It was dusty and imperfect and occasionally smelled like sewage, but it fed my traveller fire.

Unlocking the Real Lima

- LIMA, PERU -

By the time we boarded the bus back to Lima, we'd become seasoned South American bus veterans. We knew the drill. Settle in, snacks ready, accept that personal space and privacy is non-existent. Carlos, however, decided this was the moment to tempt fate and skip his motion sickness pill. It did not go well. For four and a half hours, he fought a quiet, miserable battle with his stomach while I sat beside him, completely useless, happily absorbed in a book called Modern Romance. I found it so interesting that I finished the entire book before we rolled into Lima a few hours later, which felt like both an accomplishment and a cruel contrast to Carlos' suffering.

Lima greeted us the same way it had the last time. Traffic, chaos, horns, and an hour-long Cabify ride that should have taken twenty minutes. Cars inched forward like they were engaged in a shoving match, horns blaring constantly, bumpers hovering millimetres from disaster. I remembered, viscerally, why Lima and I hadn't quite clicked last week.

I didn't know it yet, but my perception was about to change rapidly.

Wandering through Miraflores to meet Elias—an old friend I'd met years earlier while studying in Poland—I felt that surreal satisfaction of keeping promises across continents. I'd told him I'd come to Peru one day, the same way I'd once casually promised a friend in Moscow I'd visit. Somehow, I kept doing these things. Here I was again, halfway across the world, following through with my promises. Proof that younger versions of myself had meant what she said.

Elias showed us a Lima I hadn't seen before. The kind that only locals can unlock. We were whisked away to Amar de Lima, a stunning restaurant perched over the water at the Club de Regatas. That very exclusive club our tour guide had told us about the week before. Glass windows wrapped around the space, the ocean surprisingly clear below us, the city lights sparkling in the distance like they were trying to impress us. I ate roasted vegetables, we clinked *Pisco* sours, and I declare, confidently, that this was the best one I'd had so far. I was back in my happy place.

It really is true that cities come alive when you experience them through people who love them.

From there, we drifted into Barranco, supposedly home to the best bars in Lima. Last week, we'd only seen the neighbourhood during the day, so this was a new experience.

The first bar felt colonial and grand, all white columns and elegant gardens, packed with young people clutching cocktails. I'm not a heavy drinker, so it didn't take much before I was already giddy and loose-limbed. At some point, Elias' girlfriend handed Carlos and I a double shot of straight *Pisco.* Elias raised his camera, and we both took the shots.

The rest of the night dissolved into fragments. A quieter bar where the drinks were allegedly better (I was too drunk to know). My drink tasted like a milkshake. Carlos' tasted like lemon-lime bitters. I got ID'd, which felt offensive and flattering all at once. "Why?" Elias challenged the security guard in rapidly aggressive Spanish. "She looks young, but you can tell she's not eighteen." I suspect the guard was looking for a bribe since I was obviously foreign. But hearing Elias' native Spanish, he quickly gave up.

Later, and I mean *very late,* we devoured pizza, burgers, and fries, then, because we are either brave or stupid, walked home through Lima around two in the morning. Somehow, we made it back unscathed, armed with nothing but full stomachs and a growing collection of ridiculous memories. At the very least, I was leaving Lima laughing.

The next morning punished me accordingly.

I woke up disoriented, head pounding, unsure where I was or why everything hurt so much. Eventually, reality settled in: Lima. Hungover. Badly. After an hour of trying to get ourselves out of bed, we begrudgingly found the strength to adventure. This would be our final stay in Lima—we wouldn't be looping back here again—and it felt important to give the city one last, honest chance.

We started with brunch at La Lucha, recommended by Elias. The sandwiches were genuinely excellent. The place was full of tourists, but I couldn't fault it. I just wished I'd been capable of appreciating it without feeling like my head was splitting in half.

From there, we wandered along Avenida Arequipa, stopping at an EcoMarket that felt comfortingly familiar. Organic products, homemade teas, fresh food ready to go. The falafel wrap and tea worked small miracles on my hangover. Eventually, we reached Larcomar, an open-air mall perched dramatically above the ocean. Waves crashed below us, loud and insistent, while luxury stores gleamed uselessly around us. We didn't shop. We just stood there, listening, letting the view do the work.

After that, we went home, and I slept for three solid hours. A much needed nap.

That evening, revived enough to function, we walked nearly an hour to the Circuito Mágico del Agua. The city unfolded around us as we went. Bars, clubs, neighbourhoods we hadn't yet seen. The park itself was unexpectedly magical. Fountains erupting like volcanoes, lights rippling into rainbows, kids shrieking with joy as they ran through interactive sprays. Food carts lined the paths, selling everything from chicken burgers to *chicha* to *arroz con leche*. It was joyful, chaotic, cheap, and alive.

We walked home again that night, trusting our instincts and sticking to main roads. I knew Lima had its dangers, so we'd taken appropriate precautions. If something happened, it wouldn't be because we were careless. It would be timing, chance, luck. Sometimes that's all it comes down to.

By then, we were three weeks into our six-month trip, and time had completely lost its meaning. It was flying and crawling simultaneously. In such a short span, I'd crossed an ocean, flown over the Andes, explored abandoned mines, celebrated a birthday with strangers who sang to me, hurtled down sand dunes, eaten things I couldn't pronounce, travelled thousands of kilometres. At home, weeks disappeared into routine. Here, days expanded, swollen with experience.

I genuinely struggled to know what day it was at any given point. Time was measured in hostel bookings and bus tickets, rarely more than two days ahead. We had no real plan. Just backpacks, passports, debit cards, and each other. Everything else could be figured out later.

The freedom was intoxicating.

The Desert Gives Back

- ICA, PERU -

Leaving Lima felt strangely triumphant. We'd cracked the code now. Cabify was a dream, the bus station no longer intimidating, the city suddenly navigable. Peru, which had felt loud and overwhelming at first, was starting to feel navigable. On a quiet Sunday morning, the roads were blissfully empty, a stark contrast to the weekday chaos, and within ten minutes we were at the station, smug in our newfound competence.

This time, Carlos didn't gamble. He took a motion sickness pill before boarding. He learned the hard way just days earlier. He slept through most of the ride, which suited me fine. I pressed myself against the window, watching the landscape shift again. Rocky stretches melting into beaches, dunes rolling endlessly into one another. We'd taken this route twice already in the past week, but what really held my attention this time, though, were the chickens. Hundreds of them. Thousands, maybe. Crammed into visible cages right along the road, packed so tightly there was barely space to move. It was confronting. I knew, intellectually, that factory farming existed everywhere, including back home, but seeing it so starkly, so unavoidably, made my decision to stay vegetarian feel less like an inconvenience and more of a validation of my values. South America might be famous for its meat, but I felt steadier in my choice than ever.

Somewhere along that ride, I realised I was missing home a little. Not in a homesick, I-want-to-leave way, but in a reflective, grateful one. Travel has a funny way of doing that. Seeing different ways of life sharpens your awareness of what you've always taken for granted. I missed small, invisible luxuries like walking at night without my guard up, pulling my phone out on the street without thinking twice, drinking water straight from the tap, flushing toilet paper without a second thought. These weren't universal comforts. They were privileges.

If travelling had taught me anything over the years, it was that places like New Zealand, Australia, and much of Europe sit firmly in the global minority when it comes to quality of life and infrastructure. My family had never been rich by any stretch, but compared to so much of the world, we'd been incredibly fortunate simply by virtue of where we were born. I thought about kids I'd seen in poorer pockets of Chile and Peru, and about my brothers growing up in England before moving to New Zealand. Access to competitive education, stable internet, cupboards full of food. These things weren't guarantees everywhere. Suddenly, migration made complete sense to me in a deeply human way. Of course some people left countries in search of a 'better' life. Of course they chased stability. I would too. In fact, hadn't my family already done so by moving from England to New Zealand?

As we pulled into Ica, the sun welcomed us like an old friend. The town felt instantly calmer than Lima. Still noisy, still full of honking cars, but smaller, warmer, more manageable. We set ourselves the very unglamorous task of doing laundry, only to discover that laundromats were apparently a rare luxury. So we improvised. Dirty clothes went into the shower, washing powder followed, and I resurrected my universal plug, originally purchased for clothes-washing emergencies on the Trans-Siberian Railway. We stomped around like lunatics, creating our own low-tech backpacker washing machine. Clothes dried in the sun on the windowsill, then got a final blast with the hairdryer to prevent mould. I missed the simplicity of a real washing machine, but I drew the line at re-wearing underwear inside out. Some standards had to remain.

Later, we headed back to Huacachina. Our mototaxi driver warned us sternly not to trust anyone, that people would be watching us for the wrong reasons. It wasn't the first warning like that, and it wouldn't be the last, but it always lodged somewhere uneasy in my chest.

Huacachina felt different this time. Quieter. The roar of dune buggies was gone. After a multi-fatal accident days earlier, the government had temporarily banned dune buggying, and the energy of the place had shifted. Tour companies looked desperate, trying to sell quad bike rides, but tourists weren't biting. The oasis' adventurous image had been tainted. Even though it was just one reckless company, the ripple effect was undeniable. I suspected many travellers would skip Huacachina altogether now.

I was glad I'd already had my dune-buggy thrill. This time, I just sank into the oasis version of Huacachina by reading in the sun, listening to unfamiliar birds, watching locals aggressively pitch tours to the few remaining tourists. It was slower, calmer, more contemplative.

As sunset crept closer, Carlos convinced me to climb the dunes again. My calves screamed with every two-steps-up-one-step-down motion, the sand unforgiving beneath us. The sun was intense, but after grey Lima and freezing Santiago, it felt glorious. Every time I thought we'd found a good spot, Carlos pointed higher. Steeper. Eventually, we settled. We cracked open two beers, one immediately sacrificed to a thirsty and suicidal fly, and watched the sun melt into the desert. A warm orange orb sinking behind distant dunes. Around us, maybe a hundred other people dotted the landscape, all quietly witnessing the same thing. It felt shared, but still intimate. A perfect ending.

Later, at dinner, we asked for a takeaway container because we couldn't finish our meal. The server nodded, disappeared, and returned with our food tied neatly into a plastic bag. No box. Just thrown loosely into a bag. We laughed until it hurt.

White Stones and Volcanoes

- AREQUIPA, PERU -

I was actually looking forward to the long bus ride out of Ica. That might sound bizarre, but the kind of travel we were doing meant my brain was constantly switched on. Whether it be navigating, translating, problem-solving, or simply absorbing. It was exhilarating, but exhausting in a quiet, cumulative way. A bus ride meant permission to do nothing. To sit still. To catch up on life admin. To stare out the window without needing to do anything with what I saw.

For me, the hours passed quickly. I edited GoPro footage, watched the landscape roll by, and let my thoughts drift. Carlos, on the other hand, suffered. Even armed with multiple Gravol, the winding mountain roads and the driver's apparent belief that he was in a Fast & Furious audition made things rough. At least the bus itself was excellent. We were trying a new company, Oltursa. It had mixed reviews, as always, because Peruvian buses have a genuinely terrifying reputation. We'd done our research. The kind that includes reading about multiple fatal accidents at. But we were pleasantly surprised overall. The seats reclined deeply, meals were delivered to us, and movies played overhead. Honestly, South American buses had been some of the best I'd ever taken in the entire world. If only the drivers weren't quite so enthusiastic about bendy roads.

We pulled into Arequipa just after midnight, and my nerves kicked in immediately. I'd read far too many horror stories about express kidnappings by taxi drivers at this exact bus station. The hostel had told us to only take official taxis from inside the terminal. The problem was that when we arrived, the place was eerily empty. Outside the terminal, though, I could see the enemy. Dodgy taxis idling in the dark, exactly like the ones every blog and backpacker forum had warned us about.

We stood inside with our bags, unsure what to do. When I eventually wandered over to the group of taxi drivers outside the official station, they started wolf-whistling.

Great.

They were, unfortunately, our only option. We negotiated (poorly), paid double (inevitable), and got in. To top it off, the driver didn't even take us all the way to the hostel because there was a street party blocking the road. Arequipa's anniversary, apparently. Though I realised later he definitely could have gotten closer. Still, we walked the final stretch and made it back safely, which was all that really mattered.

The hostel was quiet. Our room was on the rooftop, which felt odd at first, and then the light blew and the power went out. I went to bed feeling grumpy and fragile and deeply aware that I was being a bit of a brat. I knew that if I'd read this scene in someone else's travel memoir, I would have told them to toughen up. That this was part of it. The frustration, the fatigue, the moments where everything felt slightly off. They mattered just as much as the magical highs. This was the full shape of the journey. Just roll with it.

The next morning began with an actual, audible "ahhhh."

I pulled open the curtains and was greeted by a perfectly symmetrical, snow-capped volcano looming calmly in the distance. Still active and magnificent. It felt worlds away from the chaos of the streets we'd arrived through the night before, where people had been urinating openly and vendors were selling straight spirits from carts. Arequipa clearly had layers to it.

Breakfast confirmed that. The hostel had promised the best free breakfast around, and for once, that claim wasn't exaggerated. I sat on the terrace, eating a mountain of pancakes stuffed with bananas and drowned in *dulce de leche*, staring out at colonial buildings and volcanoes beyond. The sun was already intense, a reminder that we were higher above sea level now. You could feel it immediately. On your skin, in your lungs.

We did a free walking tour that turned out to be too much talking, not enough seeing. Plus, the streets still smelled distinctly of last night's celebrations. But it started with a free cup of chocolate tea which, unsurprisingly, ended with us signing up for a chocolate-making class.

Our class instructor, Adrian, introduced himself as a "chocolate expert and beer nerd," which was printed proudly on his business card. At one point he declared, "Chocolate comes from cocoa beans, cocoa beans are fruit, and therefore chocolate is basically a f***ing salad." I adored him immediately. For over two hours, we learned how cocoa is produced, how to spot fake chocolate, and how to make the real thing from bean to bar. Adrian rubbed cocoa butter all over his face, encouraged us to inhale handfuls of cocoa beans, and radiated pure enthusiasm. We made chilli hot chocolate and left with bags of our own creations. Chilli, quinoa, coconut, sea salt. Expensive by local standards, yes, but worth every single sol.

Arequipa itself was genuinely beautiful. White stone buildings, strong colonial influences, volcanoes framing the skyline. It would be easy to mistake parts of it for Europe if you ignored the altitude and the sun. There were more tourists here, mostly backpackers, which gave the city a lively, social energy. Add the anniversary celebrations and the weather, and it was hard not to feel good. I felt noticeably better than I had the night before. Lighter, steadier.

The days that followed were wonderfully unstructured. One afternoon, we wandered through the Claustros de la Compañía, a preserved cluster of 18th-century buildings that felt almost like Roman ruins. Tucked inside was a small coffee truck boasting "the best coffee in the world." Mostly, though, we ate. A lot. We found a cosy Mexican restaurant on Calle Jerusalén where meals cost next to nothing, and we absolutely overdid it. The food coma required a two-hour lie-down, but I had zero regrets.

I noticed I was getting tired earlier in the evenings. Whether it was the altitude, the relentless pace of the past month, or the lack of routine, my body was ready for bed by nine. That wasn't a bad thing. It meant I woke naturally around dawn, just in time to sit on the terrace and watch the sunrise cast soft light across the volcanoes surrounding the city.

I was glad we'd arrived with no specific plans. Arequipa was the kind of place that didn't demand an itinerary. Its charm was in wandering. Through white-stone streets that felt vaguely medieval, hearing vendors call out for *queso helado,* watching tourists and locals weave past each other in clearly distinct ways.

I did learn one unexpected lesson. Altitude and dryness can mess with your nose. An uncomfortable, constant dryness that required endless blowing, often filled with specks of blood. Eerily similar to how my nose had reacted in Mongolia's freezing temperatures. A quick Google confirmed it was normal when in higher altitudes, and it made me even more grateful we weren't rushing straight from Lima to Cusco. There were practical benefits of taking our time as we navigated through Peru.

Lessons in Altitude

- CUSCO, PERU -

By the time we rolled toward Cusco, I had decided that paying extra for safety did not automatically translate to comfort. I'd always loved long bus rides. Those liminal stretches of time where you can reflect, read, get your life together, or at least pretend to. This one ruined the genre for me entirely. Even with the "better" seats—more recline, downstairs for less motion—the bus lurched and stuttered. I was almost grateful it was dark; I didn't need a visual accompaniment to the feeling that we were flying around mountain roads.

The cold didn't help. I understood we were cutting through mountain ranges, but surely blasting arctic air-conditioning wasn't essential to the experience. Even bundled in blankets, I kept waking up shivering, my body confused and uncomfortable. They did try, in their own way—individual movie screens (silent ones, because of course the sound didn't work), and a vegetarian dinner that appeared to be a cheese sandwich with remnants of ham stuck to the bread. Small mercies.

What amused me most was how low my standards had dropped. Despite the freezing temperatures, the jerky driving, and the sleep deprivation, my primary concern was simply arriving alive. After weeks of reading horror stories about buses plunging off Peruvian cliffs, survival felt like a win. And to be fair, Cruz del Sur delivered on that front. We arrived in Cusco breathing, which meant we were immediately off to a good start.

Cusco, unsurprisingly, was beautiful. There's a reason it's such a tourist magnet. We reached our hostel mid-morning, dumped our bags, and promptly committed ourselves to doing absolutely nothing. For hours we sat with a cheap breakfast, inhaling food and free Wi-Fi while gazing out over the city. Every guidebook screamed the same advice about altitude sickness: take it easy. We listened. The only exertion we allowed ourselves was a short walk to another restaurant, where the food bordered on obscene in its abundance. Salads, soy burgers, fried cheese, guacamole, bananas drenched in chocolate sauce. I was in heaven.

We briefly popped into our Salkantay Trek office for a rundown of what lay ahead, then returned to bed and spent the rest of the day editing videos. Sometimes the most responsible thing you can do while travelling is absolutely nothing.

The next day, we decided to ease ourselves into adventure with a Sacred Valley tour, largely because we'd been told it was a "must-do," and also because it was Sunday and there were special markets. The hostel booked it for us, with lunch included. I had seen a glossy brochure image of terraced hills that looked like they'd been designed by aliens, and while the price made me hesitate, curiosity won.

It turned out to be so much more than I expected. In a good way. After a mildly awkward start involving me accidentally wandering into someone's bedroom thinking it was the kitchen, we were off. Packed lunches in hand, rolling through landscapes that kept shifting beneath us. We started high, at an ancient church perched on a hill, where the stonework quietly revealed the collision of Inca precision and colonial force. From there, the views opened wide, mountain ranges stretching into the distance. I found myself staring at them, wondering if these were the same peaks we'd soon be climbing, and tried to not think too hard about it. I wasn't convinced I was physically ready and it made me anxious.

The day unfolded in a blur of ruins, terraces, salt ponds, and markets. We climbed the windy stone staircases of Ollantaytambo, wandered through the ruins overlooking Pisac, dipped our hands into the streams feeding the salt pans at Maras, and browsed market stalls overflowing with colour and texture. Somewhere along the way, we learned how alpaca wool becomes fabric, how cactus bugs turn brilliant red when crushed, how to spot real silver, and why aniseed shots and tea are meant to help with altitude.

What I'd initially thought was an overpriced day trip turned into a twelve-hour immersion into a part of Peru that felt entirely different from the coast and desert we'd already seen. This was all green valleys and snow-dusted peaks, vast and humbling. And even as I soaked it in, I knew it was just a prelude of what was coming.

With our hike to Machu Picchu looming just two sunrises away, nerves finally crept in. I'd trained hard—running, boxing, salsa dancing, walking everywhere, eating sensibly. Physically, I felt strong. But altitude is its own beast. Even walking up a few steps could leave your heart pounding like it was trying to escape your chest.

Still, I'd done what I could. I'd arrived early to Peru, and Cusco in particular, to acclimatise. I had coca leaves, medication, and realistic expectations. The goal wasn't speed; it was completion. And more than that, enjoyment. Fitness, I'd learned, wasn't about proving anything. It was about giving yourself the chance to actually experience what you were doing. To make sure that I could actually enjoy the hike and all its marvellous views, rather than simply surviving it.

We spent the next day ticking off logistics. Renting walking poles and a sleeping bag from a place charmingly named Speedy Gonzales, saving ourselves a small fortune in the process. Cusco, it turns out, is a hiker's dream. You can rent almost anything. Boots, backpacks, thermals, ponchos. My advice to anyone planning a trek here: don't overpack from home. Cusco has everything you need.

That evening, hunger led us into an empty pizza place across the street. The pizza and Inca Cola combination were surprisingly good. Then a crash echoed outside. At first, I assumed it was something minor. Maybe a drunk stumble. But when we looked out, a man was on the ground, seizing.

Within seconds, local young men rushed in, placing him in the recovery position, speaking calmly, taking control. No hesitation. No panic. No thoughts about their own safety, just a narrowed focus on the need to help. Medical staff arrived quickly after, and the situation was handled with care and competence. I was amazed at how quickly it all happened. I'd absorbed so many warnings about who to trust and not trust, so many quiet fears shaped by stories and stereotypes. And yet here were local strangers doing exactly what needed to be done, without spectacle or reward. They were the ones keeping people safe.

It was a humbling reminder that most people, almost everywhere, are simply trying to do the right thing.

The Savage

- MACHU PICCHU, PERU -

So, this was it. The day the seventy-seven-kilometre hike actually began. The almighty Salkantay Trek—affectionately known as The Savage—the long, slow road that would eventually lead us to Machu Picchu.

Early mornings had stopped feeling cruel by this point. Somewhere along the way, we'd slipped into a routine of waking before sunrise without resistance, so we took our time with what would be our last proper shower for several days. When the shuttle arrived, we were clean, alert, and quietly aware that things were about to get real.

Cusco's streets rattled us awake all over again. The drive was predictably bumpy, but our first stop already made the whole thing special. We visited the porter house run by our tour company, LlamaPath, and were given a glimpse into the work they do beyond simply getting trekkers from point A to point B. It was one of the reasons we'd chosen them in the first place—their emphasis on sustainability, fair working conditions, and reinvesting in local communities.

As we stepped out of the van, a pack of medium-sized dogs surrounded us, barking aggressively. My stomach dropped. The day before, we'd met someone who'd been bitten by a dog and was now navigating the nightmare of rabies shots. Fortunately, the dogs backed off as quickly as they'd appeared, and inside we listened as our guide explained how the porter house served as a base for workers from the highlands. We learned about education initiatives, schools, and even staff holidays awarded to porters, cooks, and guides who were frequently praised in reviews. Knowing how exploitative trekking used to be in this region—porters carrying absurd loads under terrible conditions—it felt good to support a company trying to rewrite that story.

The drive continued on, clinging to cliff edges as though gravity were optional. Two hours later, slightly green but alive, we reached Mollepata, a small Quechua-speaking village where trekkers traditionally fuel up before starting the trail. One tourist-friendly café offered Wi-Fi and half-English menus, but we only stopped for coffee. Our hostel had already packed us breakfast, which felt absurdly thoughtful.

Because the paved road now stretched further in the mountains, the hike itself didn't begin until Challacancha. The scene there surprised me. Hikers everywhere. Mules. Horsemen. Controlled chaos. I'd imagined isolation, silence, maybe a lone condor circling overhead. Instead, it was bustling. Then again, Machu Picchu was a magnet for adventurers all around the world. It made sense that one of the most popular, albeit difficult, routes to reach it would be crowded.

Day one was intentionally gentle. Greenery lined the path, fog rolled in and out, waterfalls appeared unexpectedly, and the incline rose slowly. The altitude made its presence known, thudding in my chest during the first ten minutes, then easing as my body adjusted. Three hours later, we reached our campsite at Soraypampa, 3,900 metres above sea level, where our tents were already pitched and lunch was nearly ready.

The routine of camp life quickly became something I loved. Before every meal, a horseman appeared with a bucket of warm water, a towel, and soap so we could wash our hands. It was such a small thing, but it felt ceremonial, like a gentle reset. Most of the staff spoke no English, which only made the smiles and quiet exchanges feel more genuine.

And the food. My god, the food. I'd listed myself as vegetarian with low expectations. Maybe extra rice, maybe the dreaded default canned pumpkin ravioli. Instead, every single meal came with a thoughtfully prepared vegetarian dish just for me. Real food. Traditional food. Food that tasted like it'd been prepared with effort and care. I felt absurdly spoiled.

We ate, napped hard, woke up to eat again, and repeated the process until dinner, which somehow included popcorn, crackers, tea, multiple mains, and dessert. Cold crept in after sunset, but with good sleeping bags, fleece liners, thermals, gloves, and hats, I was toasty. All that research had paid off. Day one ended feeling… manageable. Almost too manageable.

The next morning arrived at 4:30 a.m. with a familiar call of *"Hola, amigos"* drifting through the tent walls. Day two—the hardest day, we'd been told—had begun.

Carlos unzipped the tent and accepted two metal cups of coca tea from the horseman. Dark yellow, properly brewed, and far better than anything I'd made myself; it warmed my hands and steadied my stomach. Mornings followed a reliable rhythm—drink tea, pack up, leave our bags on a mat, then shuffle toward breakfast. And breakfast, once again, was ridiculous, in the best way. Banana pancakes dripping with *dulce de leche*, omelettes, quinoa fruit salads, hot chocolate, porridge, fresh bread. We were hikers who ate like royalty.

The trail started icy cold, all rocky terrain and dramatic glacial backdrops. Mules darted around us, manure thick in the air. For a while, it felt deceptively doable. Then the path steepened, the temperature dropped, and the altitude started taking its toll.

Strangely, my breathing was fine. Better than fine, actually. As with running, once I was moving, my breath settled into something calm and controlled. My heart, however, had other ideas. It hammered so loudly I was convinced it might burst straight through my chest.

Still, we walked. And walked. And walked. Reaching the Salkantay Pass at 4,650 metres felt surreal. People were scattered everywhere, posing with the sign marking our altitude, grinning through exhaustion. I was thrilled, and then quickly humbled by the realisation that this was only a third of the day done.

After a cheese sandwich and coca tea at the top of the mountain, we began the long descent. Seven hours of it. Loose rocks, knees screaming, constant side-stepping to avoid mules, and profound gratitude for our walking poles. I'd never had knee pain before this hike. That streak ended here.

Lunch appeared mid-mountain, prepared in a tent like some kind of magic trick. Then we descended further, entering into the highland jungle. Glaciers gave way to green pastures, which gave way to dense bush that reminded me of New Zealand. The transformation was dizzying.

By the time we reached Collpapampa in the early evening, I was exhausted but deeply satisfied. We passed campsites boasting bars, massages, and Wi-Fi, but I was relieved ours was quieter, simpler. I hadn't come here for luxury. I'd come to feel this. The simplicity of being in nature. Disconnected from the world but connected to the land.

The following day was labelled "easy," which felt like a cruel joke when roosters started crowing near our tent before dawn. Still, we slept in by trail standards, said goodbye to our horsemen—two men whose quiet pride and hard work had carried us farther than we could have managed alone—and set off again.

My knees ached deeply. Blisters were constantly on the brink of rupture. I stuffed tissues into my socks and hoped for the best. The trail rose and fell relentlessly, sometimes humid and jungle-thick, sometimes narrow and terrifyingly close to cliff edges above a winding river. Landslides scarred the path, reminding us how fragile this route was, especially in the rainy season.

Our guide spoke about fit young hikers struggling mentally with the trek, frustrated by how hard it was despite their strength. I understood completely. Back home, I was the "fit one." Out here, I was just another body adjusting, enduring. And yet, as the path narrowed, I wondered how anyone less prepared could manage it. Some sections simply didn't allow shortcuts. Not even mules could navigate them.

We stopped in a field above the river where a tiny stall sold granadilla fruit grown nearby. We bought some, cracked them open, and laughed at how enormous they were, like passionfruit on steroids. They tasted similar too. Sweet, floral, slightly citrusy. Juicy, jelly-like pulp.

Eventually, we reached La Playa, which was once completely isolated, and still semi-cut off from the world. Lunch was served. Fruits and vegetables shaped as animals appeared on plates, because apparently our chef was now showing off.

When we heard about nearby hot springs within short driving distance, it felt like a gift from the hiking gods. However, the drive there was nerve-wracking. Cliff edges, crumbling roads, near misses. But at least it was worth it. The pools themselves were surprisingly developed and well-maintained. Affordable, and blissfully hot. After obligatory Inca showers that felt like pressure washers pushing down on our spines, we sank into the hot water and let our muscles dissolve. Knees, shoulders, soul. All of it softened after days of strenuous hiking.

As the pools filled with tourists, I felt grateful we'd arrived early. By the time we left, clean and loose-limbed, the day felt complete. I realized that between the glaciers and jungle, exhaustion and awe, discomfort and deep contentment, the Salkantay Trek was teaching me a thing or two about myself. That my strength isn't just about fitness. It's also mental. It's about learning and practicing patience. It's about adjusting expectations of what I'm capable of. It's about showing up, step after step. What a great lesson it all was.

Above the Clouds

- MACHU PICCHU, PERU -

The assistant chef woke us that morning with coca tea, his voice barely louder than the birds. He couldn't have been much older than twenty, painfully shy, and earnest in the way only someone very young and very responsible can be. It was our earliest start yet—4 a.m.—because our guide was determined to get us to a set of Inca ruins high on a nearby mountain before anyone else arrived.

At first, the trail felt oddly modern. A few houses appeared here and there, which was jarring after days of isolation. It was still pitch black, so we walked by head torch, stars scattered thickly above us. I remember thinking that maybe the Mackenzie region in New Zealand didn't have such a monopoly on the world's best night skies after all.

The path itself was different too. Wide cobbled stones instead of slippery mud, steep but intentional, like it had been built to last a very long time. This route was essentially the Salkantay Trek's version of the Inca Trail, and even though we were now walking at a much lower altitude, my calves and thighs burned as we climbed steadily for hours. It hurt, but it was a good hurt. The kind that makes you feel like you achieved something.

We passed coffee bushes along the way, and at one point stopped to drink a cup of coffee made from beans picked just metres away. The coffee was black, slightly acidic, with a mild nutty flavour to it. It was the purest form of coffee I'd ever had.

There was a swing perched at the edge of the mountain, daring people to launch themselves into thin air. While I agreed to swing on it, my memories of a rope snapping mid-swing in Samoa a few months ago still felt a bit too fresh. Nevertheless, the whole experience of swinging in the jungle was magical, even if I had mild PTSD.

As promised by our guide, we reached the top of the mountain before anyone else, arriving at Llactapata.

The view stopped me in my tracks. More than 180 degrees of Machu Picchu National Park stretched out in front of us. You could see Machu Picchu itself in the distance, glaciers gleaming far off, and behind us, the ruins of Llactapata. If you lay down at just the right angle, you could see the sun peeking through the Sun Gate.

The heat arrived quickly once the sun rose fully, and I was grateful the climb had been mostly shaded. Our guide handed each of us a LlamaPath t-shirt printed with the route we'd just conquered. It felt like being given a medal at the end of a marathon. He laughed and said the trek was only for "crazy, adventurous people."

I didn't argue. In fact, I felt proud to belong in that category.

Then came the descent.

Going down is far harder than going up. Uphill burns your lungs and legs; downhill destroys your knees and your brain. Every single step demanded full concentration. One slip, one misjudged foot placement, and you'd be tumbling down a mountainside with no margin for error. But when the trees thinned, the views were unreal. Lush valleys, thick jungle, and glaciers still lingering in the distance, all somehow existing together.

Eventually, the ground flattened and my knees sighed with relief. We reached Santa Teresa, where our guide high-fived each of us before lunch. Technically, this was the end of the trek. *Technically.* But there was still the optional final three-hour walk along the train tracks to Aguas Calientes, which we chose without hesitation. After all, we hadn't come this far to quit early.

Those three hours were the longest of my life. My blisters had given up pretending to be intact. I could feel skin rupturing with every step. Tourists began appearing in droves. Fresh-faced, clean, clearly not several days deep into a wilderness hike. We must have looked feral by comparison with tangled hair, dirt-streaked legs. Like we'd just emerged from the jungle after months rather than days.

As we entered Aguas Calientes, chaos greeted us. A bus—the same kind that ferries people up to Machu Picchu all day—had tipped onto its side moments earlier. Windows shattered. Passengers being evacuated. A black screen quickly erected to hide whatever was underneath. My stomach tightened. Yet another narrowly missed disaster. It felt like a recurring theme after what had happened in Ica with the dune buggies.

Our hotel, when we finally arrived, was a surprise. Not because the tour company had planned for it to be that way, but because I'd just genuinely forgotten. It was a *real* hotel, with a real shower, and a real bed. I had somehow forgotten those things still existed. I've never gasped so loudly in a shower. After all that hiking, the hot water made me feel like I was being reborn.

That night, we gathered for our final group dinner. The restaurant was full of trekking groups celebrating similar endings. Pizza. Lemonade. Tired smiles. I felt unexpectedly emotional. Maybe it was the temporary friendships dissolving. Maybe it was the realisation that I'd just completed the hardest physical thing I'd ever done. I hadn't needed a mule. I hadn't needed oxygen.

I had done it.

The next morning came early again. Machu Picchu day.

Hundreds of people were already queued for the buses; some having waited since the middle of the night. I didn't see the point, since buses didn't start until dawn anyway. But eventually we were ushered on. The drive was thirty minutes of tight hairpin turns and steep drops, climbing hundreds of metres in altitude. Some people hiked up. I absolutely did not. After seventy-seven kilometres on foot, I was happy to sit rather than hike up something that steep.

Machu Picchu was… beautiful. Surreal. Familiar in that uncanny way places feel when you've already seen them a thousand times in photos. Clouds swept quickly across surrounding peaks. The ruins were ancient and undeniably impressive.

And yet, I felt unexpectedly calm.

I realised it wasn't disappointment. It was saturation. We had already seen so much. Glaciers, jungle, remote ruins, coffee grown at altitude, fruit plucked fresh from the land, stars blazing above our tents. Machu Picchu was incredible, yes, but the magic was the journey to it. Without the hike, you miss the point. You miss the transformation.

I knew that was ironic given that we'd skipped the last portion that morning, but at least we'd done the entire Salkany Trek to get to this point, rather than just hop on a train from Cusco. Plus, the part we'd skipped was just walking along the road going up.

We wandered for a few hours, then boarded another bus—this time with me clinging nervously to Carlos' hand—before sheltering in the hotel lobby as rain hammered down like a jungle drumbeat. The journey back to Cusco involved trains, buses, coaches, and one very lost taxi driver with no GPS. Eventually, we found our Airbnb.

Home, for the next few nights.

I pulled the scratchy woollen blankets over my aching body. After days of pushing it to its limits, I realized that not only did I have incredible memories of mountain tops, lush jungle, soaking in hot water pools, eating and drinking straight from the land. I also had a newfound appreciation, respect, and trust in my body. The quiet pride of knowing that when I had to, I could in fact keep walking. And walking. And walking.

After the Summit

- CUSCO, PERU -

The following day was dedicated entirely to rest. The good kind of tired. The "I just walked seventy-seven kilometres through mountains and jungle" tired. We woke early anyway, because our bodies hadn't yet learned how to sleep in. At least the Airbnb had two affectionate cats who seemed determined to help us recover.

Our only real mission for the next few days was returning gear. That done, we stumbled upon a slightly dodgy-looking market that became our unofficial dining room. Food stalls lined the aisles, women smiling as they cooked right in front of you, calling out for more vegetables when supplies ran low. Everything was simple, generous, fresh. A sandwich, an omelette, a mountain of vegetables. We ate perched at benches like kids at a kitchen counter.

It was cheap. It was nourishing. It felt grounding.

We bought a tourist pass that promised entry to an unrealistic number of museums, and we felt morally obligated to get our money's worth.

So we declared it Museum Day.

Armed with our non-vacationy body clocks and fuelled by breakfast from our new favourite place—the slightly dodgy market with the life-changing vegetarian sandwiches—we set out with a one directional focus. Museum by museum. In, out, tick.

Most of the museums were small. Some were genuinely interesting. Some were not. But the one that stuck with me was a collection of skulls from the Nasca region, hundreds of years old, bearing clear evidence of cranial surgery. Holes cut clean through bone. Shapes deliberately altered. And somehow, a reported success rate of sixty percent. Whatever success actually meant in that context.

I couldn't even wrap my head around modern surgery statistics, let alone ancient ones. The longer we stayed in Peru, the more I was exposed to ideas that sat well outside my usual worldview. Hallucinogens as rites of passage, creative awakenings, cosmic connections, visions of the future, communication with aliens. At first, I'd dismissed it all as nonsense. Then, slowly, something shifted. I realised I couldn't actually prove any of it *wasn't* true. And really, who am I to decide what's real and what isn't?

By lunchtime, we'd conquered the entire museum list. Efficiency at its finest. With the afternoon stretching ahead of us, we turned uphill toward Sacsayhuamán, the Inca ruins perched above Cusco. People had told us they were, in some ways, even more impressive than Machu Picchu.

They were extraordinary. Enormous stone blocks, some polished smooth, fitted together so precisely it made modern engineering feel a bit embarrassing. Standing there, staring at stones that had been moved centuries ago without cranes or machinery, I felt that familiar itch of wonder. This wasn't just a Peruvian mystery. The same question marks hovered over Stonehenge, the Pyramids, Angkor Wat, Easter Island. It all felt like evidence of a missing chapter in human history. Something we haven't quite figured out yet.

And then the sky turned on us.

Hail. Heavy rain. Thunder cracking overhead. We tried sheltering under a tree, which was laughably inadequate, then sprinted to a wooden structure where we waited, damp and hopeful. The weather teased us with a brief lull, then came back harder. Eventually, soaked and cold, we admitted defeat. Walking back down the slippery stone steps felt like a genuine death wish, so we decided to find a taxi.

We knew the going rate. Five to eight soles. So when a driver said "ten," we refused and stood stubbornly under shelter in the pouring rain. It wasn't about the money, it was about the principle. About seventy New Zealand cents' worth of principle. The taxi also looked suspiciously unofficial, which only fuelled our resolve. Eventually, he caved and agreed to eight soles. Victory. We climbed into the dodgy taxi, smug and triumphant, only to realise, at the end of the ride, that we only had a ten-sole note. With mild shame, we handed it over. He gave us change. Yikes.

Any lingering embarrassment was quickly erased by our next decision: massages. Cusco is absolutely saturated with massage offers. Every two metres, a young woman is calling out "*Masajes, masajes*!" There's clearly a thriving market, especially with so many hikers limping back into town. But given my background in people trafficking research, I was deeply uninterested in wandering blindly into somewhere questionable. So we did our homework and found a legitimate place near the Plaza de Armas called Nueva Vida.

Upstairs, it looked like a therapeutic cow shed. One large room divided by multiple curtains that didn't quite close. Bodies everywhere. Half-naked limbs appearing and disappearing. This was my first ever proper full-body massage, and I was painfully awkward. Carlos, who gets massages regularly, was completely unfazed. I, meanwhile, whispered questions like, "Do I take my bra off?" and "What about my socks?" I kept both on because his answer was so vague. But that decision did not last long when the masseuse started asking me rapid questions about my attire in Spanish.

Despite my initial stiffness—emotional, not muscular—the massage was incredible. An hour of bliss for about twenty New Zealand dollars. With my face pressed into the table, rain and thunder rumbling outside, it was easy to pretend we were alone, rather than in a room with about twenty other people. My body melted. My brain finally shut up. Ten out of ten. Would absolutely recommend.

To round out an already gentle day, we wandered into an Irish pub called Paddy's on the main square. Carlos wanted a beer. I wanted a cup of hot tea. Outside, hail rattled against the windows. Inside, fairy lights glowed, soccer played on a screen, and something in me warmed up. It had been a decade since I'd lived in the UK, but sitting there with tea and beer and rain pounding outside stirred a quiet nostalgia. Comfort in an unexpected place.

The next day arrived without a plan. Or rather, with only the loosest version of one. We had vague anchors—Spanish school in Sucre, a flight from Santiago to Patagonia, a few road trips, Christmas in Argentina—but everything in between was still a question mark. And somehow, that was becoming our strength. We were good at this now. Booking buses with hours to spare. Finding beds at the last minute. Not knowing where we'd be tomorrow, only that we'd figure it out. It was a skill in itself.

We spent the day visiting tour companies, seeing what was possible. It was exhausting. Sleazy salesmen. Inflated prices. Half-truths. I felt my patience thinning, and my lack of Spanish more acutely than usual. Even when language wasn't a barrier, there were frequent moments when I wasn't even asked my name or what I did for work. Those questions were directed straight at Carlos, which made it very clear whose opinion was being courted. The sexism wasn't subtle. I felt like I was just seen as a quiet accessory.

After hours of this, plus a free walking tour and helpful feedback that jungle tours nearby were so lacklustre you don't even see mosquitoes, clarity finally emerged. Snow was forecast for Rainbow Mountain. The jungle involved a ten-hour bus ride. Lake Titicaca began to glow quietly in our minds. Sometimes the right decision isn't the most exciting one. It's the one that feels right in your gut. So we booked a bus to Puno that evening for the next morning.

We returned to the market one last time. The women there asked if we'd be back tomorrow. We smiled. It was another goodbye for us.

Back at the Airbnb, we spent the evening tangled up with the two outrageously affectionate cats, soaking in the last of Cusco's familiar comforts.

And just like that, another chapter closed. After the crazy hike to Machu Picchu, those last few days in Cusco had been a pause *and* a pivot. A chance to rest sore muscles, question old assumptions, laugh at ourselves, and practise the art of choosing what came next without certainty. Between ancient skulls, stubborn taxi negotiations, awkward massages, and cups of tea in foreign pubs, I was proud of myself for slowly building the skill of just making it all work. I was less rushed. Less rigid. More trusting.

I was genuinely getting so good at winging it, and I really liked that about myself.

Letting the Road Decide

- PUNO, PERU -

Leaving a Peruvian city felt familiar by now. Another early morning, another cab ride, another terminal. Six soles later, we were back at the station where we'd started weeks earlier, backpacks slung over shoulders, mentally bracing for whatever version of South American transport we'd been handed this time. Because we'd booked so last minute, our options were slim. We chose the least terrifying one and hoped for the best.

At check-in, hope briefly wobbled. Our seats had been changed. Split up. Carlos argued, politely but firmly, until the woman behind the counter explained that one of their buses had broken down that morning. It was barely 7 a.m., which didn't exactly inspire confidence. Those passengers had been reshuffled and given priority. Eventually, after a bit of back and forth, she managed to seat us together again.

Honestly, things like this barely registered as stress anymore. By this point, South America had taught us to laugh first and problem-solve second. Things rarely went exactly as planned, but they usually worked out. If you liked rigid schedules and predictability, this continent would eat you alive. If you could roll with it, you'd be fine.

We grabbed a makeshift breakfast—coffee, cake, a doughy *empanada*—from a stand outside the terminal, failed spectacularly at locating a toilet, and boarded our bus. That's when we realised we'd somehow landed on a luxury tourist coach filled with other foreigners on guided tours. Plush seats. Near-bed-level recline. A driver who didn't seem intent on testing the laws of physics. We didn't arrive on time, naturally, but we arrived intact, which by now felt like the only metric that mattered.

The landscape shifted again. Drier. Barer. Women in traditional Quechua and Aymara clothing appeared along the roadside, rainbow-coloured woven bags slung across their backs, babies tucked inside. The clouds looked different at nearly 4,000 metres. Thicker, closer, almost three-dimensional, like I'd slipped on a pair of invisible 3D glasses.

We passed through a town I thought was Puno and immediately panicked. It looked brutal. Dust everywhere, rubbish piled high, only one paved street, buildings barricaded and raw. I felt my stomach drop with nerves…

then realised we were in Juliaca. Relief washed over me like I'd narrowly avoided a bad dream.

Our actual destination, Puno, didn't exactly smell like a dream either. The bus station reeked of sewage. It was intense. But I reminded myself that I'd felt the same way arriving in Ica, where we'd tiptoed around leaking sewage only for it to become one of my favourite places in Peru. First impressions weren't everything.

Puno shared some of that same unfinished feel as Ica. blocky brick buildings, dry roads, battered cars belching black fumes. But I sensed there might be something more dangerous about it. Our Airbnb helped ease my nerves. A petite, elegant elderly woman greeted us with a smile and showed us to our room. A big bed, private bathroom, TV. The shower ran so hot I stood under it until my skin turned an alarming shade of red. *Bliss.*

We wandered briefly and confirmed what we'd suspected—there wasn't much to do. Which was perfect. We were actively trying to rebalance after weeks of relentless movement. Ninety percent adventure, ten percent rest hadn't been sustainable. We found a cosy restaurant offering a tourist set menu, ate just enough, and went home to do absolutely nothing. It was exactly what we needed.

The next day, we discovered we'd accidentally landed in Puno during a public holiday—Santa Rosa, celebrating the national police. Breakfast out was humbling. Carlos' plate arrived with one single strip of bacon and what looked like two tablespoons of scrambled eggs. We laughed so hard it almost made it worth the inflated tourist price they'd charged us.

Drawn by noise and colour, we headed to the Plaza de Armas, where the celebration was in full swing. Police and military lined the square. Flags waved. Trumpets blared. Guns fired ceremonial shots into the air. Under a brutally blue sky, I wore my raincoat hood purely to save my scalp from roasting. Multiple versions of Santa Rosa herself were paraded around the square, carried like queens on thrones by dozens of people. It was strange and theatrical and fascinating, and we stayed far longer than we meant to.

Later, we searched unsuccessfully for a Cusco-style vegetable market and instead wandered into one that smelled overwhelmingly of meat and carcass. It was enough to kill my appetite instantly. Carlos, however, ordered a bowl of chicken soup and declared it some of the best food he'd had in South America. All for just eight soles.

We hadn't been there long, but Puno confused me. It forced me to slow down, which I needed. And it had fewer tourists, fewer people hustling you, less noise. But I couldn't quite imagine staying there for long. We had one more night booked, and then decisions loomed about what to do next.

When the Body Says No

- LAKE TITICACA, PERU -

By the following day, my body decided for me. I was catastrophically unwell. Weak, aching, barely able to walk. By early afternoon, I surrendered and crawled into bed, where I stayed. Curled up, miserable, unsure what exactly had gone wrong. My appetite had been fading for days, and now it felt like my body had simply hit a wall. We were meant to head to the islands on Lake Titicaca the next morning. Nothing was booked. I told myself I'd decide after sleeping.

Sleep was awful. Painful. Restless. But when morning came, I wasn't dead, which felt like progress. I dressed with the help of clothes Carlos had kindly laid out, grabbed our small day backpacks, and we set off. The port was only a twenty-five-minute walk, and we planned to be back the following evening. Manageable. Doable.

Buying tickets was straightforward. Thirty soles for the boat. Eight soles per island. The lake was glassy smooth as we pulled away, the boat slow and deliberate. The first stop was the floating reed islands also known as the Uros. Squishy underfoot. Ingenious. Ancient. These islands are man-made anchored platforms constructed from woven Totora reeds. But the whole experience was also uncomfortably performative. There was dancing, singing, demonstrations, and then pressure—try the clothes, now buy the crafts. The same crafts I'd seen everywhere else in Peru, but now triple the price. Guilt hung thick in the air, reinforced by our guide reminding us that tourism was how these communities survived. I understood that. I also understood that something about the transaction felt off and it made me uncomfortable with participating any longer.

When we finally left for Amantaní Island, I slept the entire three-hour boat ride.

We arrived to find Quechan families waiting for stragglers like us. We, and a French couple, joined a young local and trudged uphill to her family's home, every step draining what little energy I had left from my lingering illness.

The house was simple. Courtyard. Two spare bedrooms. Tiny kitchen. Solar panels. A flushing toilet. It felt like time had folded back on itself. Due to poverty, they ate mostly vegetarian food produced from the land behind their house. Ironically, it was my dream diet, though I could barely manage more than a few mouthfuls of soup and fried cheese at lunch. Tea, however, I could handle. Buckets of it.

Feeling faint and sicker than ever, I slept through the afternoon, missing the hike to the island's peaks. And then, suddenly, something changed. I woke up feeling somewhat better. Not perfect, but alive.

I wandered outside and ended up playing with the family's five-year-old, then soccer with the neighbour's kids, then chasing chickens and patting pregnant donkeys. The absurd contrast made me laugh. From bed-bound to wheelbarrow races in two hours.

At dinner, I ate properly for the first time in days. Potato soup. Rice with eggs and vegetables. Cups of tea. My appetite roared back. Sitting there, I realised how ironic it was that this "simple" way of eating—fresh, local, plant-based—was born of necessity here, while back home it was an expensive lifestyle aspiration.

I slept deeply, despite spiders and spring mattresses, grateful in a way that felt heavier than words. How lucky was I to be having such an authentic experience in the depths of Peru? Such a contrast from the Uros experience earlier.

Morning came with pancakes and tea. We said our goodbyes, paid the family in cash directly, and walked down to the port with the mother and youngest daughter, who waved as we boarded the boat. The lake shimmered. It was beautiful. But the baton of illness passed quickly. Now, Carlos was falling apart.

Taquile Island was harder than the previous islands. Rocky paths, altitude, steep climbs. Carlos barely made it, though the views at the top—deep blue water, snowy mountains, Peru on one side, Bolivia on the other—were worth it. Borders always feel strange from that height. Lines humans draw across landscapes that don't care.

We skipped lunch, found shade, waited it out. On the ride back, Carlos lay stretched out while strangers offered medicine. I watched the islands slide past, reeds thick in the water, the sun unrelenting at four thousand metres. The perfect setting for self-reflection.

Puno and Lake Titicaca slowed us down whether we liked it or not. It was a humbling reminder that travel isn't just about chasing highlights; it's about listening when your body, or the road, tells you to stop.

Between sickness, kindness, floating islands, and quiet lakeside afternoons, I realised how important it was to drop the sense of urgency to do and see it all. Instead, I had to remember that part of this adventure was also learning *how* to move through it all and pivot when needed.

Across the Lake

- COPACABANA, BOLIVIA -

Back in Puno, we walked slowly to our Airbnb, ordered pizza and fries, and collapsed. This bout of illness really was kicking our butts and we needed to rest up for the next adventure the following morning to Bolivia.

We'd read the horror stories, but we'd done our research. Instead of risking a sketchy overnight bus to La Paz, we opted for a shorter hop to Copacabana, just over the border.

The crossing itself was laughably easy. Paperwork done on the bus. Exit stamp out of Peru. Walk uphill in a weird no man's land space. Entry stamp into Bolivia. Done. Easiest border I'd crossed outside Europe. Ten minutes later, we were in Bolivia.

Copacabana surprised me. Quiet. Lakeside. Sunlit. Our hostel sat up a steep hill with llamas in the garden and a view of boats bobbing gently on the water. We checked in early, ate an unexpectedly gourmet lunch, and did nothing for the rest of the day. Fries. Pancakes. Ice cream. Hot chocolate.

Proof that we were finally learning how to rest. There wasn't much to do in Copacabana that day anyway. Short strolls, read books, eat.

By the time we left Copacabana, I'd lost count of how many buses we'd taken in South America. They'd started to blur together. Terminals, plastic bags of takeaway drinks, cramped seats. That particular combination of excitement and mild dread you only feel when your life depends on someone else's driving skills.

We were determined to have a slow morning the next day. We lazed right up until checkout and then wandered upstairs for breakfast, only to discover that in Bolivia (or at least in this restaurant), "midday closure" apparently meant 10 a.m. We stood there, mildly annoyed, hungry, and then shrugged. *Fine.* We'd go explore.

It turned out to be the best little inconvenience, because we found an absolute gem of a bakery called Pit Stop. I'm talking proper fresh sweet-and-savoury heaven, tucked near where the bus had dropped us off the day before. *Empanadas* were seven bolivianos each, which felt like an invitation to eat until we exploded. We bought six. Then we added a slice of spinach and cheese pie, a *dulce de leche* pastry, and a chocolate oat slice. I ate like I'd been starving for months, and saved the rest for the road like a smug little squirrel.

We'd booked with a company called TurisBus this time around. More expensive, good ratings. I was optimistic that we'd arrive in La Paz alive. It was funny, because months earlier, I'd pitched buses to Carlos as the authentic way to travel South America. You know, mingle with locals, see real life, absorb culture from a sticky vinyl seat. The reality was that the authentic buses were often the ones that terrified us. Too many terrible stories, too many avoidable tragedies. Speed, exhaustion, drivers high or drunk. Sure, statistically we'd probably survive. But neither of us felt like gambling our bodies on probability.

So instead of a bus full of locals, we ended up in what was basically a private shuttle. Just me, Carlos, and one other tourist. Not exactly authentic, but it felt relatively safe.

We boarded at Hotel Rosario, me wearing my backpack front-and-back like an overburdened turtle and a sweater wrapped around my head to save my scalp from being char-grilled. Definitely not the look of most glossy backpacking photos you see on Instagram.

The drive was stunning. Lake Titicaca shimmered royal blue beside us, the hills around it dry-green and yellow, and beyond that the mountains looked almost aggressive. Dark grey, sharp, snow-capped. Our driver blasted the most cliché white-person playlist imaginable while absolutely sending it down the road at around 130 km/h. And then, just when I'd settled into the rhythm of "this is beautiful but also I might die," we rolled down to the lake edge, and the driver calmly drove the shuttle onto a floating wooden platform with an engine attached.

A literal car ferry. Except it looked like it had been made in someone's backyard.

We just sat there, in the shuttle, on a slab of wood, floating across the lake alongside trucks and gigantic buses as if this was the most normal commute in the world.

That's travel in a nutshell, isn't it? The constant exposure to "wait, *what?*" moments. One day you're casually crossing a lake on a wooden raft with a rowdy engine glued on, and your brain just files it under "that time in Bolivia."

Something about it made me flash back to a bus ride years earlier through the Serbian countryside. Me alone, music on my phone, the guy beside me watching what I was scrolling. Eventually, instead of guarding my screen with paranoia, I handed him a headphone (which was corded in those days) and we listened together. I played him New Zealand music, indicating it was kiwi music by showing him New Zealand on Google maps. In turn, he showed Serbian music. We didn't speak a common language, and that was the only interaction we had. That was the kind of "authentic bus experience" I'd imagined throughout this trip in South America. And here I was in Bolivia, on a private shuttle, listening to an iPod playlist from 2009 and thinking, well… *close enough.*

A City That Refused Expectations

- LA PAZ, BOLIVIA -

We reached La Paz in record time, and I was immediately obsessed. I'd arrived with almost no expectations. My entire knowledge base was basically "Bolivia is supposedly a worse version of Peru," *ouch*. But Copacabana had already softened that assumption, and now La Paz blew it up entirely. The city spilled down into a crater-like valley, packed tight and sprawling, framed by mountains like a dramatic stage set. It looked alive.

We were starving, disoriented, and cursed with non-functional Wi-Fi in our room, meaning no frantic Googling of "best vegetarian food La Paz." So we did what we always do when technology fails. We walked until something looked promising.

We briefly considered an English pub, but it didn't feel right. Then we stumbled upon a place called Higher Ground and immediately clocked it as Australian. Vegemite toast. Flat white coffees. The whole vibe screaming Aussie expat refuge. We went in anyway and ordered like we hadn't eaten in days, including Vegemite toast on the side. Sometimes you want comfort served as salty nostalgia, even though they made the rookie error of not putting butter on first.

While I'm English and definitely sound it, I realised how much I feel at home in that down-under cultural space. Probably because New Zealand had held my adult life for so long. Sitting there with music I recognised, especially songs I'd heard back home, made me relax in a way I hadn't noticed I'd needed.

The next day, La Paz kept surprising me. It wasn't even meant to be a big stop for us. It was just a practical pause before Spanish school in Sucre. But the city had a buzz. It was messy, vivid, unapologetic. Peru had left me oddly conflicted at times, and I'd struggled to name why. Standing in La Paz, I think I finally found the shape of it.

Peru sometimes felt like it knew it was being watched. Like it performed itself a little. It was hard to get the authentic version given how touristy it was. Bolivia, at least in these first days, felt more like "this is us, take it or leave it." And that bluntness was weirdly refreshing.

We joined a walking tour with Red Cap. Again, I will always, always use a walking tour to orient myself in a city. But here, "free" tours are illegal. There was a small admin fee, and then you tip. Therefore, it wasn't free. Easy.

We started near San Pedro prison, where the guide gave a stern warning about prison tours. Apparently, it used to be a bit of a thing. Tourists partying with prisoners, dodgy people offering access, the whole situation screaming bad idea. The prison has its own internal economy; prisoners pay rent, run businesses, families can live in and come and go. Fascinating in theory. In practice? Hard pass. At the end of the day, they're prisoners, and there's no scenario where that's the quirky experience it gets marketed as.

From there we walked through the Witches' Market, which was a lot to process. Llama foetuses hung in clusters like grotesque wind chimes. The guide said they had to have died naturally for it to be a legal sale, but I found that hard to believe when there were so many of them. It turned my stomach in a way that was less "culture shock" and more "this feels wrong."

Around the foetuses were potions promising love, obedience, better behaviour. Little bottles of human desperation dressed up as magic. Souvenirs piled beside them, bright and familiar, similar to Peru. It was the strangest mix of sacred, commercial, and unsettling.

We were also warned that Bolivians are more sensitive to having their photo taken. Which should be a universal rule anyway. Ask first, always. But of course, there was a couple on our tour acting like everyone existed for their camera roll. The woman kept lifting her camera into people's faces and got everything from stern finger-wagging to outright shouting. One Bolivian woman covered her eyes with a notebook until we were gone. It made my skin crawl. Not because of the reactions, but because of the entitlement that caused them. Some people are idiots.

The tour took us through a local market that felt instantly familiar in the best way. Stalls of vegetables, juices, bits of chaos, and the kind of food you can eat leaning against a counter with your backpack still on. We found our new favourite place and returned repeatedly, buying enormous avocado-cheese-tomato sandwiches and litres of fresh juice for around a dollar each.

We finished the tour near our hostel and were ushered upstairs for a little (and secret) political talk. It was timed perfectly, because we'd had to dodge the main plaza where a big protest was brewing. We got the pros, cons, and "it's complicated" version of Bolivian politics, then ended with free shots of something delicious and fruity that I couldn't name even if you threatened me.

After that, we hopped on the Teleférico—La Paz's cable car system—and I genuinely could not stop grinning. Driving into a city in one of the poorest countries in South America and discovering a sprawling, functional cable car network used as everyday public transport was not what I expected. I'd assumed it was a tourist gimmick. Nope. It's genuinely how people commute. For three bolivianos you float over the whole city like a little human ornament, watching neighbourhoods shift beneath you for hours. It was peaceful, surreal, and completely brilliant. La Paz, again, surprised me by just how cool it was.

Rule Number One: Don't Be a F***ing Idiot

- DEATH ROAD, BOLIVIA -

And then came then Death Road, known locally as Yungas.

We hadn't planned to do it. It had always sat in the category of "cool idea until you understand what it is." But then we did last-minute research, found Gravity, which is the oldest, best-reviewed, and most expensive company. And convinced ourselves that if you're going to do something objectively terrifying, you might as well do it with the people least likely to let you die.

Gravity's vibe was very clear from the start. The guide's first instruction, delivered with a grin that wasn't entirely a joke, was "Rule number one. Don't be a f***ing idiot."

Fair enough.

We met at Higher Ground (great coincidence), got breakfast poured loosely into plastic bags (including our coffee and orange juice), and joined a big group of riders. Our guide, Noel, briefed us in the bus. We started at La Cumbre, around 4,700 metres above sea level, did a quick ritual for *Pachamama* by pouring a bit of 98% alcohol on the ground and our tyres, then taking a microscopic sip like we were tasting death itself. And then we were off. A sixty-four-kilometre bike ride along one of the most dangerous routes in the world.

The first section was paved road, meant to warm us up. It was still terrifying. We were flying downhill at speeds that made my brain scream *this is not a warm-up, this is a chase scene.* I tried to keep up, felt myself falling behind, and then was advised by the guide that the laws of physics were simply different for my smaller body. Gravity helps, yes. But it helps taller, heavier people more.

Then someone in front of me flipped over his handlebars.

He bounced on his head, crumpled into his bike, and started snoring. Unconscious, like a cartoon, except it was all completely real. My heart stopped. The guides moved instantly. Calm, competent, no panic. They controlled the scene, soothed his friend, assessed him, got him into the support vehicle. No ambulances. Just them. This was the moment it hit me. This is exactly why you pay for the legit company. It's not the gear. It's what happens when the worst thing happens.

After that, any leftover ego about keeping up vanished. I rode at the speed I needed. Brakes became my my absolute focus. Front brake: worst enemy. Back brake: the one you grab when you want to live. I stayed cautious, and I still had fun. Because even with fear humming in your bones, you can't deny how wildly beautiful it is to descend from the high, cold altitude into thick, green jungle.

We cycled through waterfalls, past valleys that looked painted, with drops so steep they didn't feel real. At one point, there was a sheer fall of around 400 metres right beside the track. My body responded by clenching every muscle it owns. One slip and that was it. I was done.

We learned about the road's history. When it was the main route north, hundreds of people a year died on it. The name *"El Camino de la Muerte"* wasn't branding. It was fact. The guides told stories. Some so dark they didn't feel like they belonged in the sunlight. And the road itself didn't need embellishment. Loose gravel, blind corners, thin edges. It all made sense.

Halfway through, everything in my hands started to ache from constant braking. My bum went numb from violent vibrations of biking over chunky rocks. This is the part people don't put on Instagram. Yes, you're doing something iconic; but you are also destroying every part of your body in doing so.

Carlos and I wore the thick, biker-like waterproof gear the whole time. Not because we were chilly, but because we'd both decided that if we fell, we'd like to keep our skin attached to our bodies. Which was smart, because near the waterfalls the rocks got looser and bigger, and that's when Carlos slipped. I'd been too scared to look back for a while, and when I finally did, he was gone. The silence was terrifying. My brain instantly leapt to the worst possible outcome. I turned around, searching for about ten minutes until eventually another couple passed and told me he was fine. Just a small accident.

Eventually I found him. Back on his bike, face pinched with pain, leg grazed. He'd pulled up his waterproof pants for air, and promptly lost traction on a loose rock. Easy to do. Too easy.

Near the end, his pain worsened and our hands were cramping so badly we had to keep stopping to shake them out. When we reached the last checkpoint, we climbed into the support vehicle and called it quits. No shame. No regrets. We'd already done the hard part and completed ninety percent of the ride. And honestly, it felt amazing to sit down and look at the landscape instead of trying not to die in it. The whole thing was another reminder of why fitness is important. It means you can enjoy your experience as much as possible with minimum fatigue and/or pain. It means more opportunities to enjoy the scenery around you.

Then, because apparently we hadn't learned our lesson about fear, we went zip lining.

I'd never zip lined before. Not even in New Zealand, where you could probably zip line to the supermarket in some towns. Our tour company, Gravity, offered it as an add-on, and we thought, well, if they're legit, surely this is legit too. But upon arrival, we noticed that the gear looked rusty and sketchy. We weren't the only ones on the tour to point that out. I had a moment of pure, primal "absolutely not. I want a refund."

And then I watched others go. Realised I wouldn't get my money back. And did it anyway.

I flew one and a half kilometres across a valley at something like 85 km/h, heart dropping through my body, adrenaline turning my blood into electricity. And then I did it again. And again. Three lines. Three separate moments of thinking, this is how people become headlines. "*Young backpackers die tragically zip lining in remote Bolivian jungle.*" And then... landing safely. Laughing. Shaking. Feeling weirdly proud.

Afterwards, we ate late buffet lunch. Pasta, salad, beer. While monkeys clambered around outside the restaurant like they were part of the décor. People watched videos of other Death Road experiences. Crashes, of bikes slipping, of everything going wrong, and I was intensely grateful we were seeing them after we'd ridden.

We merged with another group due to the earlier accident, and by the time we loaded into the bus home, everyone was buzzing: exhausted, euphoric, bonded in that way strangers become when you've shared a day of controlled danger.

And then the bus turned into a party.

Beers. *Cuba Libres.* Singing at the top of our lungs. Stars outside. Millions of them, sharp and bright away from city lights. Every time we hit one of the many police or drug checkpoints, we'd hide our drinks, sit up straight, pretend we were innocent choir kids. As soon as we passed, the bus erupted again. Drinks raised, cheers, music blasting. It was ridiculous and perfect.

The guides were the best kind of chaotic. Mountain biking guys who loved a drink and to party, but who took safety deadly seriously during the day. When things went wrong, they were professional and calm. They checked on everyone. They made sure we felt okay. They were exactly the people you want when you're doing something with "Death" in the name.

One of them was a Kiwi from Wellington, which felt increasingly inevitable. We asked how he ended up guiding Death Road tours in Bolivia, and his story started with: "Well, I'd been working for a few years, so I decided to take six months off to travel South America… and then things happened… and it's been a year and a half…"

I wondered if we'd be telling a similar story in a year or so.

By the time we stumbled back into La Paz, dusty, aching, adrenaline-sore, I felt wrung out in the best way. Like my nervous system had been through a washing machine but come out cleaner. Bolivia had already cracked open my assumptions and replaced them with something better. Sharper, more honest, more alive. This wasn't the "worse Peru" I'd been warned about. It was its own beast entirely. Raw, funny, confronting, unexpectedly modern, and absolutely not interested in performing for tourists.

Just One More Night

- LA PAZ, BOLIVIA -

By our third day in the La Paz area, we'd fully accepted that we were supposed to have left the city already, but wanted just one more night. This was becoming a theme. We'd arrive somewhere with low expectations and a tight plan, and then the place would quietly win us over, and suddenly we'd be "just staying one more night" like it was the most reasonable thing in the world. La Paz did that to us. It was fun. It was chaotic in a way that felt alive rather than threatening. And we'd fallen into a comfortable little routine of walking until our legs went numb, buying yet another five-boliviano avocado sandwich and fresh juice from the market, and topping it off with a three-boliviano soft serve from our new favourite ice cream spot.

We were also getting braver about calling people out when they tried to pull the classic tourist tax. Carlos wanted a *papa rellena*—this deep-fried ball of mashed potato with a surprise in the middle (meat, cheese, egg… essentially a Russian roulette snack). The woman told him it would be seven bolivianos. He pointed out that yesterday it had been six. She didn't even pretend to be offended. It was more like, *ah yes, you've noticed.* And just like that, it was six again. South America was slowly teaching us that prices were sometimes less like rules and more like opening offers.

With the protests settled down a bit, we finally made it to Plaza Murillo, the main square that had been off-limits earlier. It was… a lot. Not politically this time. But ornithologically. The square was carpeted in pigeons. Thousands of them, covering every inch like a living, cooing, feathered rug. We later realised it was entirely fuelled by women selling corn so people could feed them, which felt both entrepreneurial and vaguely sinister. We sat there for ages anyway, just listening to the constant coo-coo-coo like we'd wandered into a pigeon-themed meditation retreat.

Above the square sat a church with a clock that was supposedly "backwards." Something to do with symbolizing southern hemisphere identity and anti-colonialism values. Both the numbers and hand movements were inverted, so it moved from one to twelve in an anticlockwise direction. It was quite confusing.

We walked until we were properly hungry and then annihilated an entire pizza each at a cute place called Little Italy. After that, we started the slow climb to the bus station. An uphill, twenty-minute slog that was still faster than taking a taxi in La Paz traffic.

I felt a bit self-conscious, trudging along with my backpack like a turtle, after hearing that traditional Quechua/Aymara men found women carrying huge bags attractive. I wasn't sure if that was supposed to make me feel better or worse, but either way, there I was. Sexy, apparently. Struggling uphill with my gigantic backpack.

That night, we boarded the bus to Sucre with one goal: arrive alive.

The driver treated "7:30 p.m. departure" as more of a suggestion than an obligation. People kept climbing on to sell us things. Entire roast chickens (who buys a whole roast chicken on a bus?), bottled water, emergency power banks, and at one point a woman who sang for change like we were on some chaotic moving stage show. We stopped constantly. Eventually a few passengers got off to shout at the driver to get on with it because he'd literally pulled over to buy a Coke. And this bus, for added spice, had neither toilets nor seatbelts. So we made regular bathroom stops at places that looked like they were invented as a punishment for travelling by bus. One toilet stop in the middle of nowhere required you to "flush" using a plastic jug and a giant drum of water, which didn't flush so much as gently dilute your shame.

Somehow we made it in one piece.

Spanish School

- SUCRE, BOLIVIA -

Sucre greeted us with terracotta roofs and a warmth that felt like a reward for surviving the bus. We were late, obviously, and arrived with absolutely no clue how to get to our homestay. We'd signed up for two weeks of Spanish school and chosen to stay with a family, which sounded wholesome and slightly terrifying in equal measure. But the address was confusing, Google Maps was having a breakdown, and we stood there with our bags feeling like idiots.

Then a woman at the information desk saved us. She gave us directions and, more importantly, handed over the golden rule of taxis here: don't ask the price. Just hand over a ten-boliviano note at the end. We only had a twenty. Without missing a beat, she swapped it for two tens so we wouldn't get messed around. I loved her instantly.

The system worked perfectly. We got out of the taxi, handed over the ten with full confidence, and for once there was no drama. We buzzed into the building and were met by our host dad, who didn't look Bolivian at all. He greeted us enthusiastically, and we later learned he was a glorious mix of Mexican, Bolivian, and Austrian.

Upstairs, the rest of the family appeared. Host mum, three young kids, and a tiny sausage dog. It was so much better than I'd imagined. I'd pictured an elderly couple, a slightly worn spare room, polite awkwardness, maybe a crocheted doily somewhere. Instead, we landed in a warm, comfortable apartment with a young family and a genuinely nice vibe. Plus, it was only a twenty-minute walk to school.

And then came the absolute luxury. Unpacking properly for the first time in six weeks.

We hung up coats with absurd excitement. We put underwear in drawers like we were performing a sacred ritual. We placed electronics in a bedside table and just stood there, drinking in the novelty of having a place for things. It's hard to explain how thrilling it is to stop living out of a bag. In that moment it didn't matter that we were still technically backpacking. For the first time in ages, we had a "home" shape around us.

After breakfast with the family, we went to the school to sit a Spanish placement exam, which was humiliating in the funniest possible way. Carlos grew up speaking Spanish at home but couldn't really read or write it. I had done five short lessons eighteen months earlier and mostly knew how to count to ten and name a few colours. So when the test demanded tense changes and grammar rules, we both ended up laughing out loud like two idiots in detention. It obviously didn't go well. But that was also literally why we were here.

The day filled up quickly. A chaotic SIM card mission, getting trapped in traffic because a parade for the Virgin of Sucre decided to materialise around us, and then lunch of wraps, beans, vegetables, before we finally wandered out on foot to explore.

Sucre immediately made sense to me. It had that "big enough to be fun, small enough to be navigable" energy. It reminded me of a university city called Dunedin back in New Zealand in the best way. Walkable, friendly, quietly charming without needing to show off.

There was dancing in the streets, street food everywhere, and I ate the best cake of my entire life for seven bolivianos from a street vendor. *Seven* bolivianos. I have paid far more money for far less. We even found a vegetarian restaurant without trying particularly hard.

The next day was essential pre-school admin. Finalising the SIM card process. We already knew the SIM itself was five bolivianos, but the guy tried to charge ten. Carlos immediately said no. The guy immediately backtracked as if he hadn't just tried it. It was annoying in that constant, low-level way. Like being reminded repeatedly that to a lot of people, you are a walking wallet in human form.

But we soothed ourselves the correct way: ice cream.

There was a vendor called Sandra's Heladería near the main park, which was basically Sucre's attempt at cosplaying

France. There was a fake Eiffel Tower and green lawns. It was adorable and slightly hilarious. Festival energy still hummed through the streets, meaning more cake, more crowds, more chaos. We tried to go back to Condor Café—the delicious vegetarian not-for-profit place we'd already decided we loved—but it was closed, so we ate somewhere else that was twice the price and half the quality and sulked about it like proper snobs.

Then came the first day of school.

I felt like a teenager again, which was rude because I was twenty-six and should be immune to first-day nerves. Apparently not. I even had nightmares about overdue assignments and unrealistic deadlines, like my Master's degree was lurking in the shadows waiting to jump me. We woke up early, showered, and attempted the dramatic transformation from scruffy backpackers to tidy students. I brushed my hair properly. I put on mascara. I felt glamorous, which mostly meant I looked marginally less feral.

The walk to school was genuinely lovely. White buildings, terracotta roofs, the occasional cobblestone street. It felt good to have a routine. Also, the motivation was immediate and practical. Every single word I learned would probably be used in the next few months. There's no existential crisis like "when will I ever use trigonometry?"

when you're trying to order lunch without accidentally asking for something else.

The classes were intense. Four hours a day sounded manageable until I actually did it. By hour three my brain felt like it had been microwaved. We had a ten-minute break where I met Carlos for *empanadas* and ice cream, and then we were back to learning. By the end of the day, my head was buzzing in that exhausted-but-proud way.

And then Sucre turned into lunchtime chaos.

Lunch here is *the* meal. People leave work. Kids flood the streets. Everyone goes home and eats together. It's actually kind of beautiful. Like a collective agreement that food and family matter more than forcing yourself through a dreary afternoon. We ate with our host family, washed dishes, and then headed out for admin, including paying school fees, grabbing snacks, taking laundry to a laundrette.

Money was a nightmare. ATMs refused to cooperate. Banks were unhelpful and weird. One bank literally told us off for having our phones out and then locked us in for ten minutes at a time like we were inmates. Police had to let you out. It was such an oddly dramatic experience for something as boring as "please let me access my own money."

To recover, we did what we do. We returned to Condor Café for another *papa rellena.*

It was becoming a pattern. We kept thinking we should branch out, but the cheesy deep-fried potato ball had us in a chokehold. And because I have no limit when it comes to treats, we wandered down to Para Ti ("for you") and I ordered a gourmet hot chocolate so decadent it felt like I was undoing all the kilometres we'd hiked in Peru.

The next day confirmed what I'd already suspected: Spanish school is not a cute little hobby. It is mentally exhausting. My brain got headaches. I was in bed by 9:30 p.m. every night. We learned sentence structures, conjugated a whole parade of verbs, and added vocabulary at a rate that made my soul feel slightly itchy.

But something was shifting underneath the frustration. I started talking for myself more. Ordering things, asking questions. Tiny moments of independence that felt like little victories. During our break, I ordered my own pineapple juice in Spanish and felt ridiculously proud, like I'd just given a TED Talk.

Then the school sprang a surprise. Presentations. We had to interview strangers and present them to the group. We all survived, but the real horror came later when our host parents told us the school had streamed it on Facebook Live.

I wanted to evaporate. I knew I had looked like a babbling idiot.

That evening, after hours of homework that felt never-ending, we ventured out to collect laundry and, of course, more hot chocolate. We joined a school city tour that was mostly in Spanish, which meant it doubled as a lesson and a gentle humiliation. But it took us to parts of Sucre we'd somehow missed. A mock Arc de Triomphe, a market bigger than expected, and chocolate tasting at Para Ti (yes, again). Sucre was starting to feel familiar. Not just "pretty," but known.

Every day, we walked home, twice—back for lunch, then back after dinner—and every evening there were street dogs. At first, it was a handful. Then it was a pack. Then one night it was eleven. The next night it grew again. Twenty, maybe twenty-five, many of them huge and beautiful and moving with a kind of eerie elegance. Cars stopped for them. They owned the street.

For a split second I wanted to take a photo, but the instinct to keep moving was stronger. I didn't want us to be alone with them on a dim road. So we just watched them glide past like a wild, silent parade, then bombed it up the hill to our apartment.

The next day at school, the lesson became real life. A solo mission to the veggie market. My teacher sent me off with a list of items to price-check and a meeting point, which meant I sprinted around like a madwoman asking the price of oddly specific things while vendors sliced off little samples for me. Fruit, cheese, whatever. Ask the price and you'll be fed. It was delightful and chaotic.

That's where I learned a word I loved. *Caseras.* The women you buy from. And you are their *casero.* Their regular, their person. The idea is you find your favourites and keep going back. We absolutely had a favourite fruit lady by this point. We'd also started hearing about *yapa*, which was asking for a little extra for free. It felt so wrong and cheap to ask. We were psyching ourselves up to try it when the fierce juice lady called out and refilled our whole glass without being prompted.

That was *yapa.*

We sat in a café with stable Wi-Fi (a rare treasure), me sipping a bitter dark hot chocolate while dogs barked outside in Plaza 25 de Mayo. When we walked home, we saw the dog pack again. Bigger, bolder, still glorious in its own slightly terrifying way.

And then, because female hormones are real, I hit a day where I was inexplicably grouchy after school. Like a dark cloud had decided to rent space above my head. Carlos made it his mission to cheer me up, and he succeeded in two ways that felt very on-brand for us.

First: he stepped directly into a fresh pile of dog poo.

Sucre is a city of beauty, culture, and approximately fifty heaps of excrement per twenty-minute walk. You learn to watch your feet like it's a sport. Carlos apparently forgot this, and when his entire foot sank into the worst possible surprise, my mood lifted instantly. I laughed with the kind of joy that is morally questionable. The fact I grew up with five brothers was immediate apparent.

Second, *papa rellena.*

We had a cooking class scheduled, and I'd just discovered the dish we'd be making featured cow tongue and chicken. I'd been vegetarian since 2005. So we decided I needed a protective pre-class potato ball to cushion the blow. The mission: find a fresh *papa rellena* and not get ripped off.

We found a "store" that looked like it might collapse if you breathed too hard. There was a hot cabinet with a couple of *papa rellenas* sitting sadly inside, but Carlos demanded the freshly fried one still sitting in oil. The woman tried to pretend she didn't understand. Carlos held firm. Eventually she caved, and we ate what might have been the freshest *papa rellena* in all of Sucre.

The cooking class itself took place in a cozy apartment. The teacher worked at our school and was hustling on the side. We walked in and were immediately confronted by the remains of a cow's head on the table, which is one way to start an evening. Everyone was horrified, but the teacher made a fair point. It's just meat, no different to sausages or burgers. That was easy to accept in theory and much harder to accept while watching someone peel the skin off a tongue like they were removing a jacket.

Still, once it was chopped into vegetables and potatoes, she was right. It became food. We played rounds of Dos (similar to Uno), and I was pleasantly surprised that I won most rounds. The real victory came when Carlos casually mentioned how obsessed I was with *papa rellenas*, and the teacher offered to teach us how to make them the following week. I nearly cried. Imagine returning home with a new skill and a deep-fried potato legacy.

By the end of the school week, we didn't have the energy for anything dramatic. We wandered through the ongoing celebrations—music, dancing, street food smells intoxicating the air (except barbecued liver, which is a smell I will never forget). We treated ourselves to ice cream in the square and then realised Carlos had mistakenly handed over a fifty-boliviano note instead of a ten, and we were suddenly operating on a budget that could only be described as comically tragic.

We didn't want to walk uphill to the apartment to get more cash, so we decided to survive the night on the equivalent of about seven New Zealand dollars. Bolivia made it possible. Street food here was gloriously cheap. I smashed two *papa rellenas* at three bolivianos each like a champion. Carlos went for barbecued heart and some potato, then somehow also managed to scoff down two burgers with fries. We capped it off at Condor Café with a litre of fizzy drink for five bolivianos, using the free Wi-Fi and sugar to fuel our optimism until it was time to walk home.

Between the pigeons, the markets, the dog packs, the school headaches, the tiny triumph of ordering juice in Spanish, and the ridiculous comfort of a deep-fried potato ball, Sucre was exactly what we needed it to be during this stage of our trip. We weren't just racing from highlight to highlight, but building a life in one place, even if it was very temporary. It gave us a safe, walkable, warm spot to base ourselves while our brains were stretched at school.

And then it hit me, I actually had a *weekend* again.

Not a "what country are we in tomorrow?" weekend. An actual thank God it's the *weekend* weekend. The kind I hadn't felt since we left New Zealand, because up until now our life had been a long, glorious blur of buses, beds, and constant motion. In Sucre, time moved differently. School carved out structure. Homestay life gave our days a rhythm. And suddenly the weekend felt like something you earned.

We started it gently. A lie-in (a rebellious act in our new grandma-era bedtime routine), then a family outing to Para Ti's chocolate museum a few kilometres out of town. Sucre has this beloved chocolate brand, and seeing the factory felt weirdly full-circle. The tour was entirely in Spanish, which should have been terrifying, except I'd basically done the chocolate origin story already in Arequipa with Adrian the "chocolate expert and beer nerd." So I nodded along, feeling smug and fluent in cocoa facts if not much else.

There was something extra special about learning it here, where cacao isn't some abstract imported ingredient. It's grown nearby. They said Para Ti gets most of their beans from Yungas, which is where the Death Road is, and suddenly I had this bizarre mental mash-up: cyclists gripping brakes for dear life, and jungle workers plucking cacao pods off trees. Bolivia is constantly like that. Beautiful contradictions stacked on top of each other.

Afterwards we tried to be productive, bravely heading into town to drop off laundry, which felt like the least glamorous activity imaginable until I made it worse by deciding this was the day to wear a nice dress and ballet flats. I wanted to feel girly again. Mission accomplished. Unfortunately, my feet had fully adapted to running shoes and now viewed ballet flats as an enemy. Within an hour I was walking like an injured baby deer.

We didn't have long before lunch with our host family's parents up on a hill, and their house was ridiculous in the best way. Huge, European-styled, with this charming Austrian-Latin blend that somehow made perfect sense in Sucre. We ate a massive serving of Alfredo pasta, followed by homemade cinnamon buns, and I reached that stage where you're so full you can't sit upright without making weird grunting sounds.

Naturally, we followed that up with a trip to the grocery store.

We'd decided we were going to cook New Zealand food for our homestay family the next day. We wanted to properly treat them. After much serious deliberation, we landed on a menu that screamed Kiwi. Pies, kūmara fries, and afghan cookies. Honestly, the only thing missing was an L&P and maybe a chilly bin.

So we ran around the markets like stressed-out contestants on a cooking show. Sweet potato here, flour there, butter, this, that. We visited our usual fruit *casera*, the woman we'd been buying from often enough that I genuinely believed we'd formed a bond.

And then she betrayed us.

We grabbed a few pieces of fruit, and she told us it would be fifty bolivianos. *Fifty*. My entire body screamed rip-off, but I also did that thing where you doubt your gut because you don't want to become the cynical tourist who assumes everyone is out to get you. Plus, she threw in an orange as *yapa* and I let gratitude override basic math. We paid, then later asked our homestay family what they would've paid.

"Half," they said.

Half.

I felt like I'd been cheated on by a woman who'd watched me build trust, one piece of fruit at a time.

Still, Sucre did what Sucre does. It distracted us with beauty and noise. Town was absolutely pumping. Somewhere in the distance, drums were beating and trumpets were booming, the sound travelling through the city like a pulse. Men, women, and kids danced in wild costumes. Some dressed as miners, some as firefighters. Everyone moving with an energy that made it impossible to stand still. The streets smelled like fried potatoes and cake and barbecued meat and that one specific stink of barbecued liver that makes you question whether you want to smell anything ever again.

As we walked down one of the main streets, a group of communications students stopped us. They wanted to interview foreigners. We joked about how on earth they could possibly tell we weren't local (said the people wearing backpacks and who are visibly confused). They asked why we were in Bolivia and what we thought of the festival. Then they asked if New Zealand had anything like it.

I don't think I've ever answered a question so quickly. I knew the answer immediately.

No. No we do not.

That night we treated ourselves like responsible adults. Cocktails and wine. First stop was Bibliocafé, which played modern songs turned into lounge covers that made everything feel softer, slower. Like the whole room had been wrapped in velvet. I remember sitting there with a cocktail and feeling deeply, ridiculously happy. The kind of happy that makes you want to pause time.

Then we wandered down to Joy Ride, which was very obviously a tourist bar. Tours advertised everywhere, free salsa lessons, free Bolivian movie nights. But they had reasonably cheap wine, which meant they had our loyalty. We ordered a veggie burger, a glass of *vino*, and I remembered it was my first anniversary of being a dual citizen (England and New Zealand). We toasted to it, slightly tipsy and proud and a bit sentimental.

And then, because travel is always complicated, I felt that familiar punch in the gut that comes when you're having a lovely night and the world reminds you it isn't lovely for everyone.

Street children.

They were everywhere in South America, but Sucre was making it harder for me to look away. That night, two kids had found chalk and were drawing cartoons on the street. Good ones. One of them had a crumpled piece of paper he kept studying and copying, like he was doing homework in the only way available to him. We gave them a couple of coins, partly to help and partly, if I'm honest, to soothe the helpless guilt. And then I just sat with it. How easy it is back home to complain about New Zealand, and how quickly you forget what real poverty looks like until it is literally drawing pictures at your feet.

The next morning, we slept in scandalously late. I woke to the sound of kids playing and breakfast being made, and it hit a warm nostalgic place in me. Like being a teenager again, the house alive before you're ready to face the day.

Over breakfast, our host parents told us stories about child kidnappings and organ trafficking. The kind of thing you don't want to believe, except they weren't presented as rumours. A mother nearly losing her child to a guy on a motorbike. A woman in a market finding her stolen child under a blanket. Already changed into different clothes, hair shaved, identity stripped in minutes. I couldn't stop thinking about the chalk kids from the night before. How vulnerable they were. How easy it would be for them to disappear. How little anyone would do.

Then we switched gears, because we had a job: cook New Zealand lunch for the family.

And honestly? I was really proud of how it turned out.

We made a spinach and cheese pie, a meat mince pie, and kūmara fries, and they turned out beautifully, which is saying something because cooking in someone else's kitchen is hard enough. Let alone doing it at high altitude with a mystery oven that has no temperature settings. Just on/off and a dial that could mean anything from "gentle warmth" to "burn the place down."

While the family ate, we left afghan cookies baking in the oven. Big mistake. One of the kids wandered in for water and discovered the kitchen was filling with smoke. I ran in and the cookies were basically almost on fire. I stood there holding a tray of near-flaming afghans. We hadn't realised that the higher altitude meant changing up the temperature for baking.

But we were determined. Round two.

Perfect.

Like, you couldn't buy afghans that good in a New Zealand store perfect. Redemption never tasted so buttery.

When school started again, something shifted, in the best possible way. I rotated teachers and ended up with a middle-aged woman who spoke very little English, which turned out to be exactly what I needed. The previous week I'd leaned on English to ask my teacher complicated questions; now I was forced to ask in Spanish, even if I did it awkwardly, even if I sounded like a toddler assembling a sentence out of scraps.

And I was improving. Slowly. But truly.

School stopped feeling like school and started feeling like daily life. Half lesson, half comedy show, the punchlines delivered in Spanish. We played games, argued over rules, did missions that required us to speak to strangers. The language stopped being something I studied and became something I used.

And it did something else, too. It made me pay attention. It's easy to live in the future on a trip like this. Salt flats, deserts, Patagonia, Christmas somewhere dramatic. All the shiny things ahead. But the whole reason I'd crammed my life into a backpack and launched myself across the Pacific was happening right now. Walking home from Spanish school in a city I hadn't even known existed until I googled "cheap Spanish school."

Sucre was undeniably beautiful. I felt that way every time we went outside. The white-painted buildings, terracotta roofs, rolling hills, perfect weather. The streets smelled like fried meat and potatoes. Vendors sold everything imaginable. And the city had this weird organisation where certain streets were dedicated almost entirely to one trade. Lawyers, salons, prom-dress shops. Like the whole place was quietly sorted into themed sections.

And then there were the zebras.

During peak traffic hours, people dressed as zebras bounced around intersections, greeting pedestrians with absurd energy, helping manage crossings. Someone explained the zebra crossing connection and it made sense, even if I still didn't understand who employed them or how you apply for a job that requires you to embody a zebra with the enthusiasm of a motivational speaker.

Homestay life became its own cosy universe. Breakfast with chocolate milk and bread and jam, rushing home for lunch after school, kids saying grace (adorable), family meals that knocked us into food-comas, then homework for hours. Later, we'd wander back into town for dinner and Wi-Fi, and finally walk home in the dark. Safe, quiet, full of street dogs. Before collapsing into bed early with my book, like the least rock-and-roll backpacker alive.

But the street children kept tugging at me.

One day we saw the chalk kids again. They were so close to each other and yet so alone. Scruffy clothes, dirt on their skin, working. I couldn't ignore it anymore, even if I knew I couldn't fix it. So we bought them a chocolate bar and a bottle of Coke. Not necessities. Just something that might feel like a treat. I told one of them, in Spanish, that his drawing was really good. Carlos handed the other kid his share. When I looked up, the kid near Carlos smiled at me. This warm, genuine smile that hit me right in the chest. I felt like crying, partly because of the unfairness, partly because I realised I was underestimating them. They weren't just sad symbols in my travel story. They were resilient, creative little humans doing what they could with what they had, in a world that didn't feel safe.

To balance out the heaviness, Sucre continued feeding me. We'd heard about a legendary *salteña* place near school, and I was determined to finally try one. We rushed there at lunchtime, only to find it closed. I was devastated for approximately two seconds, because next door was also famous, and open. The vegetarian *salteña* was delicious, but the pastry leaned a little too sweet for me. *Empanadas* still had my heart.

That afternoon we gathered ingredients for a private cooking class, because yes, we were going to learn how to make *papa rellenas* properly. We did the market dance again. Loving the variety, hating the constant need to stay sharp. Our vegetable lady treated us fairly and gave us real *yapa*. Extra tomatoes and a random carrot, which honestly felt like winning a prize. We bought oil, hunted for cheese, decided the market cheese looked like a food safety documentary waiting to happen, and bought it from the supermarket instead. We passed eggs for one boliviano each and strawberries, twenty for ten, after watching someone else get charged first, because we learn.

We climbed to the teacher's house, arriving early, which in Latin America time is basically arriving yesterday. Inside was a warm, homey kitchen, and suddenly we were once again doing exactly what we'd been chasing. An authentic experience with locals, conducted in Spanish, involving food I genuinely loved.

I thought *papa rellenas* were just mashed potato + cheese + deep fry. Wrong. There was batter with eggs, cumin, pepper, salt, flour, and a shot of whisky. There was a sauce, with capsicum, tomatoes, onions, oil, salt, pepper. And when we finished, she surprised us with homemade tiramisu that was boozy as hell and exactly what the doctor ordered.

We did dishes, chatted in my expanding Spanglish about everything from rabid dogs to drunken brawls to travel, and ended the night playing Dos again. I didn't dominate this time, only winning one round, but it didn't matter. It was one of those evenings that glows because it's ordinary and extraordinary at once. A warm kitchen, a local teacher, the slow building of language in your mouth, and the feeling that for a moment you weren't just passing through.

Then Sucre decided to throw us a goodbye party that made every other "festival" we'd seen look like a polite community sausage sizzle. It was the Day of Students, the Day of Love (Bolivia's Valentine's), and the first day of Spring. Also, our last day of language classes. The school did morning tea with sandwiches, Coke, Para Ti chocolate. Teachers gave little gifts, we played verb-miming games outside in the sun, and sang Spanish songs like we were sixteen again on the last day before summer holidays. It felt light and golden and nostalgic, like a chapter was closing gently instead of slamming shut.

And then we went to the university *fiesta.* I packed sunscreen, a cap, water, thinking it'd be some chill Wellington wine-festival vibe. What we actually walked into was a full-blown, thousand-plus-person party in a dusty open-air venue outside the city. We squeezed onto a free bus that was so overstuffed, got wristbands under surprisingly strict security, and followed the dry track down into a sea of music and bodies and cheap beer. Beer was absurdly cheap. Massive cans for almost nothing. Giant bottles for the price of a snack back home. People were drinking rum and *fernet* like it was a national sport, but I stuck to *cerveza* because I had enough self-awareness to know that heat + altitude + "I haven't really drunk in weeks" was a perfect recipe for a drunken tourist tragedy.

Even with that caution, it was one of the best nights of the trip so far. I'd been listening to Spanish music to help with learning, and suddenly it wasn't homework. It was real life. Songs I actually knew were blasting through speakers while hundreds of Bolivians danced and shouted and jumped in the dust. When the song Felices Los 4 came on I lost my mind. It was one of my favourites and I loved singing along with thousands of others.

There were a couple of sour notes. The women's bathroom situation was feral. Door knocking, chaos, constant pressure. And men kept offering drinks in that persistent, insistent way that sets off every alarm bell you've got. Even if they meant well, I wasn't about to accept a mystery beverage from a stranger in a field in Bolivia at night, no matter how friendly they looked.

By 10 p.m. I was crumbling, so we bused back in a sweatbox of slumped drunken bodies, then walked forty minutes home to sober up. I ate an entire bag of chips like it was part of my recovery protocol and crawled into bed feeling dusty, happy, and weirdly proud of myself for surviving a *fiesta* without becoming any consequence.

The next day was our final day in Sucre. We wandered through Parque Simón Bolívar one last time. Past the fake Eiffel Tower and fountains. Then home for the dreaded ritual of packing. Packing is my love/hate relationship. It always feels like my bag grows overnight just to spite me. It's an endless game of travel Tetris where nothing fits and everything is somehow heavier than yesterday. I tried to be extra careful this time, telling myself Future Me would thank me. I even threw a couple of things out. It made no difference.

As we finished up, a dark heavy cloud gathered over the mountains, and our host dad casually predicted rain based on the warmth. He was dead right. We watched lightning crack in the distance, so far away it was silent, and hurried into town for dinner before the storm hit properly. It poured with rain, and then hail joined in. The city was strangely quiet for a festival weekend. Maybe everyone was hungover. Maybe we'd just gotten used to living inside a constant parade. Either way, it felt like Sucre was exhaling.

Sucre had given us so much: forty hours of Spanish, cooking classes in real homes, markets and *yapa* and dodgy *casera* heartbreak, street doughnuts, festivals that made New Zealand feel aggressively tame, and a rhythm of daily life that felt almost *normal.* It was the kind of stop that sneaks up on you. Not flashy, not on the top of everyone's list, but quietly transformative. We came for language school, and we left with a little pocket of Bolivia stitched into us. The terracotta roofs, the afternoon chaos of lunchtime streets, the kindness of strangers, the ache of things we couldn't fix, and the warmth of a place that made us feel, for a while, like we belonged. And as we zipped our bags shut, again, somehow fuller than when we arrived, I realized Sucre hadn't just taught me Spanish. It had taught me how good it feels to stay still long enough to live somewhere, not just pass through.

Salt and Sky

- UYUNI, BOLIVIA -

We were back on the road. The kind of "back" that involves hoisting backpacks onto sore shoulders like you've willingly signed up to be a human pack mule again. Sucre had spoiled us with routine: breakfast at a table, a fixed walk to school, a bed that didn't move. So when we said goodbye to our homestay family, with real, long hugs, the kind that make you realize you've crossed from "guests" into "friends", it felt like leaving a small sanctuary we'd accidentally built in the middle of Bolivia.

Our homestay family insisted we eat one last breakfast with them before we were driven to the bus station and boom, back to reality. The sleazy kind. The "cover your pockets" kind. The kind that makes you miss your safe little apartment and your bread-and-jam mornings immediately.

We'd debated breaking the journey in Potosí, but the mines weren't calling our names. We'd been in mines back in Chile, and once you've seen one set of dark tunnels and heard one "this is how people die slowly" story, you don't exactly need a sequel. So we committed to the full eight-hour ride straight to Uyuni.

The bus turned out to be tourists-only. Although the company had mediocre reviews, it was in decent shape by Bolivian standards, and the driver didn't seem to be treating hairpin corners as a fun little challenge. Still, the road was so windy it felt like someone had drawn it while riding a rollercoaster. I'm not even a motion sickness person, but this route humbled me.

We stopped out in the countryside and two women climbed aboard selling snacks. I heard "*empanadas con queso*" and immediately said yes like an idiot because what I got was sweet bread with a stingy smear of old, sad cheese. An *empanada* in name only. I took one bite, felt betrayed, and spent the rest of the ride trying not to throw up from the deadly combo of bad food and nausea. At some point I gave up and slept.

Miraculously, we rolled into Uyuni on time. The first bus on this entire continent that respected a schedule.

Uyuni itself looked like a town built out of low confidence. Nothing was taller than a single storey, like everyone had collectively agreed that ambition was dangerous. Yet it was very obviously a tourist hub. Tiny streets filled with cosy-looking restaurants, travellers wandering around in big backpacks and llama-print jerseys like it was a uniform. We walked through the centre to our hostel, dropped our bags, paid for the tour (because in Uyuni you basically arrive to do one thing and one thing only), and then wandered around trying to figure out where to eat while I was still bunged up with a cold.

And this is where I learned something important. Sucre had been lovingly cradling us in a cheap, gentle hug. Whereas Uyuni slapped us across the face with prices.

In Sucre, we could find meals for 25 bolivianos anywhere we went. In Uyuni, everything seemed to start at 70. We ended up at a place called Lithium, and I ate what may genuinely have been the worst pizza of my life. It had peas on it. *Peas.* Like someone looked at pizza and thought, "You know what this needs? PEAS." Still, I got a hot chocolate out of it, and with the cold air biting at my cheeks, that alone felt like a win.

Because Uyuni was *cold.* Really cold. Sucre had felt like mid-summer. Whereas Uyuni felt like we'd stepped into a barren, windblown nowhere where the sky was big and the temperature had plummeted. I dug out my big woollen snood for the first time in weeks and suddenly felt like we were gearing up for a different kind of adventure.

The next morning, shockingly, we didn't have to wake up at a disgusting hour. The tour didn't start until ten. We even had time to wander Uyuni for last-minute souvenirs before meeting at the agency directly across the road from our hostel.

There were heaps of people waiting around, and I felt that familiar travel-panic flicker: Please let us have chosen the right company. We'd read too many stories about dodgy operators, accidents, and guides who treat safety like a suggestion. The roads ahead were salt flats and mountain tracks. No room for "she'll be alright."

We met our guide, Freddy, and chose to do the tour in Spanish partly because I wanted to practice (two weeks of school and I was not about to lose it all immediately), and partly because it was cheaper. Our little crew ended up being a perfect mix. Us, a Uruguayan couple, an Irish guy, a Croatian guy, and Freddy at the helm. Seven seats. Seven strangers. One shared destiny of salt.

I thought we were heading to the Salt Flats, taking the classic "I'm tiny next to a dinosaur" photo, and then spending the rest of the time driving through emptiness.

I could not have been more wrong.

The tour opened with a train cemetery, which felt like Bolivia's way of easing us in with something weird. Old trains rusting in the middle of nowhere, people climbing all over them like metal playground equipment. It was cool in theory, but there were so many tourists it became this chaotic game of "how do I take a photo that doesn't include seventeen strangers in matching llama sweaters?"

Next was Colchani, where we watched salt being processed, bought garlic salt in a colourful knitted bag, and wandered past craft stalls selling the same bright woven things we'd seen across Peru and Bolivia. The village was basically the gateway to the Salar, and not long after we left, after being delayed by approximately fifty llamas sprinting across the road like they were late for something, we hit it.

The Salar de Uyuni is the world's biggest salt flat, but that description doesn't prepare you for what it feels like to actually be on it. It was like driving on a blank canvas. White stretching in every direction, sky so blue it looked edited, mountains sitting far off like a painted backdrop. The salt was so bright it felt actively aggressive, like it was trying to burn the retinas right out of your skull. Sunglasses became non-negotiable.

At one point we stopped near a patch of shallow water that looked like bubbling hot springs. I poked it and nearly laughed, because it was actually ice cold. Freddy explained the bubbling came from oxygen pushing up from layers below, not heat. Even the science was surprising out there.

We drove on the flats for hours. Not ten minutes. Not a quick loop. Hours of white and blue and horizon, like we'd entered another planet with better lighting.

Lunch was at Playa Blanca, which is a salt museum on the flats. It's surrounded with hundreds of flags snapping in the wind outside. We tried to spot New Zealand, couldn't, and then later discovered a giant All Blacks flag we'd somehow missed. Inside we ate like we'd been starved. Mountains of potato, a terrifying amount of quinoa, vegetables, lollipops.

After lunch came the Instagram moment. Perspective photos. The famous ones. People in Pringles cans, dinosaurs attacking, giant hands holding tiny humans. At first, we were left alone and I thought, *Cool, five minutes, easy.*

It was not easy. It's actually extremely hard to coordinate forced perspective when you're standing on a blinding white sheet of salt with wind in your face and strangers watching you squat and point and yell, "No, move LEFT… Your other left!" in Spanish.

Then Freddy stepped in and, with the calm competence of a man who has watched thousands of tourists fail, turned us into a professional production. He had props. He arranged us like chess pieces. He filmed. He photographed. He directed. Suddenly we were being attacked by dinosaurs, dancing out of Pringles cans, and holding each other like miniatures. I laughed so hard I cried. Proper tears. The kind you wipe away with your sleeve.

And that's when it hit me. People travel to Bolivia for this. This is the iconic thing. The postcard. The bucket list flex.

But the wild part was realizing it was only a fraction of the tour.

Bolivia kept doing this to us. Quietly outperforming expectations. Country after country requires weeks and flights to show you that kind of variety. Bolivia served it up in a three-day loop.

We stopped at Incahuasi Island. An actual little cactus-covered island sitting inside the salt flats like a glitch in the landscape. Dry, rocky, bristling with cacti, surrounded by endless white. We paid to enter, climbed up through the crowd, and got this ridiculous panorama of salt and sky and distant mountains. It felt impossible.

Then we chased the sunset.

We drove back out into the flats, pulled over in what felt like the coldest conditions we'd had yet, and stood shivering while the sun sank fast. The day had been hot, almost summery. Then night arrived like a punishment. Carlos, who had worn shorts because the flats were warm, instantly regretted every choice he'd ever made, and we all mocked him mercilessly because that's what love looks like on a tour.

That night we slept in a salt hostel in a little village. Salt floors. Salt walls. Salt everywhere. Three toilets for what felt like fifty people. Two showers you had to pay extra for, which meant the baby wipe wash reigned supreme. We'd heard horror stories about freezing nights and people sleeping in thermals, hats, gloves, like they were preparing for an Arctic expedition. But our room was surprisingly warm. We used our sleeping bags like extra blankets and slept fine. It was proof that living in New Zealand had accidentally trained me for poorly insulated buildings. If anything, I'd slept colder at home.

The next morning started with bread and fruit and an early departure into wind that could've peeled skin off bone. We began the day staring at volcanoes, then bounced from lagoon to lagoon, each one a different colour like the landscape couldn't commit to a palette. Some were so striking they didn't feel real. One was full of flamingos.

Bright pink and red against water that looked like it belonged in a painting. Freddy warned us not to throw stones at them, which horrified me because who does that? But clearly someone had. Thankfully, people were respectful, quiet, careful. It was one of those rare moments where tourism wasn't entirely awful.

We detoured to see the Stone Tree, and the desert around it. The boulders scattered like someone dropped a giant handful of rocks across a flat plain. It was stunning. We climbed between them, squeezed through narrow pathways, watched sandy whirlwinds in the distance, and chewed coca leaves as the altitude crept higher.

Then Laguna Colorada stole the show. Red water because of algae. *Literally red.* Freddy said wind can shift it toward orange by mixing minerals, but on that day, it was unapologetically crimson. Flamingos wandered through it, almost camouflaged against the red backdrop. It was like nature had decided subtlety was overrated.

We arrived at the second hostel, and it looked, from the outside, like a Call of Duty map. Dry, barren, crumbling, post-apocalyptic. But inside the dining room was warm from a plastic roof trapping sunlight, and we immediately claimed it as our sanctuary. We'd heard this would be the coldest night, and just stepping outside made our bones ache. We ran out to buy wine (twice the Sucre price, of course. Uyuni pricing strikes again), then retreated back into the warm dining room like survivors, drinking wine at nearly 5,000 metres above sea level with a table full of other travellers. A strange little luxury. Freezing desert outside, laughter and glasses clinking inside.

Then came the brutal morning.

We were up at 4:15 a.m., eating breakfast at 4:30 a.m., stumbling around with cloudy heads (possibly from two glasses of wine at altitude, who knows) and pancakes that were cold and chewy until drowned in *dulce de leche*. By 5:10 a.m. we were outside, and the air hit like a slap. It was around -10°C and had dropped even lower overnight. Everything ached. Snow spiked up from the ground like daggers. Wind-carved and sharp.

We reached the geysers before sunrise. Steam centralized into a steady plume, bubbling mud pools, ground soft enough to be dangerous. It was beautiful, but I couldn't help thinking, New Zealand has this too, except with fewer frozen toes and less chance of passing out at nearly five thousand metres above sea level.

After an hour of freezing, we drove to the hot pools. Everyone's first reaction was "absolutely not." The idea of stripping down in that cold felt like voluntary hypothermia. And then I remembered we were on an adventure. And, this is important, we have a long-standing travel rule: *when there's a safe option and a crazy option, you usually pick the crazy one. If nothing else, it makes a better story.*

So I changed into a bikini while my feet froze to the ground and basically dive-bombed into 37°C water. For five seconds my whole body screamed like it was on fire, and then it shifted into bliss. Warmth sinking into my skin, steam rising around us, the lagoon sparkling behind. I felt clean and alive and absurdly proud of myself for choosing discomfort in pursuit of joy.

Getting out was awful, obviously. We forgot to unpack our flip flops, so our feet were punished again, there were only two changing rooms, and I set a personal speed record changing behind a curtain.

From there the world shifted again. Salvador Dalí desert, warm sandy reds and browns, volcanoes dotted across the horizon, the landscape flattening out as we dropped toward the Chilean border. We paused for photos at lagoons, did the last group shots, and then our tour split: the "on to Chile" people and the "back to Uyuni" people. We were "on to Chile," which meant crossing another border.

Bolivia's side was straightforward. Stamp, a mysterious fee which was probably a bribe, done. Then five minutes through no-man's land, and suddenly Chile was very much in our face and intense. Every bag emptied and searched manually. I had that familiar land-border whiplash. One moment you're in Bolivia, a place that feels rough around the edges in a way you can't ignore; the next you're in Chile, which feels like the "Germany of South America," and it's only minutes apart. Even the landscape changed dramatically as we descended. Rocky freezing highlands giving way to endless flat desert.

It felt like we'd been dropped into a new chapter without even turning the page.

By the time Bolivia vanished behind us, the salt had started to feel like more than scenery. It was a reminder of why we travel the way we do. Shuttling across continents in buses that make us nauseous, sleeping in weird hostels, accepting cold mornings and dodgy food and endless packing. Because then you find yourself laughing so hard you cry on a white expanse of salt under a blue sky, or slipping into steaming water while the world is frozen around you, and you think *"Oh. This is it. This is why we keep choosing the hard, weird, inconvenient option."*

Moon and Mars

- SAN PEDRO DE ATACAMA, CHILE -

We hit San Pedro de Atacama so quickly it almost felt suspicious. Like Chile had briefly decided to be efficient just to mess with us. The only hiccup was a sudden police drama mid-journey. A random car of cops pulled the bus over, hauled the driver out, and marched a dog down the aisle like it was auditioning for Border Security.

They were intense. Not a single smile. Not even a pity-smile for the tourists trying to look innocent while sweating through their shirts.

When the dog nosed into my bag, my brain instantly did that thing it does when it's bored. It invents a crime. I suddenly couldn't remember if I'd actually thrown out all of our coca leaves or if they were lurking in a pocket. The last thing we needed was me thrown in a Chilean jail for accidental drug smuggling. Then an officer leaned toward the girl behind us and, in Spanish, casually asked if she'd smoked marijuana.

She said no.

He walked off. Like that was the end of his shift. So strange.

The bus dropped us near the station, and we walked three dusty blocks to our hostel. One we'd booked because the reviews were so glowing they basically promised enlightenment. But the place itself wasn't flash. Our room was claustrophobic, and we didn't even get our own bathroom.

It was the common area was doing all the heavy lifting. A pool, bonfire pit, picnic tables, a bar, hammocks… and, most importantly, cats. Hostel cats. Including one who'd had kittens a few weeks earlier. Honestly, you could've charged me extra just to sit on the ground and get emotionally attached to tiny desert kittens.

San Pedro itself was odd. A tiny town sitting in the middle of the world's driest desert, surviving almost entirely on tourism. It was like someone plonked a Wild West set down, dusted it with hipster vibes, and then filled it with pale tourists in linen. Ten white people for every local, easily. Restaurants charging extortionate prices with a straight face. We wandered around in that dazed post-border state, half-planning, half-decompressing, then retreated to the hostel to sit in the sun with beer and catch up on writing.

The past few days had been a complete whirlwind. Salt flats, volcanoes, freezing mornings, border stamps. So this little dusty town felt like someone had turned the volume down. We welcomed it.

And then our first full day arrived, and I remembered "oh right, this is the Atacama. This place has a reputation. People speak about it with this reverent tone, like it's a rite of passage for anyone doing the Peru–Bolivia sprint. San Pedro looked like Uyuni's cousin. Low adobe buildings, brown everything, dusty roads, the sense you're wandering through a movie set. Nothing taller than one storey, walls that looked like they'd been glued together with dirt and optimism. Everything was the colour of sand. Except the volcanoes in the background, which were angry-black with streaks of snow like eyeliner that had run.

The sky was an unreal blue. No clouds. Not even a polite little wisp. I'd heard parts of this desert haven't had rainfall in recorded history, and standing there, squinting at the dryness of literally everything, I believed it without question. Yet for all its barrenness, the town had a cool, hippy hum to it. Small resident population, massive tourist population, everyone drifting around on a slow current of sunburn and adventure.

We decided to do a bike ride to the Valle de la Luna. The Moon Valley. Because if you're in the driest desert in the world, of course you should go pedal yourself into a landscape that looks like another planet.

We found a rental shop called "Rent a Bike Emily" that felt refreshingly unpretentious. Because there were three of us (one of the guys from the Uyuni tour tagged along), we got a discount, and I immediately loved Chile for that. In

Peru and Bolivia, a discount is something you have to wrestle out of someone. Here, it was just given. No drama. No suspicious math. No one pretending not to understand their own pricing.

We cycled out of town, onto the main road, and west for about half an hour, thirteen kilometres of sun and dust, until we reached the entrance. Even the park entrance surprised us. Another discount, again without us asking. It was like Chile was quietly reassuring us, *Relax. We're not dodgy.*

From the entrance building to the actual heart of the valley was another twenty-minute cycle on paved road. The first stop was the canyon and the salt cave, and I was instantly grateful I wasn't alone because caves + earthquakes = my worst nightmare. Right as we reached the entrance, I said, out-loud, because I can't help myself, "Have you seen that movie where people go into a cave and get killed by creatures?"

"The Descent?" Carlos replied immediately.

Why was I like this.

But we went in anyway. And it was fun. The kind of fun that involves crawling through salt caves, using phones as torches, and feeling very aware of your own mortality in a way that's probably not necessary on a holiday. I cracked my phone screen holding it in my mouth like some kind of budget caver, and then we had to climb up a sharp rocky wall to get back out. There was a moment where I honestly felt like Lara Croft, except with worse core strength and more anxiety.

Afterwards we wandered the canyon, then returned to the bikes and immediately tried to murder ourselves cycling up a steep hill. I gave up and pushed mine because heatstroke felt like an embarrassing way to die. But once we crested the top, it was only ten minutes to the next stop to a *mirador*. A lookout that was about forty minutes return.

We locked up the bikes and started walking.

At first, it was gentle. Soft sand underfoot, rugged cliff rock on one side, rolling dunes on the other. And then, about ten minutes in, the landscape shifted like someone changed the set mid-scene. The path turned into a roller coaster. Up, down, up, down. Through jagged formations that looked less "moon" and more "Mars." The palette narrowed into reds and browns and shadow, and the edges dropped away sharply enough that one wrong step would've turned my memoir into a tragedy.

But the views at the end. *Wow*. I'd been in deserts before, the soft-dune kind, the postcard kind. This was different. This was the "I'm on another planet" kind. The kind that makes you feel small in a way that's both unsettling and thrilling.

By the time we biked again, we were ready to call it. We hadn't even reached the end of Valle de la Luna, but we'd seen enough, and we had to return the bikes by 3:20 p.m. We'd been in direct sun for almost five hours. No shade. Peak heat. I was reapplying sunscreen like it was a full-time job, but I could still feel the burn hovering at the edges of my skin like a threat.

The ride back hurt more. The seat was so stiff it felt like my butt was actively on fire, and every bump in the rocky path sent pain shooting through me like punishment for my earlier confidence. Still, going back was faster, because the hills that had nearly killed us earlier now became downhill relief. We regrouped, drank water, shook out our limbs, and made it back with ten minutes to spare.

On the way we passed bus tours heading out toward the valley, and I was so smug about our choice. There are other ways to do it. Bus, shuttle, cycle just the interior. But I loved being able to say, "I cycled to and through Moon Valley," instead of, "I sat on a bus." It felt earned. We'd beaten the crowds, too. Seven people, max, the whole time we were out there.

Active bodies, empty landscape, planet-Mars views. Worth every sore muscle.

The next day we shifted gears into something I still didn't fully understand. Glamping. I'd done a *ger* in Mongolia in winter once, which is basically glamping's rugged ancestor. Romantic in theory, brutal in practice. This was the opposite. The Atacama Loft looked expensive for "sleeping in a tent," but I kept reminding myself you're not paying for canvas. You're paying for the experience.

Google Maps told us it was a fifteen-minute walk from our hostel, which made no sense. San Pedro is tiny, yes, but surely glamping isn't meant to be basically downtown? We started walking with our bags in the heat, and then the directions dissolved into nothing. We reached the end of what we thought was the route and had absolutely no bloody idea where we were. Dust. Heat. No Wi-Fi. Just the sensation of potentially becoming a news headline. *Backpackers found dead in Chilean desert.*

Then a local saw us floundering, asked where we were going, and half-laughed, half-gasped when we told him. The good news was that it was near his place. The bad news was that it was another two kilometres away.

We followed him like ducklings, and the further we went, the more obvious it became we never would have found it alone. The streets thinned. The paths disappeared. It got quiet in that "if something goes wrong, no one will hear you scream" way. His timing was pure luck. The kind of travel luck you don't appreciate until you're safely inside somewhere with water and shade.

And then we arrived, and it was gorgeous.

Rustic charm. Dirt paths. Wild gardens and weeds that made it feel like you were living inside an overgrown secret. Staff came out immediately, greeted us by name like we were expected guests at a wedding, kissed our cheeks, and told us our tent was ready early, even though we were four hours early. I could've wept from gratitude.

Glamping is such a weird concept. It's slumming it with boundaries. You get the romance of "nature" without surrendering the things you didn't know you were emotionally dependent on. Things like clean toilets with seats. Toilets that flush. Sinks with paper towels. Proper showers. I'm not exaggerating when I say I wanted to write a thank-you note to every toilet I saw.

Our tent was huge; with the comfiest bed we'd slept in on the whole trip so far. Pillows like clouds. A table and chairs. A plug-in heater. Outside, there were more chairs, an outdoor couch with cushions, and towels for both shower and pool. There was a fully equipped outdoor kitchen and nearby bathrooms that felt like a spa compared to what we'd just survived in Bolivia.

And the Wi-Fi. Oh my god, the Wi-Fi. Strong enough that you could actually use it from bed. This ridiculous first-world luxury, the ability to lie under blankets and scroll, suddenly felt like heaven. At home, I'm strict about devices out of the bedroom. On the road, I'd been craving nothing more than the ability to read the news or research the next leg from the comfort of being horizontal. I got so excited I even watched talk show interviews with our Prime Minister like it was a special treat. It says a lot about how travel rewires your priorities.

We lazed by the pool. It was ice cold. Desert heat doesn't mean warm water, and I couldn't bring myself to get in. Carlos eventually did after a full motivational speech to himself, and promptly sunburned his shoulders in the time it took to psych up. I stayed on a mattress in the sun, adopted by one of the resident cats, and felt utterly content doing nothing. The site in front of me was mostly empty, but even if it hadn't been, it was spread out enough to feel calm: table tennis, trampoline, bikes… and me, reading and writing and watching the mountains turn red as the sun sank behind them.

When the temperature dropped fast, because desert nights don't gently cool, they plummet, we bought a bottle of wine from reception. We turned it into mulled wine with a bit of Mai magic, and carried our mugs out to sit by the pool under a sky packed with stars. Tour companies in San Pedro sell stargazing like it's a once-in-a-lifetime exclusive experience, complete with telescope time, hot wine, and fancy moon photos. But it cost around 18,000 pesos on the cheap end. Instead, we had a stargazing app, homemade mulled wine, and the clearest night sky imaginable, and we were already sitting in it. Also, the moon was bright, which means fewer stars anyway. So we did the sensible thing and opted out of paying for someone to point at the sky we were already under.

It was one of those quiet travel victories. Choosing not to do the obvious tourist thing, and realizing you've accidentally made something better.

The next morning, we woke in a tent that had an electric blanket on a timer. Desert-cold night outside, warm bed inside. Check-out was at noon, breakfast was included. It was incredible. Fresh bread was delivered from a French bakery, fruit and vegetables laid out like we weren't actually scruffy backpackers. We took our sweet, sweet time with it all. Sunrise, slow packing, savouring the novelty of not being in survival mode.

Then we crossed the road. Literally just over the road to get to our AirBnB. The luck of it felt ridiculous. Five-minute walk. Place to ourselves for the first time since Santiago. I was so ready for privacy.

But the AirBnB slowly revealed itself to be not so great.

It began with no Wi-Fi, despite the listing saying there would be. Normally I can roll with being off-grid, but we had admin to do. Buses, bookings. And there's a difference between choosing disconnection and being tricked into it.

We'd hauled back groceries from town, made sandwiches, and tried to settle anyway. Cable TV helped. We cracked a beer and watched the All Blacks vs Pumas rugby game live, and I had this warm, unexpected wave of feeling. Seeing "my" people on a screen, in this foreign desert, singing the anthem and doing the *haka*, reminding me how deeply New Zealand had become home for me. It hit in that soft way homesickness does. Not painful, just tender.

Then we woke up the next day to no electricity and no hot water.

At first, we tried to be reasonable. Desert. Things happen. We waited. Nothing. We knocked on a neighbour's door. No response because they'd been drinking late. And then finally trudged back to glamping site to ask if they were having issues too.

Nope. Business as usual.

We messaged the AirBnB host, irritated now. Not just because our food was warming in the fridge, but because it was becoming a pattern. No Wi-Fi, no warning, and now this. The receptionist at the glamping site casually told us it had been a scheduled town-wide power cut, and it had just come back on.

Scheduled.

Meaning the host knew. Meaning she didn't tell us. Meaning we were *done.*

To her credit, the host was reasonable and agreed to cancel the night ahead with a full refund. So we did a quick little victory walk back across the dusty road to our glamping haven, like we were returning to the promised land of clean toilets and reliable electricity.

And we didn't feel guilty about barely "doing" San Pedro. Because we'd already done so much of what this area sells, just on the Bolivian side, for cheaper, with more weirdness and more reward. San Pedro became our vacation from vacationing. A pause. A breath. A chance to stop sprinting through experiences and just sit in the desert warmth watching the sun set over the mountains dividing two countries.

That evening we opened another bottle of wine and joined a campfire lit by fellow travellers. Soon there were six of us around the fire, drinks in hand, chocolate passing around, eyes drifting up to the stars. The conversation was almost entirely travel, because what else do you talk about when you've all somehow ended up drinking together in the driest desert in the world? You trade stories, plans, mistakes, near-misses, places you loved and places you'd skip. You recognize the hunger in each other. The same itch that makes stability feel comforting but never quite enough.

And one woman, twenty years older than me, with a whole life of travel in her voice, talked about continuing to move even with a three-year-old in tow, as if adventure wasn't something you aged out of but something you carried forward, reshaped, refused to surrender. I hoped I held her mindset if children ever entered my future.

I went to bed feeling calmer than I had in days, and also strangely charged. It reminded that the road isn't just the pretty landscapes, it's also about the people you brush against briefly. The little sparks they leave behind. San Pedro had been dusty and touristy and overpriced, yes. But it also gave us this: a place to slow down after a whirlwind adventure, a private sky full of stars, and a campfire conversation that made the future feel wide open again. Maybe travel didn't stop once you had kids after all.

PART II

Flying South

- SAN PEDRO DE ATACAMA, CHILE -

Seventy-one days in, and October arrived like a quiet marker in a life that didn't have room for calendars anymore. Still, a new month. A tiny hinge. A breath before the next swing.

We were leaving this part of the continent today, and when I tried to hold the last few weeks in my head, it was almost laughable how much we'd packed into such a short stretch of time. Old friends. Vineyards. Sandboarding down dunes taller than buildings. That relentless 77-kilometre grind to Machu Picchu. Chocolate and cooking classes. The 64-kilometre mountain bike ride on the Death Road. Ziplining. Spanish school. A *fiesta* with a thousand bodies moving as one. Uyuni, white infinity and ridiculous photos. Hot pools in minus-ten at almost five thousand metres. Glamping under the kind of stars you'd swear weren't real.

Just a few things.

I woke up absurdly happy. The kind of happy that feels slightly unreal, like you'll jinx it if you move too fast. Sunrise spilled over the mountains bordering Bolivia, warming the inside of our tent in slow gold. The electric blanket had been on overnight, so the bed was still cosy. Desert-cold outside, secret warmth beneath us. One of the resident cats did a casual patrol of our tent like he owned the place, and at some point, we gave in and let him in for a proper snuggle. Then breakfast arrived. Eggs, cheese, vegetables, fresh bread delivered that morning from the French bakery.

We delayed leaving for as long as we could. We didn't want to trade our little slice of heaven for a dirty bus ride.

The reception kindly offered us a ride to the bus station for free. We saved ourselves 3,000 pesos and got a gentler goodbye. A small act of kindness that made everything feel more human. We left Atacama Loft without a single negative thing to say.

Ten minutes later we were at the "bus station," which turned out to be more like a strip of little offices lined up beside each other. Every office was drowning in Chilean flags. Twenty flags for one ticket counter, flailing like the country was trying desperately to convince you that it existed. It was oddly intense.

We walked in, bought tickets for the next bus, and found out it left in half an hour. Perfect. We parked ourselves and made ourselves at home in the warm air. No air conditioning, doors and windows wide open, and still the only breeze was hot. But it wasn't uncomfortable. Just… desert.

And then, the Chilean bus.

It was almost funny how quickly you forget what "fancy" looks like until you're back in it. Signs reminding us to wear seat belts. Seat belts that actually existed. A toilet on both levels of the bus. No one yelling "*peepee* only." The bar for luxury had shifted dramatically.

The ride to Calama was short. Under two hours. San Pedro didn't have a major airport, so the process was bus to the main terminal in Calama, then a ten-minute taxi to the airport. Simple. Clean. Chile doing what Chile does: quietly functioning in a way that makes you feel like you've stepped into a different continent.

Outside the window the desert stretched forever. A couple of wind turbines. And more flags. Always the flags.

Somewhere in all that emptiness, politics floated in too. I learned that Bolivia was pushing its claim at the International Court by wanting a corridor to the sea again. They claimed they wanted back what was lost after the War of the Pacific. Bolivia used to touch the ocean. Chile took that, and Bolivia became landlocked. Chile had offered other land once to keep things calmer, but Bolivia wanted the stretch from near San Pedro all the way to Antofagasta. It would mean port access, leverage, a way to export without paying Chile for the privilege. Especially now, with gas contracts shifting and Bolivia needing options beyond South America.

It's strange, the way a landscape can look so empty and still be thick with history and tension. It explained why there were so many flags though. Most of the locals fiercely identified as being Chilean rather than Bolivian.

The flight to Santiago was at sunset. The desert below turned into layers of red and brown, broken by smaller salt flats and clusters of cone-like volcanoes that looked extinct and ancient and stubborn. I wanted to be reflective. I wanted to write. I wanted to sit with it.

But my stomach had other plans.

The longer we travelled, the more sensitive my motion sickness seemed to get, like my body was slowly deciding it had had enough of constant movement. Flying used to be a calm pocket of journaling and thinking. This time, I spent the short two hours bracing myself and trying not to throw up. It scared me a little, because we still had so many buses and flights ahead. So much movement still to come.

Still, we arrived in Santiago in one piece.

And somehow it felt like coming home.

It was our third time in the city now, and stepping into it again felt familiar in a way that surprised me. We grabbed our bags and went to figure out the easiest way to get to our apartment. A taxi was 20,000 pesos. Day light robbery! The bus counter nearby sold us tickets for 1,800 pesos each, dropping us ten minutes from our AirBnB.

Familiar Ground

- SANTIAGO, CHILE -

Being back in Santiago was like sliding into a jacket you forgot you owned. It had been two months since we were last here, and even though our previous visits were short, we already had bearings. Recognising corners. Knowing which streets would feel busy. Understanding the rhythm.

This time we'd found an apartment in a neighbourhood called San Diego. It was central-ish, more university energy, cheap restaurants and beer, and still walkable to the middle. And we'd snagged it for NZ$20 each per night for the whole apartment, which felt like robbery in the opposite direction. It was west-facing on the 24th floor, which meant two things. City views all day, and sunsets around 8:30 p.m. that were almost violently beautiful. Purple and red smeared across the sky by pollution like the city was painting over itself.

We weren't here for the obvious tourist loop anymore. We'd done the basics, like San Cristóbal, museums, plazas, the free walking tour. Now we were here to be less touristy. To live slightly like locals. To shop for groceries. To map things out. To stop moving long enough that our belongings could spread out without consequence.

That's the hidden workload of travel, isn't it? The less glamorous side of it all. You're not working a job, but you're always planning your own survival. Booking buses. Booking beds. Chasing good Wi-Fi. Scheduling your life in four-day chunks. Exhausting and exhilarating at the same time.

And then, fate.

We hopped on our laptops and booked tickets to see Maluma live in Uruguay.

Felices Los 4, the song that had already become a strange little anthem for me, wasn't just on my headphones anymore. It was going to be a real crowd, real speakers, real bodies moving to it. We'd met that Uruguayan couple on the Uyuni tour, and they'd mentioned he'd be playing in their city, Montevideo, in November, right around when we planned to be there. It was one of those moments where travel feels like it's lining things up for you.

I'd had a mental bucket list for this trip. Machu Picchu, Spanish classes, homestays. But I also wanted more specific things. A Spanish-language concert. A running event. Little proof that I wasn't just passing through places, but actually stepping into them.

This one fell right into my lap.

There were two things left on my Santiago list. The first: the Museo de la Memoria y los Derechos Humanos, which in English is the Museum of Human Rights and Torture. The second, wandering the fancier suburbs eastward, the ones everyone says feel more "expat" and polished.

Today was the museum. It was about five kilometres away. We could've taken the metro, but after all the sitting during glamping and road-tripping, we wanted to move our bodies. Five kilometres was nothing compared to the Salkantay days.

We walked. Got a Chilean SIM card. Watched someone getting arrested by the *carabineros*, who looked absurdly dramatic on their big horses, like they'd been copy-pasted from a different century. Then we kept heading east, and the city shifted around us.

The route was charming and gritty in equal parts. Street art everywhere. Real art, the kind that gives a place character and makes you stop to look. It distracted from buildings that looked like they were held together by habit. Cracked churches, damaged apartments, the subtle evidence of earthquakes. It got quieter too, eerily so, until we reached one of Santiago's "busy pockets" near a metro station again and felt that immediate relief of bodies and movement.

And then the museum.

Free entry. I paid 2,000 pesos for an English audio guide, because I wanted to do it properly, and because my Spanish had limits when it came to complex pain. I kept accidentally switching the device into German or Spanish and having to get someone to change it back, which was embarrassing in that uniquely "I'm trying to be competent" way.

It was interesting. And it was brutal.

I've done my share of dark places. Auschwitz in Poland, Sarajevo's Galerija 11/07/95, mass graves in Slovakia. Because I believe those experiences are compulsory. Not for shock, but for memory. For context. For the blunt understanding that humans are capable of horrifying things, and that comfort makes you forget.

Chile's dictatorship hit differently because it wasn't "far away history." It was close, ending only in 1990. It was personal to the people still living around you. Seeing children's drawings of fear. Seeing manuals on torture. Seeing a map of known torture camps across the country.

It gave me a deeper understanding of Chilean identity. Not just *empanadas* and *completos*, but resilience. Pride that had been earned. And it made "Chile feels fancy" land differently too, because development isn't just economics; it's also institutions, stability, trust. You can even trust the cops here, and it's wild to realise how meaningful that felt after months in places where you never fully relax.

That night we met up with Carlos' cousin, Maribel. She was in Santiago to pick up a new passport, and we hosted her in our apartment, proud of the views and slightly ashamed of the chaos. Clothes everywhere, shoes airing out on the balcony, leftover pasta in the fridge. Backpacker domesticity.

We opened a 1.5-litre bottle of Cabernet, talked for hours, then moved the night to a cosy Italian place nearby with outdoor seating and a fountain. Pizza and jugs of beer. My Spanish warming up slowly with each sip. The restaurant tried to rip us off on the bill, and we ended the night walking her to the station, past the grand *bandera* in the Plaza de la Ciudadanía that wasn't even flailing because there was no wind.

The next day was stifling hot. The kind of heat that feels like someone is blow-drying your face. Not cute shorts weather, but humid city heat. Yet we still committed to a massive walking day. Time to explore Providencia and Vitacura.

We walked for hours, mostly in sun. The city transformed again. Shiny skyscrapers, brisk men in suits, women in polished outfits that screamed "I live east." Providencia felt modern, alive, full of restaurants and beautiful streets. It made me understand, for the first time, how expats could settle here. I'd fantasised about living in South America once, but Peru and Bolivia had made me doubt it. Providencia nudged that door open again. Not because I suddenly wanted to settle, but because it showed me that South America wasn't one thing. It was contradictions stacked side by side.

In Vitacura it got even more polished. Boutique stores, restaurants that looked like they'd fit on the shores of Lake Wakatipu, Queenstown. And then, on the way back, a woman behind a convenience store counter laughed kindly while I fiddled with my padlock. She told us she knew backpackers who'd had their bags slashed open while they wore them, items removed without them noticing.

So we wore the backpack on our fronts going forward, taking turns looking vaguely pregnant, guarding our tiny amount of valuables. The GoPro, the SD card full of memories, the cash.

By the time we reached the San Diego neighbourhood again, the sky was full of little fluffy clouds like someone had ripped open a pillow and thrown the stuffing above the city. The sunset bled orange and red and warmth, and even though it was still too hot, I had only good things to say about Santiago.

By October 5th, it clicked why Santiago felt so good. It gave me a taste of normal life. Not the office-desk grind, but the simple luxuries: hanging clothes, doing a proper grocery shop, having a place to ourselves, dancing in underwear without packing looming in the background. I knew I'd miss the chaos the moment I got home, because I always did, but right then, stability felt like an exotic treat.

The next morning, we woke to protest sounds, loud even from the 24th floor. From the balcony we watched the street fill with bodies, placards, flags, music. A stage. Dancing. Vendors selling everything from handmade trinkets to marijuana cakes to *sopaipillas* deep-fried in a makeshift fryer inside a shopping cart.

Later I'd learn it was linked to teachers. Organizing, striking, fighting for something practical and urgent. It made me laugh in a bleak way. New Zealand wasn't the only place where teachers had to protest to be treated properly.

The next day was quieter. Me in bed devouring books, travel memoirs mostly, because reading other people's journeys made mine feel sharper, like I was watching my own evolution from the outside. Carlos ran around doing admin and laundry. Later we headed out to Providencia again to watch the UFC at a pub.

The Irish bar was three storeys, surprisingly empty at 8 p.m., and we felt smug when it filled up later because we'd secured a prime spot near a heater. Carlos drank beer; I tried to stay awake with a hot toddy and then coffee. Deep-fried cheese *empanadas* and chips soaked in balsamic. Hours passed. The main fight ended late and weird, and we rushed out for an Uber before prices spiked.

And then, nothing.

My screen showed Ubers nearby, but no one accepted. One driver accepted then cancelled. People around us got rides easily. We stood there confused for half an hour before someone finally picked us up. The driver told us to get out on the same side when we arrived.

Later I googled and realised that Uber wasn't technically legal in Chile. Suddenly the earlier weirdness made sense. I'd switched payment to cash to avoid card scams, but that probably made it riskier for drivers because cash = obvious transaction = harder to pretend you're "just giving a friend a ride." And the "get out on the same side" request? A quiet little strategy. Less obvious. Less visible.

It was one of those travel lessons you learn sideways. Even in the "Germany of South America," there are still shadow systems humming underneath, and you're always moving through them whether you understand them or not.

And that was October so far. Leaving the desert in a blaze of sunset, returning to a city that felt like home, and remembering, again, that travel isn't just landscapes. It's logistics, politics, discomfort, small joys, strange risks, and the sudden sweetness of simply having somewhere to put your things down for a few days.

From Wine Cellars to Sea Air

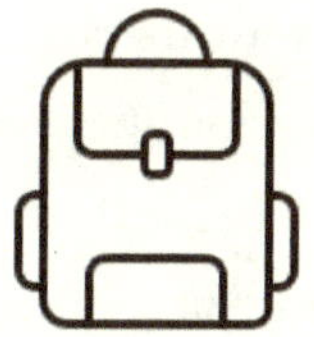

- VALPARAÍSO, CHILE -

One hangover. One single drink. One very late night. That's how I knew I was getting old. Or at least getting so tired that my body had started treating a harmless sip of booze like a full-blown crime scene. My throat was dry, my head was pounding, and I had the vague sense I'd been awake for three days straight even though the evidence suggested otherwise. But there was no room for self-pity. Today was important.

Today, we were renting a car and going on a road trip.

It had been two and a half months since either of us had sat behind a steering wheel, and after weeks of white-knuckling buses and trying not to vomit while strangers took corners like they were being chased, the thought of having control again felt like a luxury on the level of hot showers and flushing toilets. We showered, cleaned the apartment like the good little renters we were, and drove ourselves out of Santiago with the kind of giddy, slightly feral energy you get when you've been living out of a backpack for too long and suddenly you have a trunk.

Our first stop was down through the wine country to a place that had been whispering to me from supermarket shelves back home for years: Concha y Toro. And before I go any further, yes, I am aware that if you're from Uruguay, "*Concha*" is not a family-friendly word. I'm sorry.

As the city thinned behind us, the roads narrowed into something that felt weirdly like New Zealand. Rolling green. Big, snowy mountains sitting smugly in the distance like they owned the place. Vineyards stretching out on either side. It was comforting in a homesick way I hadn't expected, like the land itself was saying *"there, there. You're not lost. You're just far away."*

We grabbed cheap, impossibly fresh *empanadas* from a roadside stall and arrived in time for our booked tour. I'd been prepared to be underwhelmed because I'd heard Concha y Toro wasn't necessarily the best wine producer in Chile, it was just the most famous, the one with the export empire. I didn't care. Their Casillero del Diablo was my weekly, faithful, delicious vice back home, and here I was, in Chile, about to drink it where it was born.

The tour wasn't the bike-and-cheese-and-olive fantasy I'd once pictured for myself, and it also wasn't like the Peru winery tour where we'd basically been force-fed wine and pisco at the pace of a frat initiation. This was slower. Polished. A stroll through perfectly manicured gardens and a man-made lagoon. A tidy history lesson about how the business started in the 1880s, the French grapes, the brand mythology. We walked through cellars. First the air-conditioned one above ground, then down into the Devil's cellar where the lighting turned moody, a video played, and a dramatic little light show tried its best to convince us Satan had taken up residence among the barrels. There was a huge cobweb hanging in the gloom like a prop that had got a bit too enthusiastic, and at the end of a corridor, a devil's shadow waited behind locked bars.

It was honestly very well done. And when I lifted the glass to my mouth and tasted that deep Chilean red—my familiar favourite, but fresher, smoother, more alive—I had one of those quiet travel moments where you're hit by how absurd your life has become. I wasn't just drinking wine. I was drinking a piece of a place, a story, a whole climate and culture in liquid form. For a wine lover like myself, it was basically a pilgrimage.

Then the day pivoted from vineyards to coastline, because we were determined to make our first solo road trip a "why not do everything" kind of day. We ate lunch across the road, and then we drove west toward the ocean.

I was excited in a way that surprised me. I hadn't realised how much I'd missed sea level until I knew I was about to have it again. We'd spent the last two months living between 2,500 and 5,000 metres, and even though I hadn't had any dramatic altitude sickness moment worthy of a cautionary tale, it had taken its toll. I'd been exhausted to the core of my bones and had endless nosebleeds. I was a sea-level creature. A person who had almost always lived close enough to smell salt in the air and feel that damp ocean chill creep into your clothes even on a "nice day." I didn't even swim much back home. too cold, too lazy, too busy. Yet the ocean had always been there in the background like a security blanket. The idea of smelling it again made me feel oddly emotional.

The landscape changed in layers as we drove. First, foggy valleys that looked like they'd been wrapped in cotton wool, then dense forest that reminded me of those early-trip Chilean bus rides down near Arauco, and then suddenly we were arriving in coastal cities built on endless hills. Hills on hills on hills, dotted with hundreds of bright little houses like someone had shaken a box of crayons and everything spilled out onto the slopes. Viña del Mar, and then Valparaíso, glittering and chaotic and impossibly colourful. I wanted to know who decided to build a city like this, and why, and how anyone got groceries without developing calves of steel. We then arrived at our Airbnb. A room within a family's home in Viña del Mar. Our base for the next few nights.

The next day, we drove into Valparaíso with equal parts excitement and caution. It was the city everyone told you to visit, and the city everyone told you to watch your stuff in. By this stage we'd collected more safety warnings than souvenirs, and we'd learned the difference between "use your common sense" and "this is genuinely not a good idea." Still, I couldn't help noticing the tourists who walked around with phones dangling out of pockets like they were trying to donate them to the universe. I had to physically restrain myself from tapping on their shoulders to caution them.

The driving itself was intense. Winding roads, fast merges, everyone moving like they were part of a synchronized dance where hesitation meant death. It was hectic enough that I was relieved not to be the one behind the wheel, especially because we were also dealing with the extra layer of being on the right-hand side. Being from England and New Zealand, I'd only ever driven on the left. Carlos drove like he'd been born in it, but every now and then we'd weave between cars, and I'd imagine us careening off into the harbour. Yet we didn't crash. Because in places like this, chaos isn't chaos. It's a system you don't understand until you're inside it. I started to realise that driving "properly" might actually be more dangerous because it would put you out of sync with the flow.

We'd been relying on free walking tours as our favourite way into new cities. Instant orientation, instant context, instant human. We found one, tried to be the kind of people who show up at 10 a.m., failed spectacularly, and arrived closer to midday after doing endless circles trying to find parking. Somewhere in that chaos, we had a moment that jolted me upright. I became almost certain we were being followed.

It started at a petrol station café where we bought coffees that tasted like toilet water. A man stared at us too long, which caught my attention. Then he left and got into a black car just out the front. We got into ours. The black car ended up behind us. It followed us through several blocks.

We looped around a car park. It stayed with us. My paranoia went from 20% to 95% in under a minute, and I decided to very visibly write down the license plate in my notebook while making eye contact with them. Eventually, after more turns and more loops, he continued straight while we turned off, and just like that, the tension snapped. Maybe I was paranoid. Maybe I wasn't. Either way, my body had gotten the message: Valparaíso might be beautiful, but it was not a place to let your guard down.

We paid for secure parking. Expensive enough to hurt, but not as painful as a stolen car. And joined our tour at a plaza that may or may not have been the "real" main plaza depending on which local you asked. From there, Valparaíso unfolded like a story with a dramatic rise and an equally dramatic collapse.

The city boomed because it was once a key port for Europeans travelling by boat to California during the Gold Rush. It became a glamorous, important stopping point. So important it rivalled other major South American ports. Many migrants stayed, bringing European architecture and communities that shaped the city's bones. And then, politics and geography did what they do best… The Panama Canal opened, ships no longer needed this long detour, and Valparaíso's lifeline thinned. The port traffic dropped. The economy suffered. Unemployment rose. Crime became part of its reputation. The city that had once been the obvious place to be slowly became a place people warned you about.

We learned about the fires too. How the dry terrain, ocean winds, dodgy cables, and building materials made

Valparaíso frighteningly flammable. So flammable that major fires used to be almost weekly at certain points in history. I couldn't stop thinking about it, especially because that morning I'd noticed something unsettling in our own accommodation: no sprinklers. Not a single one. In New Zealand, the regulators would have a panic attack just looking at it.

At some point the tour involved a trolley bus ride, and then we were in the central zone for nightlife and food. Our guide gave us a rundown of local must-tries, including the infamous *terremoto* drink. Basically sugar and booze designed to knock you sideways. Also, *chorillana*, which sounded like fries that had been lovingly smothered in every possible food group (onions, meat, cheese, eggs).

Then we took one of Valparaíso's historic lifts, the kind that hauls you up steep hills so you don't have to climb like a mountain goat. It held maybe eight people, creaked upward with the slow determination of something that had survived a hundred years of human impatience, and delivered us onto the hills where the city's colour really begins.

The murals hit me first. Every surface seemed to be painted. Piano stairs, giant cats, iconic movie scenes, political commentary. Art everywhere, unapologetic and alive. I'd walked into the city ready to call it graffiti, but this was something else. Later I'd learn there are categories. Tagging, graffiti, murals. Technically, a lot of this art existed in a legal grey zone because the country still operated under an outdated constitution from the dictatorship era, but

Valparaíso had its own unofficial rule. If you had permission from the building owner, you were safe to paint. Owners even helped pay for materials sometimes, because a mural was a protective charm. Better a beautiful painting than the kind of ugly tagging that announces neglect.

Then there was the corrugated metal. So many buildings were made from container ship materials, which made sense for a port city where containers are basically local wildlife. I heard later about a guy from Christchurch in New Zealand who'd been living here for years and inspired Valparaíso's container creativity based on what he saw after the 2011 Christchurch earthquake. There, he saw an entire mall made from containers, so he took the idea back to Valparaíso to encourage container-based community spaces instead of letting containers rot by the coast. That little detail filled me with ridiculous pride. Yes, my tiny country in the South Pacific, quietly leaving fingerprints on the world.

UNESCO protection hovered over the place too, with its own complicated blessing. It meant money for restoration and an emphasis on maintaining facades. It also meant tourism… The lifeblood. But it came with rules, and it drove property prices up, often out of reach for locals. Even when a place is "saved," you start to wonder who it's being saved for.

Throughout the tour, a fluffy dog followed us with the commitment of a paid employee. He knew the route, appeared at every meeting point like clockwork, and seemed to view us as *his* tourists. Everyone wanted to pat him because he was friendly and smiling, but the guide kept shooing him away because he also had a history of biting passers-by in his overzealous attempts to protect the group. Valparaíso, in dog form. Gorgeous, loyal, a little unpredictable, and not to be underestimated.

After the tour, we made the most of having a car and did what we couldn't do when we were bus-bound. We chased the coastline. We drove through resort areas full of towering hotels, neon restaurant signs, and more seafood menus than I knew what to do with. We wound the windows down and let months of altitude finally rinse out of our lungs. The sea smell hit like memory. Salt, spray, that particular dampness that makes you feel like the world is still turning properly.

We climbed the Concon dunes with a romantic plan to watch the sunset and a practical realisation, minutes later, that wind on sand at dusk is unpleasant. The view was worth it. Huge waves smashing against rocks below. But we retreated to a more sheltered beach for the actual sunset, because although we were adventurous, we liked being warm.

And then there was Reñaca. Reñaca surprised me. People were working out everywhere. On the sand, in parks full of exercise equipment, like the whole suburb had collectively decided fitness wasn't optional. I was impressed.

The next morning, we redeemed ourselves and made it to the early tour, because we'd been told it was a completely different route. More off-the-beaten-track, more history, more dictatorship context.

We headed straight into the neighbourhood every blog told you to avoid. Safety in numbers, we told ourselves. And also, there was a friendly cop nearby, which gave us some comfort. The contrast between the plaza we saw yesterday and the one today was sharp. One polished and tourist-friendly, the other visibly frayed at the edges. Sculptures missing limbs. Areas cordoned off. A police car sitting and waiting for something to go wrong. People asking for money. It wasn't subtle. It wasn't somewhere I'd wander alone, and definitely not after dark.

To get to the hills, we took a bus that drove like it was on a schedule set by the devil himself. The guide warned us to sit down and hold tight because drivers have strict time frames and they treat corners like vendettas. Honestly, it felt a lot like taking a bus through Wellington's hills—Mount Vic, Brooklyn—so in a weird way it made me feel at home. I've been trained for this.

On that same bus, I heard a familiar accent and my brain did a little glitch. Carlos and I looked at each other and mouthed, *kiwi.* Of course there were New Zealanders on the bus with us. There were always New Zealanders. We spoke to them and discovered they lived in Wellington and one of them worked opposite our apartment. The world is so small.

One of the stops that lodged in my chest was the prison on Cerro Cárcel, used during the dictatorship years for political prisoners. It was a place of torture, overcrowding, executions. The kind of history that feels like it should belong to centuries ago, not within living memory. The building is open now, functioning as a public space, with information and photographs that make you stop and swallow. What struck me wasn't just the horror. It was the closeness of it. Not even thirty years since the dictatorship ended. Not even long enough for the story to become "history" instead of "lived experience." There are still people alive who remember before, during, after. There are still shadows in the architecture.

We planned to visit one of famous poet Pablo Neruda's houses afterward. La Sebastiana, the poet's view-filled perch over the city. But our plans were derailed when we learned Carlos' friend was arriving in Santiago earlier than expected. So we pivoted. *Empanadas*. Wine. Back to Santiago.

The drive felt faster now that we knew the route, and even more beautiful because the fog had cleared and the valleys rolled out in full green confidence, vineyards stretching like endless patterned quilts. We timed it to avoid the worst of rush hour, which was a small victory, until we hit the wall of Santiago parking.

Our next AirBnb was central, because we'd booked it before we extended the car rental, and suddenly we were cursing our own optimism. Street parking was impossible. Private lots were charging truly offensive rates. Eventually, Carlos found a homeless man with a limp who offered to watch the car. When asked what he charged, he shrugged and said it was up to us.

It was perfect. It was also, in its own way, a quiet little lesson in trust and the strange systems cities build when formal systems fail.

Back upstairs, we sorted through our bags to decide what we needed and what we didn't for the remainder of our trip. I had a friend in Santiago willing to babysit a bag of our stuff. My backpack could finally zip without me having to sit on it like a feral suitcase wrestler. We delivered the bag with a bottle of wine as a thank-you, because some debts can only be paid in Chilean red.

That night was a whirl of airport pickup and reunion. Friends arriving from Canada, the ones we'd be road tripping with down in Patagonia. We cracked open another beautiful bottle of wine and demolished the *empanadas* as if we hadn't eaten in weeks. And then, because life refuses to let you linger in any one moment for too long, we had to go to bed.

I lay awake longer than I wanted, mind fizzing with plans and logistics and the low hum of excitement. In a few hours we'd be up at 4 a.m. for a 6:35 a.m. flight to Punta Arenas. Another chapter. Another landscape. Another version of ourselves. It was time for Patagonia.

We'd moved from wine cellars to sea air to hillside murals to the dark bones of history, testing our own bravery in small ways. Trusting the road, trusting the city, trusting our instincts, trusting that we could keep carrying our lives on our backs and still find joy inside it. Between the *empanadas* and the paranoia, the ocean and the art, I could feel a chapter ending. Away from the cosy routines we'd built in Santiago and toward something wilder and much, much further south. The world kept opening, and I kept meeting it with equal parts gratitude and disbelief, as if I was still trying to convince myself that this was really my life.

The Edge of the World

- PATAGONIA, CHILE -

I wanted to die.

Three and a half hours of sleep is not enough for anyone, least of all someone trying to pretend they're energetic, functional, and emotionally stable. I faked it anyway. Dragged myself into the shower, swallowed a cup of tea, shouldered my bag, and reminded myself that we still had to get gas, return the car, and make it to the airport in what felt like ten minutes flat.

Somehow, we did.

Bags checked, security conquered, we made what I considered to be a fatal mistake of stopping at Dunkin' Donuts. There was a boarding queue already forming and my brain immediately jumped to catastrophe. I watched the women behind the Dunkin' Donut counter move at a pace

I can only describe as leisurely, attempting to make food, coffee, and conversation simultaneously. Carlos calmly pointed out that the gate didn't close for another fifteen minutes. I calmly did not believe him. I'd seen this movie before. Friends missing flights for coffee, luggage disappearing into the abyss, financial ruin. Internally, I was unravelling. I walked to the gate and back. Twice. While Carlos and his two friends leisurely waited for their coffee's and donuts.

In the end, I was wrong. We made it to our flight easily. Everyone else got sandwiches and croissants. I got a sad little donut because I couldn't handle the emotional weight of waiting for a coffee. I boarded thirsty, exhausted, and full of regret, watching the others eat and enjoy their hot beverages.

I'd planned to sleep on the flight, but guilt got the better of me. Writing on planes is one of my favourite rituals. Plane journeys feel almost spiritual sometimes, either the beginning or the end of something important. I was determined not to lose that to motion sickness or fatigue.

It was the right decision. The view outside was unreal.

Snow-covered mountains punched up through the clouds, so high I wondered how the plane managed to clear them. The snow looked impossibly white. So fresh that Carlos briefly mistook it for sand. Glaciers crept through valleys, and the further south we flew, the more it sank in how remote this all was. Peru and Bolivia had felt isolated at times, but this was different. This was the edge of things.

Chilean Antarctica-adjacent territory. Wind, cold, and nothing else to soften it.

You could even see the difference between Patagonia on either side of the border. Chile's jagged, snow-heavy mountains versus Argentina's vast, flattened plains. Geography as personality. I was grateful we'd flown. This was meant to be seen from the sky. A little turbulence on descent made me think of my friend's warning about the winds. I laughed it off. We're from Wellington, after all. How bad could it be?

Bad.

The moment we stepped outside in Punta Arenas, the cold slapped us in the face, and the wind tried to physically remove us from the country. The warnings had not been exaggerated. I was deeply grateful for my thermals and boots, and mildly alarmed to learn the city had installed ropes for pedestrians to cling to during extreme winds. Casual. I knew then that the next few weeks were going to be chilly.

Still, Punta Arenas surprised me. I'd imagined a tiny outpost of wooden huts and fireplaces, but it was a full-sized city, humming along on oil, tourism, and its port. Not a destination in itself, but a launchpad. We wandered briefly. Maps, phone credit, food. Before deciding to squeeze in a short hike. If we were about to spend hours in a car, moving our bodies felt necessary.

The trail was modest, icy in parts, exposed above the tree line just long enough for the wind to remind us who was in charge. Mostly, though, it was sheltered and manageable, which suited me fine. I was still acclimatising to the cold after deserts and cities and sunshine.

From there, the road pulled us north toward Puerto Natales. The Ruta del Fin del Mundo, the "Road to the End of the World," lived up to its name. Coastline first, dark and forbidding, then mountains rising sharper and angrier with every kilometre. By the time we arrived, we were wrecked. Late night, early start, flight, hike, drive. Our Airbnb host ran out to greet us with hugs and kisses, as if she'd been waiting all day. Inside, there was heat, space, and a fluffy cat. Then she reappeared with a basket of eggs from her chickens.

That night was wine, pasta, and panic-planning. We had done almost no research for Torres del Paine National Park and were suddenly confronting the reality of camping in Patagonia. Hypothermia loomed large in my imagination. Thankfully, our host and her sister stepped in with advice, reassurance, and offers of cutlery. We decided to sleep on it, literally and figuratively, and deal with logistics in the morning.

The town of Puerto Natales turned out to be far prettier than I expected. Wooden buildings, mountains on the horizon, icy air that somehow felt festive. But there was no time to linger. Carlos' friends were only with us briefly and Torres del Paine waited for no one. Everyone had told me you had to book camp spots, camping gear, and ferries far in advance.

Except, we hadn't.

Cue frantic laps of town, tourist offices, and whispered prayers. The woman at the information centre was an angel. She explained entry fees, hikes, transport, and the two companies that effectively run accommodation inside the park. From there, we went straight to their offices. One involved a man drinking *mate* in a warm room who calmly explained that yes, we could camp, yes, everything would be set up for us, and no, we didn't need to lug equipment.

I nearly hugged him.

Suddenly, we had a plan. A loose, ambitious, slightly insane plan. But a plan, nonetheless. Lago Grey. Icebergs. Torres Base. Boats. More glaciers. Possibly pumas.

At the park entrance, we were handed a waterproof guidebook and casually informed where coffee could be found and where pumas had recently been sighted. Instructions followed on what to do if you encountered one. Apparently, only one person had ever been killed and eaten by a puma in a national park.

Her final words of "Good luck!" did not help ease my nerves.

The park was overwhelming. Ice-blue icebergs floating like sculptures. Wind that forced you to lean into it just to remain upright. Mountains that looked violently beautiful. And tourists in jeans, which baffled me entirely. Inside the overpriced mini-market, a bag of chips nearly gave me a heart attack. Thank god for our grocery shop back in Puerto Natales.

That first walk was short but powerful. Standing above Lago Grey, learning that what we could see was only a fraction of the iceberg's true size, spotting the glacier in the distance that we'd soon hike toward. It all felt surreal.

The drive to camp was equally distracting. Snow, turquoise rivers, waterfalls. When we arrived, the tent was ready, sleeping bags warm, and miracle of miracles, hot showers and toilet paper. Luxury. We celebrated with wine, scotch, and fiercely competitive rounds of Uno while the wind battered the tent. Inside, we were cosy. Outside, chaos.

The next day's hike to Mirador Las Torres, the Base of the Towers, humbled us.

It wasn't the gentle stroll we'd been promised. It climbed, dropped, climbed again, threw waterfalls at us, and demanded full concentration on the descent. It was a twenty-two-kilometre hike over the course of about ten hours into some of the most beautiful scenery I'd ever seen. Jagged mountains, streams you could fill your water bottle from, fresh snow, windy valleys. But it was hard, especially because the boys were hungover. In the end, we'd had to turn back before reaching the base, choosing time and safety over stubbornness. It was too bad, but I didn't regret it. Not when a massive condor glided overhead, wings stretching wider than felt reasonable, watching us like potential snacks.

By the time we collapsed into the lodge for coffee and sugar, I realised how much the previous months had trained my body. The distance and elevation that once would have crushed me now felt… doable. My feet disagreed. Blisters were brewing. But I was proud. In some ways, I barely recognised myself. I was becoming the kind of person who could hike mountains with ease and who others struggled to keep at pace with.

We made the ferry, survived the waves, laughed over a mistranslated menu item that briefly made us think sitting down cost money, and drove back toward Puerto Natales with no accommodation booked and no cell service to sort it out on the road. Somehow, a warm, wood-scented hostel appeared just in time. Pizza was inhaled. Wine was poured. Stories spilled out.

Torres del Paine was done.

Paperwork and Other Near-Death Experiences

- PATAGONIA, ARGENTINA -

We woke up with one urgent mission. Recover the infamous PDI immigration card. The flimsy little "receipt" Chile expects you to guard with your life like it's a birth certificate. Fortunately, it turned out to be almost offensively easy. We wandered into an empty police station, a man in uniform appeared, printed a replacement on the spot, and laughed like this was his main hobby. We laughed too, but with the strained energy of people who'd been carrying the weight of a potential US$100 fine over one stupid scrap of paper. Crisis averted. Paper resurrected. Onward.

Next stop: Argentina.

Crossing a border always feels like a tiny plot twist. New language rhythms, new road rules (or lack thereof), new snacks, new ways to get confused. The Chilean side started with a familiar dose of chaos. A busload of Australians was ushered straight past the queue, and the rest of us stood there in that particular kind of shared human misery where everyone is trying to be polite while also fantasising about becoming a lawless vigilante. A little drama unfolded about the queue skipping. The Australians played the innocent "we're just doing what we're told" card. The people who'd been waiting twenty minutes did not find this compelling. Somehow, our initial line of six ended up watching twenty people drift in front of us like migrating geese.

The Argentine side, on the other hand, was a breeze. We drove five minutes into the middle of nowhere, bounced onto gravel and potholes that immediately made the car feel like it was being shaken for loose change, and then got our passports stamped within two minutes. No bag checks. No questions. No suspicious dogs. Just a couple of officials who seemed keen to get back to whatever people do at a border post surrounded by emptiness.

The drive to El Calafate was long and gorgeous in that stark Patagonian way. Chile's dramatic mountains and moody clouds off to one side, Argentina opening out into rolling plains that made you feel tiny on the other. We could see angry grey weather looming above Torres del Paine behind us, like the park was finally exhaling now that we'd escaped. Ahead, I wasn't sure whether the road was trying to murder us with potholes every few metres, or if our friend's driving was deadly erratic. Nevertheless, the sky stayed kind. Thank God. We'd had enough near-death experiences recently without being taken out by a crater in the middle of nowhere.

And then, just as we pulled into El Calafate, *ta-da*, our Airbnb didn't exist.

The first red flag had been the lack of an address, just coordinates and photos. But we were seasoned now, right? Coordinates were normal. Pictures were normal. Slight chaos was normal. We found the house, matched it to the photos, tried calling the owner. He answered once, hung up, then went mysteriously silent while still showing as "online" on WhatsApp. The neighbour wandered over and delivered the final blow with the casual brutality of someone who's seen this play out before. The owner had sold up, moved to Colombia, and the place wasn't being rented.

We stared at each other in that stunned, almost impressed silence.

We had been scammed. *Properly* scammed. Our first real South American scam. Two and a half months in, just shy of the halfway mark. It almost felt like a rite of passage, like the continent had finally stamped us back. In all honesty, I was laughing and actually happy it happened. It was another story to be shared.

And here's the thing, it worked out perfectly.

We didn't even linger long. We drove straight into town, fed ourselves, walked into a hostel, and checked in. The place was only slightly more expensive, but it was central, practical, and came with the holy trinity: laundry, Wi-Fi, and a tourist information centre basically at our feet. Even better, we learned that if we paid by credit card, tourists could have a chunk of tax knocked off the price. Some convoluted economic crisis solution that somehow resulted in us getting a discount. Had we not been scammed, we might never have discovered this. Life is chaotic, but occasionally it's chaotic in your favour.

That night became a little celebration of things falling into place. We supermarket-sprinted for a DIY cheese platter, then camped out in the kitchen, played Uno, and I made mulled wine. It was warm and comforting. Patagonia had been testing us, and we were answering with carbs, cheese, and competitive card games.

The next day we meant to do glaciers, but our thermals were still in the wash and none of us felt like proving ourselves through hypothermia. So we explored El Calafate instead, and it surprised me completely. After visiting Buenos Aires two years before, wild and colourful and occasionally sketchy, this town felt like a quaint winter postcard. Everything looked like a wooden lodge. The air was crisp and dry. It made you crave Christmas markets and cinnamon and the kind of mulled wine you drink out of a mug while pretending your life is a movie. If someone had plonked me there without context, I genuinely might have assumed I'd accidentally wandered into Europe.

Even the tourists were different. Up north, it had been mostly young backpackers stretching coins, trading tips, living on rice and optimism. Patagonia drew a different crowd. Older, well-off, often American, often on short trips. Patagonia isn't cheap. It felt like the continent's luxury appendix. Safer, shinier, more expensive, and full of people who could afford to treat it like a once-in-a-lifetime highlight reel.

We walked to Laguna Nimez, a little sanctuary a short stroll from town. It was windy and cold, but the lake beyond it, Lago Argentino, was so intensely blue it looked like someone had attacked the landscape with a highlighter. We looped the reserve, spotting black swans and flamingos, reading the information boards, enjoying the simple miracle of stretching our legs without having to summit something. Not every day needs to be a mission. Sometimes it's enough to stand in the wind and watch birds carry on with their important bird business.

That evening, we joined a bizarre excursion that promised Indigenous history, ancient cave paintings, and most importantly, according to Carlos, dinner in a cave with wine. A Land Rover picked us up, the driver apologising profusely for being late. He had bright blue eyes that didn't match my mental picture of "typical Argentinian," and then we were off, rattling over rough tracks while Carlos' motion sickness once again tried to ruin his life. Every time we stopped, the view punched us in the face; Lago Argentino glowing under the setting sun, vast and cold and unreal.

We got split into language groups. Our English tour was just the four of us, led by a Bosnian guide, which made the whole thing feel strangely intimate. The cave paintings themselves were a little underwhelming. A few stick figures, some of faded remnants, a lot lost to time and animals. The cave was soot-black, supposedly from centuries of fires, and the most compelling part of the entire history segment was how our guide, someone who'd lived through brutal war, could say almost nothing about it and still make you feel its weight in the background. When Carlos' friends mentioned they were heading home soon, the guide said, "It's never long enough, is it?" and Carlos and I practically snorted. Six months was *absolutely* long enough. We'd already agreed there would be no more trips of this length unless we were secretly relocating or had lost our minds. Four to six weeks? Perfect. Anything longer? I better have a job, a lease, and a toothbrush with a permanent home.

Then the cave dinner happened. We were served pumpkin soup in metal containers, instant defrosting for our freezing hands, followed by bread bowls. Actual bread bowls. A whole sourdough loaf hollowed out and filled with hearty food like the cave was running a rustic little Michelin star. The boys got lamb stew, us girls got garlic vegetables, and it was exactly what you want when the wind off the lake is slicing through you. The red wine kept flowing, topped up constantly. Candlelight flickered. A man played gentle guitar. The smell of stew lingered in the air. We warmed from the inside out, wrapped in that cosy, slightly unreal feeling that travel sometimes gifts you, like the world has paused just to set a scene, until we eventually made our way back home.

Our hostel became its own kind of heaven. Underground heating meant we could lay clothes on the floor at night and wake up to them toasty warm. Breakfast was all breads and pastries and jam, with eggs if you wanted them. The kind of comfort that makes you feel briefly domesticated, like you might start doing yoga and journaling about gratitude instead of panic-booking accommodation the night before. It was a comforting pace to lean into.

And then, the Perito Moreno Glacier day.

We drove out, paid the fee, caught a boat that slid past blue ice chunks floating on milky grey water, and pulled up near the face of the glacier. I'd been carrying a weird little grief about missing the "proper" view of Grey Glacier in Torres del Paine, but this felt like the universe making it up to me in the most dramatic way possible. Not only could we see the glacier properly now, we were about to hike on it.

They strapped heavy crampons to our boots, gave us a safety briefing, and then we stepped onto the ice like we belonged there. Crampons were instantly life-changing. Not one slip. Not even a wobble. I became evangelical about them immediately, wondering why they weren't standard issue in countries with harsh winters like Canada.

The glacier itself was otherworldly. The sun came out despite forecasts threatening rain, and I peeled off layers because although I was hiking on ice, I was sweating, which feels like a contradiction you can only experience in Patagonia. We saw caves so blue they didn't look real. Deep, electric, almost glowing. We walked through smooth ice hills and jagged towers, past clear streams where people refilled bottles with what had to be the freshest water on Earth. And then, as if someone in the sky was writing this trip like a TV show, we rounded a corner and there was a table set up. Glasses. A guy smashing glacier ice into a bowl. Whisky being poured. Chocolates offered. We clinked glasses and drank whisky cooled with ice from the glacier we were standing on. *Salud.*

It was absurd. It was perfect. It was the kind of moment that makes you forget that your bank balance is quietly weeping.

We still weren't satisfied, apparently, because after that we walked along wooden boardwalks on the far side, watching and listening as the glacier cracked. Sometimes pieces calved off with a thunderous roar, collapsing into the water right in front of us. Sometimes it seemed internal. Deep groans and sudden cracks that made the lake ripple. You could stand there forever, waiting for the next boom, hypnotised by the slow violence of ice moving.

That night, because we clearly had an "ice theme" going, we went to an ice bar.

Polarbar was ridiculous and hilarious; ten-ish dollars, twenty-five minutes inside, unlimited drinks. Drinks came in ice glasses, and I drank so fast I couldn't even think of what I wanted next, so I told the bartender to surprise me. I got everything from coffee liqueur to something grapefruity and bubbly to one drink that tasted like thick Listerine and regret. We left the bar, peeled off the giant fur-lined coats that had been provided to us, stood outside under the late evening sun, and realised, oh. We are *drunk.*

We continued anyway, because it was our last night together as a group of four. We drank at a bar that reminded me of home, then wandered into a posh restaurant while definitely wasted, like four idiots cosplaying as functioning adults. I have no idea how I successfully ordered anything. I do know the food was incredible. I do know we bought more wine. I do know at some point I looked up and the entire staff were standing at the bar watching us, and the restaurant was empty. Midnight had arrived like a slap. The night had vanished.

On the way out, we fell in love with a pack of street dogs outside the restaurant. Sober, we would have avoided them out of fear of bites and rabies shots. Drunk, we were rubbing bellies and calling them angels. One dog rolled onto his back, feet in the air, growling with happiness—until Carlos' friend suddenly lunged through, lost his balance, and basically startled the dog back into reality. It was one of those moments that's impossible to explain and hysterical for years afterwards. We laughed about it at least twenty times like it was a treasured family story.

Then morning came, and it was time to say goodbye.

That week had been a gamble. Travelling with friends can either bond you for life or quietly destroy everything you once loved about them. But it had worked. We'd encouraged each other into adventures we might not have chosen alone. Road trips through emptiness, hikes through world-famous landscapes, glacier trekking, endless wine, shared exhaustion.

It had been expensive, yes. Patagonia always was. But it felt worth every cent. And I realised something else too. I'd always thought I preferred travelling alone, but on this trip, I'd come to love the shape of our little unit. Carlos and I moving together through the mess and magic of it all. His friends had added energy and boldness. They nudged me into moments that probably wouldn't have happened if it were just me and my overthinking brain.

After the airport drop-off, Carlos and I were back in that familiar state: winging it. Plans shifted. Ushuaia suddenly seemed far and ferry-filled and unrealistic with the time we had left on the rental car. So we went north to El Chaltén instead. Famous for epic hikes and mountaineering. And arrived with absolutely no intention of doing either. We just wanted to wander, breathe, and recover like we were on a spa retreat, except the spa was a windy mountain town and the treatment was *empanadas*.

El Chaltén was adorable, smaller and rougher than El Calafate, with that "peak season will be chaos" feeling even though it was quiet now. We found a bakery and bought *empanadas* for a price that felt like a gift after El Calafate's crazy expensiveness. Then I bit into one and immediately spat it out in horror.

Beef.

My first bite of meat in thirteen years. Whoops.

I tried another. Pork. Also whoops.

Eventually I went back inside, asked very clearly for *empanadas* with no meat, and left with a caprese one.

We slept deeply that night. Fluffy bed, some heat, the kind of rest that feels medicinal. In the morning, breakfast appeared despite being "not included," which felt like a tiny miracle. The hostel was almost empty, and I could picture it swarming in summer with hikers from all corners of the world gearing up for trails.

Not us. The only thing I planned to stamp my boots into was grass near a coffee truck and then the passenger seat of our rental.

We had a long drive ahead, back toward Puerto Natales, retracing roads we'd already taken, but under a sky so clear it made everything sharper. The lakes were bluer. The mountains looked closer. We'd finally figured out the iPhone cord in the car, which meant we spent six hours blasting a top-2000s playlist like teenagers, except tired, slightly hungover teenagers with joint stiffness.

With the better weather came more roadkill. Rabbits, a guanaco, guts spread across the road. A sheep and lamb sprinted in front of us at one point and we slammed on the brakes while they panicked and paced like they were also surprised to have bodies.

We crossed the border again, this time from a slightly different angle after a wrong turn, and got pulled over by cops. My nerves flickered (Argentina had felt less predictable), but these guys were friendly. One officer even grinned at Carlos' Spanish name and proudly pointed to his badge because his name was the same, like this was the highlight of his shift. At immigration, things were calm and quiet. Argentina stamped us out quickly. Chile searched our bags, as expected. We'd eaten our fruit, but a mandarin had hidden in the bottom of a backpack like a stowaway. The Chilean guys were surprisingly chill and waved us through with that kind of gentle understanding that makes you feel both relieved and mildly guilty for assuming the worst.

By the time we reached Puerto Natales, I felt oddly at home. I knew the streets. I knew where the best *empanadas* were (or at least I thought I did, until my favourite bakery was tragically out of cheese ones). We checked into a hostel that looked like a run-down tin shop from the outside but was gloriously warm inside, thanks to a constantly blazing fire that felt both comforting and like a potential insurance nightmare. And then, we both fell into a much-needed deep slumber.

And somewhere between the clear sky, the familiar roads, the almost-missed mandarin, and the disappointment of no cheese *empanadas*, it landed... We were halfway through the trip.

Halfway.

It didn't feel like a neat milestone. It felt like standing on a ridgeline. Behind us, deserts and salt flats and high-altitude breathlessness; ahead, whatever else this continent still wanted to throw at us. The more we "winged it," the more I realised we were building a strange kind of competence. Messy, accidental, fuelled by wine and optimism, but real. We weren't just moving through places anymore. We were starting to trust that even when plans fell apart. When borders were chaotic, Airbnbs were fake, weather threatened, or a mandarin tried to sabotage us, we'd figure it out. And somehow, that made the world feel bigger and safer at the same time.

Climbing sand dunes in Huacachina, Peru.

View from our homestay bedroom in Sucre, Bolivia.

Palafitos in Chiloé Island, Chile.

View of Machu Picchu, Peru.

The many bottles of wine we bought on our bike ride in Mendoza, Argentina.

View after hiking on the Perito Moreno Glacier in Patagonia, Argentina.

View of El Valle de la Luna in San Pedro de Atacama. We'd just completed a twelve-kilometre bike ride in desert heat to get there.

Sitting in the darkness in our farm stay in Tacuarembó, Uruguay. We had back-to-back storms all day and it wiped out the electricity.

Our cycling group posing at the Curva Clasica on the Death Road, Bolivia.

The road between Santiago, Chile and Mendoza, Argentina via the Andes.

Carlos fully immersing himself into his Uruguayan heritage with his thermos and *mate* in Montevideo, Uruguay.

Our hiking group at the peak of our trek to Machu Picchu. 4,600 metres above sea level.

Relaxing in Miguel's parents pool in San Nicolás de los Arroyos, Argentina.

Carlos and Rosemarie exploring Punte del Este, Uruguay.

Playing at the beach in Arauco, Chile.

One of the many *asados* cooked on a *parrilla* for us by Rosemarie's friends in Libertad.

Halfway, Somehow

- PATAGONIA, PUERTO MONTT & CHILOÉ ISLAND, CHILE -

By the time we hit Punta Arenas again, Patagonia had started to feel weirdly familiar. Which is an outrageous thing to say about a place that can casually fling 130km/h winds at your face and call it a nice day. But there we were, limping out of Puerto Natales with groggy eyes and stiff bodies after a truly stupid decision to turn off the heater overnight because I was convinced it would set the bed on fire. Our perfectly planned early start immediately collapsed into reality. Late wake-up, rushed packing, and the kind of grim determination you only achieve when you're running on caffeine and regret.

We pointed ourselves along the dramatic-sounding "Route to the End of the World," which honestly felt accurate. Not because it was ominous, but because it kept stretching out into this massive, open, windswept nothing that made you feel like you'd driven past the edge of the map. The sky was absurdly clear. Not one cloud. The kind of day where everything looks sharper and brighter, like someone has adjusted the contrast settings on your life. The grass was greener, the lakes glittered, and even the roadkill, still everywhere, still grim, felt like part of the landscape's blunt honesty. Patagonia doesn't really do delicate.

Somewhere on that drive, I had time to reflect. We'd had a blast up north in Peru and Bolivia, but there had been culture shock lurking under the fun. Things you only realise were heavy once you're standing somewhere else feeling lighter. In Patagonia, I kept catching myself thinking, *Oh.* This is what comfort feels like. Not comfort as in "I'm at home in my own bed," but comfort as in "my nervous system is not constantly bracing."

It made me grateful for the earlier chaos and also acutely aware of it. Travel is sneaky like that. It teaches you in hindsight, long after you've stopped noticing you're learning.

The drive itself was almost too easy. Smooth roads, clear weather, a quick couple of hours. And suddenly we were back in Punta Arenas, dumping our bags at an Airbnb and dropping off the car. Handing the keys back felt like giving up a privilege. After months of buses and horrific driving, having a little four-door bubble of control had been pure luxury. We could stop when we wanted. We could pull over for views. We could blast music. We could be humans rather than luggage with feelings.

Back on foot, Punta Arenas felt a little rougher around the edges than the Patagonia postcard towns we'd just visited, and our Airbnb was far enough out that we did that classic traveller thing of squinting at the street like, "*is this dodgy or is this just… normal?*" But "dodgy" in Patagonia didn't ping my alarm bells the way it might have elsewhere. We did a very grown-up supermarket shop. Fruits and vegetables. Then immediately counteracted our efforts with a bakery trip next door. Balance.

That night, the bed saved us. A proper double. Multiple blankets. One with a whole layer of wool sewn underneath like it was designed specifically for people who'd spent the last week being tenderised by wind. I slept so hard I swear I time-travelled.

In the morning, breakfast was waiting downstairs, and it gave me that cosy, home-stay feeling I'd been chasing since I started planning this trip. I'd wanted local families and kitchen-table conversations and small domestic details that make a place feel real. And fortunately, private-room Airbnbs were giving us exactly that. Often more than hostels did. We sat at a sturdy wooden table in an oversized kitchen with chequered tiles, eating bread rolls slathered in homemade jam made from some native berry I'd never heard of, sipping a tea I also couldn't name, and demolishing a bowl of sliced fruit like we were trying to reverse months of *empanada*-based decision-making.

Our host loved to talk. And normally I live for that. The problem was I understood roughly five percent of what she said. Which was kind of depressing when you consider I'd been in Spanish-speaking countries for months and had convinced myself I was becoming some sort of semi-fluent explorer. No. Down here, the Spanish felt faster, harsher, more swallowed, like all the consonants had been removed. I kept wondering if it was a dialect thing. The further south you go, the trickier it gets. But mostly I just sat there smiling awkwardly while Carlos translated, feeling simultaneously grateful to have him and mildly betrayed by my own ego.

Politics came up almost immediately. She had the kind of passionate, sharp energy that makes you picture family dinners exploding into arguments and someone storming out dramatically. I wanted to understand every word because this is absolutely my jam. But the language barrier turned it into this frustrating blur where I could only catch scattered keywords and vibes.

Then she brought up the Falklands War. Several times.

From what I could piece together, she believed the islands belonged to Chile, which was a new one for me. It was also painfully awkward because she knew I was British, and I'd already clocked that a lot of South America carries a simmering resentment about England's claim to the cluster of islands floating off Argentina's coast. I didn't have the language skills to debate geopolitics over breakfast even if I'd wanted to, so I did the next best thing. I nodded politely, took another bite of toast, and mentally filed it under *Do not touch this topic unless you want to ruin your entire day.*

Later, I did what I always do when I feel out of my depth, I researched. I knew the basic outline… A war in the 1980s between England and Argentina, a messy colonial legacy, emotions still running hot. I knew it personally only in weird fragments. My dad being in the region for Antarctica work at the time, and an Argentine friend once telling me his dad was in the army, and us laughing awkwardly like, *So… are we enemies?* The more I read, the more I concluded that this was the kind of topic you don't "win" in casual conversation. It's not trivia. It's identity and history and pride and pain all bundled up together. The safest plan was simple: educate myself quietly, hold my opinions gently, and avoid having a breakfast-table argument that ends with someone throwing jam.

By the afternoon, it was time to leave again. We had a flight to catch. Booked just two days earlier, somehow still reasonably priced, and it felt like another little travel miracle. Two hours in the air instead of three full days on buses? It was an easy decision. We could have flown straight back to Santiago, but there was another region of Chile calling my name, and I wasn't ready to trade wild landscapes for city streets just yet.

As we headed toward the airport, I realized that our Patagonia chapter was fully closing. It was a chapter that had soothed me in some ways. A chance for my nervous system to finally let its guard down, even though much of the trip was still unknown. Patagonia had been cold and expensive and exhausting, and yet it had also given us this steady, almost comforting and familiar kind of beauty. The kind that makes you breathe deeper without noticing you're doing it. It left me feeling both tougher and softer at the same time. I might still be struggling with the language, but I had surprised myself by how physically strong I was, and that made me feel alive.

Puerto Montt greeted us like it had been offended by our recent happiness. Rain, thunder, and a bolt of lightning that seemed to flirt a little too closely with the plane on the way down. We arrived late enough that "sightseeing" became a tomorrow-problem, except the next morning, the rain was crackling against the single-pane window like it was trying to get in. We hadn't seen much rain in months, and I can't say I'd missed it, but I'm English. Rain is basically a family member.

Downstairs, our host had laid out bread, ham, cheese, and a box of teabags in a way that felt quietly caring rather than Airbnb-performative. I liked her immediately. She had that lonely, empty-nest softness, like our presence was as much the point as the payment. She'd picked us up from the airport, fed us, and then offered a driving tour of the city, which is the kind of generosity that makes you want to do your dishes without being asked.

The tour didn't last long, because Puerto Montt wasn't really putting on a show. It felt run down, not in a romantic "gritty port city with character" way, but in a "someone slapped corrugated metal over a wound and decided that counts as structural integrity" kind of way. You could see the German influence in the bones of some buildings, but it was like they'd been built in the 1800s, partially burned down at some point, and then everyone collectively agreed to just keep living in them anyway. It had a shady little edge to it. Valparaíso vibes, but without the murals and the tourists and the unofficial agreement that art would keep everything afloat.

Still, we wandered. We walked along the pier, up into the suburbs, and got approached by a handful of drunks asking for money or a lighter. Nothing dramatic. Just that faint sense of being watched by the town itself. Our host warned us not to go out at night and said if we were going to have trouble, it would likely be near the bus terminal in the centre.

Naturally, that was exactly where we needed to go.

We bought bus tickets for the next day and promptly decided we were going somewhere that sounded like it had been invented by a novelist: Chiloé Island. The ticket price was almost comically reasonable. The journey included a ferry across the strait, and the island was advertised with the kind of marketing line that makes you instantly suspicious and instantly sold. A land of myths and legends, unique folklore and culinary traditions. It also promised incredible seafood, which mattered greatly to Carlos and not at all to me, the vegetarian who continues to travel through seafood capitals. But I was in. Mythical island? Yes. Even if my contribution would be cheese and carbs.

The moment we rolled onto Chiloé, the first thing I noticed was colour. The island was saturated with it: rich green fields, tiny trees, yellow flowers like someone had dropped handfuls of sunshine across the hills. Even the houses looked like they'd been designed by people who believed joy was a civic duty. Colourful wooden homes with shingled sides, the kind that make you want to slow down and start describing things as "quaint" without irony.

We passed through Ancud first, small and sweet, with wooden churches that looked like they belonged in a storybook. And then I learned one of those facts that makes a place feel instantly more magical. The island is dotted with around seventy churches protected by UNESCO. *Seventy*. On one small island.

Castro, the main town, was a ten-minute walk from the bus stop and already felt different. There was a softness to it. Like the island's history of being tucked away from the mainland had seeped into everything. We dropped our bags and went on a mission. Apple *empanadas*, supposedly made with a local apple that Chiloé does in a way the rest of the world cannot. Naturally, every single place had sold out.

So we wandered to the plaza instead, passing a sunflower-yellow wooden church that looked like it had been painted by someone who genuinely liked happiness. The plaza itself was smaller and quieter than the grand, dramatic city squares we'd been seeing elsewhere, but it had the feeling of somewhere that could swell in summer. This was an island getaway for Chileans, I'd heard. Especially those fleeing Santiago when it got too loud. And I could see why. Castro didn't shout. It didn't demand your attention. It just existed. Calmly. Colourfully. Like it had all the time in the world.

Down by the port, the water was glistening. Fishing boats bobbed. A few brave kayakers cut through the cold like they'd made a mistake but were committed to it now. And then the smell hit me like a memory. Crab, fish, sea salt. It was exactly the smell of my childhood in England.

Carlos grimaced. I, on the other hand, was instantly transported. I could practically see myself at Lymington Quay with my bright orange crabbing line. Bacon on a hook, net in hand. Running crab races with my brothers like it was an Olympic sport and the fate of the nation depended on it. Two decades later, I was on the other side of the world breathing in the same salty stench, living a completely different life. Those full-circle moments sneak up on you and make you go quiet for a second.

Our accommodation was near the water too, which meant waking up to that view: boats on glassy blue, the town still sleepy and colourful. The house was wooden like most of the island. Exposed floorboards, thin paint in places, a fireplace positioned like a guardian between the bedrooms and the cold. We were staying with a local family. Two kids, parents. The mother had the kind of warm smile that made me absolutely certain she could bake an apple pie that would end wars.

The next morning was one of those mornings you want to bottle. No wind. Sun out. Boats reflected perfectly beneath themselves like the water was showing off. The air had a slight chill if you leaned into it, and everything smelled like salt, fish, and woodsmoke drifting from chimneys. The only thing that screamed "developing continent" was the tangled mess of cables outside our window, like a bird's nest made of electricity.

We tried the apple *empanada* mission again, because I am nothing if not stubborn about snacks. I finally found one at the bus terminal from a kiosk run by several women. They ripped off tea towels with aggressive efficiency and barked options like I was interrupting something important. It was intimidating, like tossing a chip into a pack of seagulls. But the *empanada*? Worth it. The dough was the best I'd had on the continent. Flaky, rich, absolutely delicious.

After that we went hunting for Castro's famous *palafitos*. The colourful stilt houses you see on Instagram, hanging over the water like they're trying to be both home and postcard at the same time. We walked and walked along the waterfront, seeing clusters of them but not the famous view, until we finally found it. A pastel rainbow of houses reflected perfectly in still water, the kind of scene that makes you suddenly understand why people become annoying online about travel. I stood there having one of those tiny internal battles where part of you wants to be present and part of you wants to take seventeen photos.

Chiloé, it turned out, was too big to understand from one town. So, we rented a car for the next day. We learned quickly that traffic here was basically theoretical. "Giving way" meant waving at the one other car on the road and carrying on. It was all very relaxed.

We drove northeast to see one of the island's famous churches. Bold blue, stars painted on it, sitting in the middle of nowhere like it had been plonked down by a whimsical deity. Churches kept popping up everywhere, and it started to make sense. This island holds colonial history and local Indigenous tradition in the same hands. Tangible evidence of two worlds layered on top of each other.

Then we went looking for a waterfall. Getting there meant navigating flooded stretches, gravel tracks, potholes. We parked, walked the last stretch, and paid an entrance fee at someone's house (after waiting around and patting a tabby cat who clearly ran the place), then got absolutely tormented by mosquitoes while taking in the view from above. From below, the waterfall was powerful, less "cute photo spot" and more "washing machine of death." Skinny dipping would not have been a good idea.

Midday, we had a brief detour back to town because I hadn't charged anything and needed my power bank, only to realise I'd padlocked my bag and lost the key. I tried to pick it with a hairpin like I'd been trained by the CIA, achieved nothing, and then Carlos took over and popped it open immediately like this was a normal skill he'd been casually withholding. I laughed so hard I couldn't even be mad.

We drove west along roads lined with fluorescent green hills that looked almost edited, like someone had boosted the saturation settings and then forgotten to turn them back down. We stopped at a rustic café by a dark lake where a horse-sized dog barked at us like we were intruders in his personal kingdom. A scruffy guy assured us he was harmless, so we tiptoed past anyway. The coffee was a rip-off. Small drip coffee for the price of a small mortgage. But it did the job.

By the time we arrived at Cucao, the air felt different again. There was a hippy vibe I couldn't quite define. Like the atmosphere itself was wearing patchouli. We skirted the edge of the national park, found sand dunes, and stood facing the ocean. It was cold, but it made me weirdly happy to think that if you kept going in that direction long enough, you'd eventually hit New Zealand. Home tugged at my brain for a second, like a familiar hand on your sleeve. Then I remembered home was still months away, and the whole point was to stay here, now, in this misty, mythical corner of Chile.

That's how we ended up hiking to Muelle de las Almas, a place we'd only half understood from a blog. We paid the fee, parked the car, and set off expecting a short stroll. Instead, it turned into a full two-hour trek over planks laid across thick mud, through dense forest, up and over and on and on until we reached the cliffs. And there it was. Ocean and sharp rock faces and fresh air so clean it felt like it reset something in my chest. The wind had died down, the view was enormous, and I felt that deep, simple satisfaction of earning a place with your legs.

But now, it was time to move on and head to our next destination. As we drove back to Castro, Carlos and I debriefed about our time in Chiloé. It wasn't flashy, and it didn't shout about its beauty. It just quietly offered it, through woodsmoke mornings and apple *empanadas*, through pastel houses on stilts and blue-star churches in the middle of nowhere, through landscapes so green they looked imaginary, and a hike that refused to be as short as advertised. After Patagonia's wild drama and the rough edges of the mainland, the island felt like a fairytale with muddy boots: gentle, strange, comforting, and just unpredictable enough to keep you paying attention.

And now we were back to the reality of two buses, eight hours on the road, and the kind of travel day where time becomes an abstract concept and your brain starts buffering.

Sea Lions and Volcanoes

- VALDIVIA, VILLARICCA, PUCÓN & ARAUCO, CHILE -

The bus from Castro zipped across the island, rolled onto the ferry, and spat us back out in Puerto Montt where, in theory, we had a tiny window to make our connection. In reality, the bus was late, so we did that classic bus-terminal hover—loitering with purpose, clutching our bags, trying to look like we definitely knew what we were doing.

Once we finally got moving, I did the thing I always do on long rides. Shoes off, headphones in, face pressed towards the window like a golden retriever who has discovered scenery. The sun was out. Mountains started to appear. And then a couple of them looked suspiciously… volcano-y. Perfect cone shapes. Thick snow. Just sitting there like they were posing. Later, I looked them up and discovered they were Volcán Osorno and Volcán Calbuco. It was instantly obvious we'd entered Chile's lake-and-volcano territory.

I hadn't really heard much about Valdivia, which meant I had no expectations to crush me. The city felt young, leafy, and safe, in a way that was hard to articulate but instantly felt in my bones. It had that university vibe. Parks, trees, a kind of casual energy. We were confident and felt safe enough to walk the thirty minutes from the bus terminal to our Airbnb. Here, cars actually stopped for us at crossings and waved us across like we were their honoured guests. I was almost suspicious of their kindness at first.

We wandered into the riverside market and discovered that Valdivia is basically a wildlife documentary. The market was bustling. Fish being gutted, fruit piled up, crafts laid out—and behind the fish stalls, fishermen tossed scraps. Birds swooped and strutted. Pelicans, vultures, everything with a beak and an opinion. And then the sea lions.

So many sea lions.

Not politely in the distance either. These were sea lions living their best lives right beside the market, roaring like disgruntled old men, flopping around like giant lumps of lard with inexplicably good mobility. I watched them for ages. One of them launched itself off a pier with a two-metre drop like it was doing a dramatic stage exit. I stood there, transfixed, wondering how something so enormous could move with so much confidence.

We crossed to another market, poked at adorable souvenirs (teas, hats, little Chilean games I didn't understand but wanted to pretend I did), and then found *sopaipillas*. I'd been quietly collecting *sopaipilla* moments like treasure because I knew they were a Chilean thing, and we were heading back into Argentina soon, where my beloved oily dough discs would become a distant memory. When the guy charged us 500 pesos each, I thought, *rude, that's expensive.* But then he handed us *sopaipillas* the size of my head, dripping with an entire bottle's worth of oil, and I suddenly felt like I owed him an apology.

Later, we made a pilgrimage to Kunstmann Brewery because Valdivia, plot twist, is a beer city. A continent famous for wine, and here we were getting educated about IBU bitterness ratings like we were attending Beer University. The bus driver kindly kept an eye on us and told us when to get off, which I appreciated. The brewery was wildly German-looking, and the bus stop was shaped like a beer barrel.

We ordered a tasting board of sixteen little beers in shot glasses, laid out like a science experiment, complete with alcohol percentages, ideal storage temperatures, and food pairings. My meal even had beer in it. Falafel patties drenched in a honey-beer salsa.

The next morning, I woke up with a single mission. Sea lions. I could have watched them all day. Sea lions rolling in the river, pelicans gliding onto roofs, vultures standing with wings spread like they were airing out their grievances. It reminded me of a trip to Samoa earlier that year, of standing on a balcony at sunset watching turtles surface in a milky lagoon. Except here it was sea lions popping up instead, and the soundtrack was market chaos and barking dogs and the occasional human swinging a handbag like it was a weapon.

Because it was drizzling, we declared it a museum day and went searching for culture. The Contemporary Art Museum took us through derelict, graffiti-coated university buildings. The building itself was half-ruined. Apparently cursed by fire and then wrecked by the biggest earthquake ever recorded in the world (a magnitude 9.5!), now a skeleton filled with art. Down in the basement, it was freezing and lined with hundreds of Mapuche masks that stared at us with a level of judgement that made me wince. There were tunnels at the back. One dimly lit, one pitch black. I don't know if walking into a dark tunnel counts as contemporary art, but I wasn't keen on exploring it any further.

The other museums stitched together pieces I'd been holding loosely—migration histories, German influence, the fact that there were significant German communities here long before the post-WWII Nazi-escape narrative that everyone loves to mention in whispers. Valdivia started to make sense. The architecture. The beer. It was like I'd been walking through a place with a question mark over it, and suddenly some of the punctuation clicked into place.

And then we left. Midday bus, drizzle, grey sky. I didn't even mind. I was in that weird state where I felt so alive that I struggled to sleep, like every day was Christmas and my brain was refusing to power down because what if it missed something. I found myself thinking about how wild it was that I hadn't been that interested in South America before. I used to be obsessed with Eastern Europe, Soviet history, bleak cities, and the lingering ghosts of Cold War politics. That obsession had led me to a semester abroad in Poland, an internship in Montenegro, a solo adventure on the Trans-Siberian Railway, and more. And yet somehow, my "first date" with South America, an accidental week-long stopover in Buenos Aires two years before, had teased me into wanting more. I'd promised I'd be back. And here I was, not on a one-year working holiday like I'd once planned, but also not on a fleeting visit. Somewhere in the messy middle, which is arguably where the best stuff happens.

The bus ride to Villarrica could have been described as grim. Heavy cloud, rain slamming the windscreen, the driver peering through a watery blur. But I was happy anyway. I settled into my seat, watched green fields and pine trees slide by, and let myself reflect. Carlos, due to motion sickness pills, was out cold, which meant I got to have a quiet little internal monologue with the landscape.

Villarrica felt like the calmer, less polished sibling of the famous Pucón. Charming, lodge-like, more "real Chile" than tourist brochure. When we arrived, rain was still pouring, and halfway through hauling our bags, someone shouted Carlos' name. For a second I thought it was coincidence. His name is everywhere on this continent. But it was our Airbnb host, swooping in like a wholesome guardian angel with a car. Our place turned out to be an extension of a cosy home: small kitchen, bedroom, private bathroom. We'd paid for a private room and basically got our own little apartment. Warm. Quiet. And guarded by a hilariously fat, fluffy cat called *Rotonda* who threw herself onto the ground dramatically whenever you patted her, rolling with the full commitment of a creature who knows she is adored.

Then we checked the forecast.

Rain. Every day. *For two weeks.*

Villarrica was adorable, but it was the kind of rain that floods roads and makes trees look like they're drowning. The kind of rain where one minute outside means you're wringing out your clothes like you've just crawled out of a lake. We waited for a break, spotted a shift from "we might actually drown" to "temperamental drizzle," and sprinted out in raincoats and hiking boots like we were making a daring escape. The village was tiny, quiet, not particularly touristy. I liked that. We wandered markets, found a *sopaipilla* spot, and tried to see the famous volcano, also called Villarrica… which was somewhere around us, presumably, hiding behind a wall of cloud like it was playing a long and extremely committed game of hide-and-seek. Villarrica is one of Chile's most active volcanoes, and something I was hoping to summit in the next few days.

Strangely enough, in between the drizzle and the craft markets, I caught myself daydreaming about a future house. One where I'm not living out of a suitcase, not counting grams, not mentally calculating if I can justify buying a souvenir. A house where I could fill shelves with teacups from Iran, Serbian stone candle holders, *mate* cups from Argentina, Russian dolls that could hide mini vodka bottles. All the things I kept gifting other people because I loved them but couldn't carry them. I loved travel, but I also liked the idea that one day my home could be a story too. Layered with little objects that whisper, you were here, you loved this, *you lived.*

When the weather eased slightly, we took a bus over to Pucón. The touristy cousin we'd been warned about. It took half an hour to confirm everything we suspected. More hotels, more restaurants, more money floating in the air. Signs appeared announcing volcanic danger zones, which felt thrilling in theory, except the volcano was still hiding. I really wanted to hike up it, but the weather was not working in our favour. Instead, we sat down for coffee, hot chocolate, and a small portion of churros and got slapped with a NZ$20 bill like a gentle reminder that we were no longer in "quiet village" territory.

Still, the lake was lovely. We walked along the edge, passed teenagers smoking marijuana, families photographing themselves in front of the big town sign, and a hostel called "Chile Kiwi Hostel" with a logo of a kiwi bird snuggled up to a chilli. An identity crisis I found deeply relatable with my mixed upbringing between England and New Zealand. The black sand under our feet was a quiet clue. A volcano nearby, even if it refused to show itself. The water was ice cold, but I could imagine this place in summer. Warm enough to swim, sunny enough to convince everyone life is perfect, tourists spilling in.

Back in Villarrica, the lake looked calmer, milky silver under the cloud, and for the first time the clouds thinned enough that we could see the lower half of the volcano. Its base, the snow line cutting a sharp horizontal seam across it. It wasn't the dramatic reveal I'd been hoping for, but it was something. Progress. A promise. We walked by the water, got eaten alive by midges, and told ourselves tomorrow would be clearer. Tomorrow would finally give us the full volcano moment.

And even if it didn't, I still felt this steady hum of contentment underneath everything. The bus terminals and the rainstorms and the missed views. Because this whole stretch, from Chiloé's fairytale calm to Valdivia's sea-lion chaos to Villarrica's soggy charm, held the same emotional truth. We were learning how to let places surprise us. How to accept that sometimes the best moments are the ones you didn't plan. The oversized *sopaipilla*, the beer flight that turns into a lesson, the cat that flops over like a furry sack of joy, the volcano that makes you wait. It was messy and ordinary and magical all at once, and somehow that blend made me feel more alive than any perfectly sunny postcard ever could.

Nevertheless, Villarrica sent us off with one last little joke.

The morning we were leaving, the sky finally cleared, and instead of the thick, moody cloud blanket I'd been grumbling about, there was crisp, brutal cold. I woke up shivering and immediately realised the clouds had been doing us a favour. Typical. And even more typical, the volcano was finally in full, glorious view. Not a vague suggestion of a snow line. Not a "maybe that's it behind the grey." No, there it was, towering over everything, casually dwarfing the mountains I'd previously thought were the main event.

We stuffed ourselves full of road-snacks—*empanadas*, nuts, iPad charged—and climbed onto the bus with the kind of optimism you only have when you've convinced yourself that the travel day is "simple enough." It was meant to be one long ride to Concepción, then another to Arauco. Easy. Efficient. Beautifully logical.

I'd downloaded a few episodes of *Suits* like a guilty secret. I'm usually annoyingly puritanical about bus rides: they're for staring out the window and contemplating the meaning of life, or writing, or reading, or editing videos, or doing something vaguely productive. Watching Netflix always felt like wasting time. Why watch fictional drama when I'm literally living inside my own travel memoir?

And then I watched Netflix.

And my god. I get it now.

The hours evaporated. I did a brief, dutiful half-hour of window-gazing. Winding rivers, emerald hills, that wet-green Chilean countryside that always looks like it's been freshly washed. Then I slipped into a book, and then into

Suits, and suddenly we were rolling into Concepción like someone had fast-forwarded the day. I'd been so committed to "productivity" when the actual gift was simply giving my brain a break.

Concepción felt instantly warmer and louder. We'd been there before, but the bus station was new territory, which meant that familiar little travel-itch: Where do we go? Where do we stand? How do we not miss the next thing? We did quick bathroom stops, grabbed yet another *empanada*, and started asking strangers where the buses to Arauco left from.

We found the stop and walked straight into chaos.

It was Valparaíso energy, but with fewer murals and more horns. Buses pulling in and peeling off again like they were playing a game of chicken with time. Drivers beeping at each other, yelling, gesturing wildly. The kind of place where by the time you've processed the destination sign, the bus has already launched itself into the distance. It felt like the drivers were on some contractor system where lateness isn't an inconvenience, it's a threat to your pay cheque and livelihood. The result was manic efficiency and a lot of panic.

We did manage to catch our bus in the end. Bags still on our backs, bodies moving on instinct. The assistant on board immediately grabbed my backpack and basically yanked it off me with my arms still through the straps. For a second I felt like I was being mugged by public transport, but no, he just threw it onto a front seat with a few others like it was a sack of potatoes and we were off again.

The bus was empty at first. Two stops later, it was full. Or so I thought.

Then it got fuller.

And then it became one of those buses where "full" is not a limit, it's a challenge to be tested. People kept climbing on. Bodies pressed in. Carlos gave up his seat for a pregnant woman, which meant he joined the standing sardines. The woman had a little white spaniel with her, and at some point this dog ended up sprawled across my lap like I was its personal sofa. I patted it happily while we bounced along for two hours.

Rolling back into Arauco felt oddly like returning home, maybe even more than Santiago had. Santiago was familiar now, sure, but Arauco was where we'd truly taken a breath and started. And here we didn't just have a city, we had people. A home. A family rhythm we could step back into. When the bus dropped us off, we didn't need directions. We just walked the twenty minutes to the house without thinking, backpacks on, stretching our legs in that satisfying way you only appreciate after a full day of sitting.

Picnics with the Dead

- ARAUCO & CONCEPCIÓN, CHILE -

And then it was Halloween.

So after we dumped our stuff, we went out with Carlos' cousin, Maribel, and her son, who was dressed as Predator, which felt both terrifying and hilarious on a small Chilean street, to do a bit of trick-or-treating. Kids were everywhere in costumes, bouncing from house to house, the air buzzing with that sugar-high anticipation.

But we were also a little disappointed that not many homes seemed to be into it. Back home, Halloween is mostly "here's some candy, please don't egg my house." Here, I quickly learned they actually mean the trick part. The evidence was the teenage-looking kid at the local store buying a bag of ten eggs with the guilt of someone who has done this before.

The next day, it was a strange relief to wake up in a familiar bed. Not just because it was comfortable, but because my brain, ever the overachiever, decided to gift me a new paranoia. I'd recently read about Airbnb hosts illegally filming guests. Sometimes "innocently" in living rooms, sometimes… not innocently… in bedrooms and showers. I lay there thinking about how many places we'd stayed in, how many rooms we'd walked around in barefoot and unguarded, and I had a brief, private shiver.

That day happened to be All Saints' Day, and we'd accidentally timed our return for a long weekend. In Chile, it's a day when families visit the graves of loved ones. At first, the idea sounded morbid to me. I'm not sentimental about graves. I've always been very clear about my own preferences. Donate my organs, burn the rest, scatter me in the ocean. No boxes, no worms, no expensive plot of land, no grief tax for my loved ones. Let me be ash and salt and movement. Let me keep travelling.

But the cemetery wasn't what I expected.

There was a market outside, huge and lively, selling toys, fast food, cosmetics, clothes, flowers. It felt like a community event. And inside, it wasn't suffocating sadness. It was strangely uplifting. Graves were decorated beautifully, and families weren't just standing and crying, they were sitting together, sharing food, talking, remembering. It wasn't about tragedy. It was about presence.

We had strawberries and *nalca*, which I'd seen before down south and had assumed was some kind of sea-plant. It turns out *nalca* is Chilean rhubarb, and to me it tasted like rhubarb and celery had a slightly confusing baby. I wasn't convinced it was any good until someone sprinkled a mix of salt, chilli, and *merkén* over it. Then I was hooked. So there we were, picnicking among graves, eating fruit, laughing quietly, remembering people in a way that didn't feel heavy. It made me think we could use more of that back home. The permission to celebrate someone's life without having to drown in sorrow to prove you loved them.

Somewhere around then my thoughts drifted to writing.

It was the international month of writing, an event my mum loved, because she's always been a writer, and it made me reflect on how obsessed I am with keeping records of my life. I've written about nearly every trip I've taken, and I regret the ones I didn't, like moving to New Zealand as a teenager, and my first Australia trips when Brisbane felt wildly exotic. It's almost funny now to think I once saw Australia as some far-off adventure, when since then I've trained through Siberia, learned about war and human trafficking in Bosnia, gone to a wedding in Samoa, ridden camels in the Middle East, road-tripped New Caledonia. My definition of "exotic" has been dragged around the world and stretched like taffy.

I'd always thought I might write my travel memoir during this trip. I had everything documented, after all. But the truth was: even without work, my brain felt like it was exploding. New settings every couple of days. New language. New social rules. New food. New bed. I was having the time of my life, but it still took a ridiculous amount of energy just to keep absorbing it all. I needed to cut myself slack. Creativity isn't always something you can squeeze out at the end of the day when your head is already full of everything.

And I kept telling myself there wasn't much to write about anyway, because things had gone smoothly. No dramatic muggings, no unexpected romances, no cinematic turning points. Mostly just fun and adventures. But even as I thought that, I could feel the counter-truth forming. Sometimes you don't see the lesson while you're in it. Sometimes you need distance. The meaning shows up later, quietly, like the volcano finally revealing itself the minute you're leaving.

Back in the household rhythm, the cultural misunderstandings started up again too, particularly my ongoing South American battle with vegetarianism.

"Do you want a salami sandwich?" Maribel asked.

"No, it's meat. I don't eat meat."

"Salami isn't meat."

This happened constantly. Part of it was language because *carne* often meant beef specifically. So when I asked for something without *carne*, people would reassure me cheerfully, "*No! Es con jamón y pollo!*" as if ham and chicken are simply different categories of vegetable. Later we all laughed about it at the table, and Maribel declared that if something is red, it's probably meat. Her son then pointed at the capsicum jam and told me I shouldn't eat it because it was red, which honestly felt like the most accurate summary of my dietary experience on this continent.

We did a day trip to Concepción, again. This time because Maribel wanted to bulk buy nuts for her school. And as we drove, the conversation drifted into corruption in South America, the way people talk about it with a casualness that still surprises me. Apparently Chile, not so much. Argentina and Uruguay? More normal. The rest of the continent? Don't be naïve! They were ridden with it.

I found it endlessly fascinating, this generational layering: people who lived before dictatorship, people who lived through it, people who grew up after it. I wanted personal stories, not museum panels. I remembered a man who ran a hostel in Bosnia telling me about the 1990s war, and the one detail that lodged in my brain like a splinter. That there was more sex than ever during the war, because it was the only distraction from the horror. Human beings are strange and resilient and messy. It was a lot to hold in your head on a short drive to buy nuts.

The markets in Concepción were pleasant. No aggressive haggling. No constant pressure. Everything was priced. One price for everyone, no opportunity to boost it because of my accent and obvious whiteness. After months of markets where you had to brace yourself, this felt like luxury.

On the drive back, the outskirts of the city looked rougher. Withered apartments, areas described as *peligrosa* at night, stories of people throwing stones at traffic. A dry, dusty soccer pitch. A collection of shacks. Chile is more developed than many parts of the continent, but it still has edges that remind you where you are. It's never just one story.

That night, Carlos and I were getting snappy at each other, which pushed me into doing something I hadn't done since leaving New Zealand. I went for a run. It had been over three months. I couldn't believe it. And it felt amazing. All the walking and hiking had kept me fit enough that it wasn't as brutal as I expected. I got odd looks. Some Mormon missionaries even preached at me mid-run, because apparently running in Arauco is an invitation for spiritual guidance. But I realised I'd missed that feeling. The simple, clean sensation of moving fast on purpose, of shaking something loose in your body and letting your thoughts settle.

And that was the emotional pulse of coming back to Arauco. The comfort of familiarity, yes, but also the reminder that travel doesn't pause your inner life. You still carry your anxieties and your ideals and your tired brain and your creative guilt. You just carry them through different landscapes. In Arauco, with family around us and routines briefly returning, it felt like a place where everything could land for a moment, where the trip stopped being a blur of bus stations and started to feel like something I could actually hold, examine, and eventually, one day, write into meaning.

We hit one of those glorious travel days where the only achievement is existing. No dramatic itinerary. No "must-see" list. Just us, in Arauco, doing absolutely nothing, and somehow it felt perfect.

This was meant to be our launch day toward Mendoza, but with our accidental timing to return to Arauco with a public-holiday weekend, it was too good to rush. We didn't really have deadlines anymore, just one loose anchor in the distance: we wanted to be in Montevideo in a few weeks. But everything in between was negotiable. And honestly, after weeks of wind-whipped Patagonia and constant motion, the luxury of slack time felt like being handed a soft blanket.

Still, I could feel myself itching for the next chapter. We'd been in Chile longer than I'd expected, and as much as I adored it—its warmth, its steadiness, how homey it could feel—I was ready for something new. I was ready for Argentina prices again, for more predictable weather, and for "*Argentina*-Argentina," not just Patagonia's polished, expensive corner.

It also made me laugh at how naive my pre-trip brain had been. I'd honestly lumped the whole continent into one big mental file called South America, like it was a single flavour of salsa. As if everyone spoke the same Spanish, looked the same, ate the same things, danced the same dances, lived the same history. Meanwhile this "far away continent" was quietly holding hundreds of languages, endless mixtures of ancestry, and faces so distinct you could start to guess where someone's roots might be—Peru/Bolivia, Chile, Argentina/Uruguay—without even meaning to. Assuming "South Americans all look the same" is about as ridiculous as assuming all Europeans do. Travel has a brutal way of showing you what you didn't know.

And that's why the world is a better classroom than any lecture hall. University memories blur into panicked essay-writing and exam cramming, but travel sticks, because you tie the information to a street smell, a face, a conversation you didn't fully understand, a moment you felt small or brave or stupid. New experiences keep colouring in parts of you that you didn't realise were still blank.

The next day, our laziness peaked. Getting up before 10 a.m. now felt like a hate crime unless absolutely necessary. But the weather finally decided to behave, and Arauco was sparkling, so we dragged ourselves into the daylight like two sleepy cats and wandered down to the Plaza de Armas.

The square was bursting in that specific small-town way. Children sticky with ice creams, parents lingering in the sun, street dogs casually treating the fountain like their favourite water bar. We joined in by slurping freshly made strawberry juice, which tasted like summer and happy memories.

And then, *nalca.*

We'd become mildly obsessed with this "Chilean rhubarb," and we found a man selling piles of it on a corner like he was dealing contraband. Next to him sat an older woman with a completely deadpan expression, chewing *nalca* with the calm authority of someone who has never once cared what anyone thinks. Without changing her face, she announced, *"es delicioso."*

We bought two sticks and the little salt-and-*merkén* mix, and then she stared at us, same expression, same tone, and asked if we were Chilean and where we were from. The whole interaction was so flat and so unintentionally funny that I had to escape quickly before I burst out laughing right in her face.

After a quick grocery run, we did the school pickup with Maribel, and it hit me how much the seasons had shifted in just a few months. We'd done this exact same walk in winter, at the exact same time of day, and back then it had been dark and viciously cold. Now it was still bright daylight, and I was overheating in a t-shirt while shoving a *sopaipilla* into my mouth outside the school gates. Perfect kiosk placement for hungry kids and equally hungry adults doing pick-ups.

We finished the day with the beach. I'd never pictured Chile as a beach country, even with that absurdly long coastline, but Arauco's beach was breathtaking. The ocean was calm, the waves soft, the kind that whisper instead of roar. And right at the entrance were kiosks selling the most cliché Chilean lineup imaginable. *Empanadas* (cheese for me, crab for others), *completos*, and *sopaipillas.*

We couldn't eat too much because we had a farewell dinner ahead—homemade *completos.* Carlos and I made a grave mistake last time by purchasing hot dog buns from the supermarket as our contribution, which turned out to be a cultural crime. This time Maribel insisted, firmly, that we buy the proper bakery ones you pick yourself from the bins. She was not negotiable about it. And she was right. The bread was fresher and softer. I swapped the hot dogs for vegetarian *milanesa*, added homemade pickled eggplant and capsicum, and genuinely felt like I was eating happiness in a bun.

Then it was time. Our bus was leaving at 11 p.m., and our taxi ride to the station became its own weird little episode. The driver asked the usual friendly questions. Where are you from, do you like Chile. And then went from 0 to apocalypse in one breath, announcing the world was ending because of drugs and launching into a rapid-fire monologue about how dangerous everything is, including Arauco, where apparently you can't even walk at night. This was news to me.

But we survived the prophecy, escaped the taxi, and flung ourselves onto the bus with that last-minute adrenaline that always makes you feel like you're starring in a slightly low-budget action film.

The overnight ride to Santiago was suspiciously fine. Gravol knocked me out fast. I fell asleep early and woke up just as we were sliding into the outskirts of Santiago. Carlos was completely out cold. He'd taken two pills, I'd taken one. And I pulled back the curtain to a pastel-pink sunrise. Santiago was apparently having one of those brutal heat spells, mid-thirties for days with radiation warnings, and I was deeply grateful we were passing through in the cool early morning.

We barely had time to breathe before the next bus. Coffee, breakfast, bathroom, a quick leg-stretch. We heard an announcement, and Carlos thought our bus was delayed until a ridiculously specific time. I assumed it was actually just the platform number. I was right. I guess my Spanish was improving after all.

And then our bus arrived, and it was fancy. Wide leather seats that reclined nearly flat, movies playing, an attendant who clearly took pride in making the whole thing feel clean and calm. It was like someone looked at our passports and decided we deserved an upgrade to Tourist Mode. And honestly? Driving through the Andes like that felt like being handed a gift.

PART III

Wine and Ride

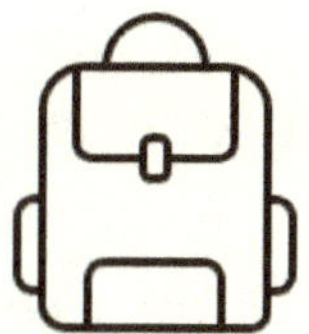

- MENDOZA, ARGENTINA -

The ride between Santiago and Mendoza was one of the best bus journeys of my life. At first, I was distracted by my book about an Aussie couple motorbiking through the Americas, describing this exact route from Santiago into Argentina. Eventually I put it down because the view in front of me was better than anything printed in words. Vineyards stretched for miles below bright blue skies, dwarfed by snow-capped mountains that made Santiago's skyscrapers look like toy blocks. As we climbed, the landscape dried out. Vineyards giving way to cactus and dusty hills. And the engine sounded like it was working overtime just to breathe.

The Andes aren't just beautiful. They feel powerful in a way that makes you quietly respectful. I kept seeing signs of rockfalls, shrines on the roadside, sudden drops into deep canyons, and it made my brain do that unhelpful thing where it imagines earthquakes at the worst possible moment. The road wound into a series of looping hairpin turns, the bus painfully curling around each one, and the highway below us looked like a long snake laid across the mountains. Genius engineering, borderline terrifying, utterly mesmerising.

Higher up, angry black rock appeared under lingering snow. Waterfalls battered the cliffs. Evidence of melting as warmer months edged in. We moved through tunnels, horns echoing inside like some chaotic mountain symphony, and in the longer ones the bus bounced like a sugared-up child. I tried not to think about fault lines and confined spaces and what-ifs.

Carlos, meanwhile, slept through most of it as always. He missed the whole spectacle, but in fairness, that was preferable to him vomiting into my lap, so I decided to call it a win.

And then, Argentina.

It looked instantly different. Red earth. Dust. Rocks in shades of rust and clay, rapids running reddish like the whole landscape had been stained. It was almost Martian. There were occasional shacks, kids on cheap bikes, low-hanging haze that might've been fog or smog, and the poverty felt more visible right away. The contrast hit hard.

We arrived in Mendoza earlier than expected, argued about directions (yikes), and then found our Airbnb was bigger than the photos suggested, which was a win. We dumped our bags and went out for dinner and drinks.

The night ended with one of those travel coincidences that makes the world feel tiny. We met up with an Irish guy we'd travelled with from Uyuni to San Pedro de Atacama. It was the third country we'd seen each other in. We swapped stories, laughed at how we'd kept just missing each other by days, and said goodbye with that quiet understanding travellers have. That we'll probably run into each other again, somewhere ridiculous, when we least expect it.

And then Argentina did the thing Argentina does. It made me feel slightly guilty for how cheap everything was. Meals for the price of a coffee back home. Beer that didn't make me wince. Our walking-tour guide called it "adventure tourism" in the economy, because the currency swings so wildly it becomes part of the experience. You could feel the crisis in the background: people coming up to tables, placing candy or cards down, returning a minute later for a donation. But you could also feel this strange, resilient joy. Like people here have survived the rollercoaster before and know how to keep dancing while the ground wobbles.

I also became quickly aware of something else. The men were… more pervy. More forward. That aggressive "no just means try harder" vibe that I'd read about and now recognised. It wasn't constant, but it was enough to register, to make me more alert in my own body. Travel doesn't just change the scenery. It changes how you move through space.

Still, Mendoza itself made me happy. Even with cloud cover hiding the mountains, the plazas were lovely, the Italian influence was everywhere. Names, food, that particular musicality to the language. And there were little architectural echoes that reminded me how tangled histories really are. Arabic influence braided into Spanish, Spanish braided into South America, geometric patterns and floral motifs showing up where you don't expect them. Once you know to look, the world starts connecting itself.

And then came the day I'd been fantasising about. Wine biking in Maipú.

I'd pictured it like a movie scene. Cute bikes with baskets, gentle pedalling through vineyards, casual sips of Malbec, me being effortlessly charming and not at all sunburnt.

Reality began with a rattling old trolley bus and cycling through Maipú's sketchy streets with partially destroyed pathways, and drivers who seemed offended by the existence of cyclists. I genuinely wondered how anyone made it back after a full day of tastings. But we'd committed.

We rented bikes from a place called Wine and Ride, run by two young Argentinians who were still hauling bikes outside when we arrived.

First stop: an olive oil factory, as a sensible attempt to line our stomachs before the wine avalanche. We tasted seven different olive oils. Lemon, garlic, rosemary. Plus spreads and olives so good I swear we were making involuntary pleasure noises. The best part? It was free.

FREE. We immediately planned to come back later like greedy little goblins.

Then came the vineyards.

A smaller one first, charming and chaotic and a tour in Spanish, with generous "tastings" that were absolutely not the measured polite pours I expected. I learned random things I didn't know I'd ever need. Like the different ways to make rosé, and that some red wines can be served cold. The wines were thick and syrupy in an Italian style that wasn't really my preference, but I was grinning the whole time because I love learning through doing, and wine is basically history and chemistry you can drink.

Next was a slicker, more modern vineyard with plush couches and perfectly aligned vines under a blue sky. The vineyard you imagine when you imagine vineyards. We sipped merlots and carmenères, posed for photos like we were in a travel brochure, and Carlos bought several bottles to enjoy later.

By the time we aimed for the organic vineyard, the day started to wobble. Literally. We took a wrong turn, ended up on a highway with massive trucks, cycled around a roundabout the wrong direction, got honked at aggressively, and had to concentrate so hard on riding straight that it felt like a cognitive exam.

The organic vineyard was worth it. They talked about pest management by planting fruit trees to distract insects, and about labour practices that suddenly mattered more once I'd read about migrant exploitation in the region. The tasting, however, lasted approximately one hundred hours.

The pours were generous. Everything became hilarious. We ordered too many tastings, bought too many bottles, and somehow ended up with a dusty bottle from 2005 that looked like it had been excavated from an archaeological site.

We stumbled out, discovered I'd been searching for my helmet while it was still on my head, dodged smoke from a paddock fire started by someone's discarded cigarette, and then sprint-cycled back to the olive oil place like we were on a mission. I tried to act sober and realised I wasn't the only one failing. There were packs of middle-aged American tourists also attempting to walk in straight lines back to their shuttles. I sat down and demolished a whole tub of trail mix while Carlos bought olive oil like a man who has discovered religion.

Then we remembered the deadline: bikes back by 6 p.m.

We thought we had it. Six kilometres. Easy. Except it was over 30 degrees, we were sun-cooked, wine-soaked, already twenty-plus kilometres deep, and the path back was so rough we had to hop off frequently to avoid smashing the bottles we'd shoved into our bags like reckless squirrels hoarding for winter.

We rolled in at 6:30 p.m., sweaty, euphoric, late, and a little ashamed. What a combination.

The Wine and Ride office was packed with other cyclists, all glowing and exhausted, celebrating with another glass of wine from the little bar inside. Which is genius, by the way… Ending a drunken cycling day at a wine bar is either brilliant hospitality or a safety hazard, depending on how you look at it.

I looked at us. Sunburnt, tipsy, laughing, carrying bottles like trophies. And thought *this is it.* This is the feeling. Not just the big mountains or the famous landmarks, but the full-bodied absurdity of a day where you plan for romance and end up with chaos, generosity, wrong turns, unexpected lessons, and a silly amount of joy.

The day Mendoza decided to humble us, it did it before sunrise.

"F***!"

I shot upright in the dark like a meerkat who'd heard a predator sneeze. It was pitch black, my brain still somewhere inside a wine-fogged dream, and Carlos was already moving like he'd been launched.

It was 5:30 a.m.

He told me the apartment had flooded.

Not with normal, innocent water either. It was black-and-gold, oily, thick in places like mud.

The neighbours had warned us the day before. Apparently, it had been happening daily, like a scheduled feature of the building since Monday. But I was already on thin ice emotionally because the "repairs" had been going on until a disgusting hour the night before. When I finally fell asleep around 1 a.m., they were still drilling and hammering behind the kitchen wall, every jolt and scrape vibrating through the apartment as if someone was trying to tunnel into our life.

Now we had an industrial swamp creeping across the floor and the occasional ominous splat. Four distinct bursts, like a floodgate opening and snapping shut again, just to keep the tension alive.

There was nothing to do at that hour other than accept our fate and try to sleep through it.

We then woke at 10:30 a.m. to violent knocking.

Carlos answered the door in his underwear, and a man handed over a slip of paper and announced we were forbidden from using any water. Building-wide rule. No showers. No cooking (because washing dishes would require water). No toilet flushing.

We brushed our teeth anyway and spat into the toilet like guilty animals. Then we escaped the apartment in search of breakfast and a sense of normalcy.

We went straight to Beirut, which was a café we'd discovered thanks to a voucher from a walking tour we'd done a few days ago. It was bright, colourful, and tucked into a corner of the Plazoleta Pellegrino like a little hipster oasis. The menu was quirky and vegetarian-friendly, there were homemade juices, and the furniture looked like it had lived at least five previous lives in various homes and garages. It reminded me of Wellington in the best way. Like you could order something with three kinds of fermented goodness and no one would blink.

Carlos ordered an "*Ensalada Zonda*," and the waitress explained that *zonda* was the name of the hot winds that whip off the mountains. We were feeling them that day. This warm, dry gust that blew straight at your face like a hairdryer. It reminded me of those northerlies in New Zealand that make you feel like you're walking through invisible heat.

We weren't trying to be ambitious. After the glorious chaos of wine biking and the lingering hangover that clung to me like a needy child, we wanted an easy day. Light strolls, greenery, something sweet, maybe some people-watching.

Also, we couldn't exactly relax at home while it flooded with greasy liquids and sounded like a construction site.

So we drifted through parks instead, watching end-of-year high school kids doing what high school kids do everywhere. Smoking cigarettes, kicking footballs, strumming guitars, being heartbreakingly young and confident in their own immortality. I felt ancient. Which is funny, because I was only 26 years old. But something about watching teenagers live their little dramatic lives makes you feel like you should be holding a cup of tea and muttering about "kids these days."

We did have to make an important decision, though. Without water, the apartment was basically a glamorous camping situation with none of the nature. No shower, no toilet, no ability to wash anything. We started weighing up whether we should pack up and find somewhere else for the night.

And then our Airbnb host offered to pick us up and take us to her place for the night so we could shower, use a toilet, and cook dinner. We accepted immediately.

She arrived looking impeccable. Toned arms, perfect makeup, Spanish laced with the occasional Italian word in that way that makes Argentine Spanish feel so distinctive. Like it's got a little extra swagger built into the vowels. We drove south for twenty minutes through pretty neighbourhoods, and I expected maybe a normal apartment, a modest house, something… regular.

Instead, she pulled into a place with a huge security gate—two metres high, "you shall not pass" energy. The car rolled up the driveway, and I caught a glimpse of a swimming pool and kayaks lounging on the grass like they belonged in a lifestyle catalogue.

The house was gorgeous. Old-school wood, high slanting ceilings, and a kitchen that hadn't been modernised in decades but somehow still looked charming rather than sad. She had five kids, some of them home, plus two overly friendly dogs who acted like we'd been away at war and had finally returned.

She showed us to a room with a king-sized bed and its own ensuite. It was almost entirely covered in family photos and religious decorations. The shower had excellent pressure, which felt incredible, until we noticed an ant infestation gathering in a corner of the ceiling like they'd called a meeting about us.

That was the moment I realised, I would rather stay unshowered than spend the night wondering if an ant would crawl into my mouth while I slept.

Thankfully, before we had to commit to any ant-related decisions, her son casually announced the building leaks had been fixed and we were safe to go home. A full day of ups and downs over something as basic as water, and suddenly it was resolved. It was stressful, but it was also one of those situations that you know would make a great story.

The next day felt like Mendoza apologising.

It was cooler than the previous few days. Still warm, but less like being baked. I was reminded just how happy this city is as a place. Sunlight everywhere. Trees everywhere. Green threaded through streets and plazas like the city was quietly determined to soothe you. It made sense why people rave about it. Mendoza has that easy, liveable charm that makes you want to stay longer than you planned.

But we had a bus to catch, so the day was mostly logistics. Filming a couple of little videos around the centre, prepping food for the journey ahead, and then returning to Beirut café again. We'd checked out of the Airbnb and didn't want to loiter at the bus terminal like lost baggage, so we set up camp on the colourful couches outside the café, sipping fresh juice, and watching palm trees sway gently in the plaza.

It was *siesta* time and Mendoza was eerie in the best way. Shops closed, streets oddly empty, like someone had turned the volume down on the city. If you didn't know better, you'd think it was dawn on a Sunday. Sitting there, in that quiet warmth, felt like being given a pause button.

And then, like the universe was being annoyingly poetic, one of my happy songs started playing from inside: "Lover's Carvings" by Bibio. The kind of song that makes you smile without meaning to. Like you're on your way home after something good, something that shifted you slightly. It landed perfectly in that moment—us perched in the shade, bus-bound, sun-tired, full of memories and the faint thrill of the next place waiting.

We walked to the bus terminal with our bags on our backs. They weren't heavy, but the heat was still in the thirties, and I could feel sweat sliding down my skin as if my body was slowly liquefying. Cycling shorts, vest, minimal clothing. It didn't matter. The city held its warmth like a grudge.

The overnight bus to Buenos Aires was the kind of decision you make when you're tired of decisions: just get it done. AndesMar turned out to be an absolute dream of a company. They fed us constantly—snacks, drinks, full hot meals like we were on a plane—and at one point they even organised Bingo on the bus, with the winner scoring a bottle of Mendoza wine.

Sleep was rough. Outside, a lightning storm lit up the distance like a silent film. Beautiful, unsettling, impossible to ignore. The bus stopped in the middle of nowhere a couple of times, that classic long-haul mystery where you wake up and think, *Is this a stop? Is this a breakdown? Is this a dream?* But we kept moving.

We were crossing a whole country. West coast to east coast. Mountains to plains. Vineyards to whatever waited in Buenos Aires. It felt huge and ordinary at the same time.

Where It All Started

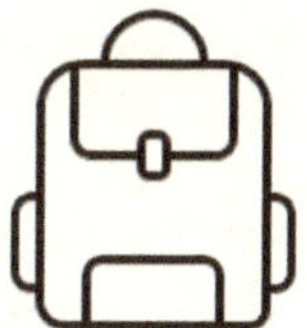

- BUENOS AIRES, ARGENTINA -

We rolled in slightly late, and the first thing I noticed about Buenos Aires was the wetness in the air. Evidence of rain overnight. It threw me, because my last memory of this city in 2016 was basically sun. heat. sweat. repeat. Apparently, November is the rain season.

Getting out of the bus terminal turned into its own mini thriller. We didn't want a taxi. Partly because I'd heard the horror stories, and partly because the taxis themselves looked super sketchy. There were shady guys hovering near the taxi entrances, circling like they could smell fresh arrivals and weak boundaries. They offered us rides, we said no, and suddenly it felt like we'd offended the entire taxi industry.

So, we ordered an Uber.

Which sounds simple. Except it wasn't.

The first driver accepted, then declined. The second accepted, then drove right past us like we were invisible. The third accepted and finally pulled in. Rushed, stressed, engine still running like he was ready to launch. As the car slid to the curb, I saw those same sketchy guys pointing toward it and moving in, fast, like they'd done this many times before. We flung our bags into the trunk at record speed. They reached the window just as we were already peeling away from the curb.

A genuinely lucky escape.

The driver filled in the context we'd been missing. Uber versus taxis here isn't just a mild professional rivalry, it's a war. Uber drivers get followed, harassed, sometimes attacked. He told us we should have left the terminal and ordered from outside. Lesson learned. Sometimes it's not paranoia, trust your gut instinct when something feels a bit off.

By the time we arrived at our Airbnb, all I wanted was a shower and a horizontal surface. Carlos did the sensible thing and slept. I did what I tended to do when my brain is too tired to be "productive" but too awake to fully rest. I watched Netflix and wrote, floating somewhere between exhaustion and the warm comfort of being in a place that already felt familiar.

Later, when we finally emerged into the city, we managed to latch onto a walking tour. The city centre unfolded in big, satisfying landmarks. Congress, murals, Plaza de Mayo, Avenida 9 de Julio, the Pink Government

House. Places that look like they've been built to make you feel small in the most theatrical way possible.

The guide pulled us through the stories Buenos Aires carries in its bones. The dictatorship, the disappearances, the economy, the politics. Everything heavy and complicated and never quite finished. It was a lot, but also exactly why I like this city. Buenos Aires isn't just pretty. It's layered.

We walked the hour home afterward, partly because we like walking and partly because walking is how a city starts to stitch itself together in your head. How one neighbourhood melts into the next, how the architecture changes, how the mood shifts block by block. I was stupidly happy to be back here. Buenos Aires had been my first taste of South America. It had hooked me two years ago and left me itching for more. Now I was returning after three months on the continent, and everything felt different. Not because the city had changed, but because I had.

Dinner was a simple win. An Italian place called Belén with cheap prices and the rare miracle of accepting credit card (withdrawing cash from ATMs was next to impossible in this economy). We left with pizza-filled bellies and that calm, contented feeling of "yes, we are exactly where we're meant to be."

The next morning, we were sprinting to a walking tour in Recoleta like we were late for a job interview we didn't even have. We passed through an area where the Jewish presence was instantly visible. Men in *kippahs*, a huge synagogue. And it struck me again how multicultural Buenos Aires is. I hadn't known before that there were major waves of migration from Eastern Europe in the 1800s, but the city doesn't exactly hide its histories. It wears them, proudly, in its buildings and its neighbourhoods and its accents.

Recoleta itself was elegant in that slightly intimidating way. Like it expects you to have your life together and also to own a silk scarf. The tour took us to a memorial for those lost in the Falklands War. The list of names was longer than I expected, and it landed oddly in my chest. It was personal, but in the opposite direction. I'm British. My dad was in the region when it was happening. Listening to it from Argentina's side was… confronting, fascinating, and uncomfortable in a way that made me want to be careful with my opinions and gentle with my identity. The strangest detail was the mini–Big Ben sitting right across from the memorial. A gift from England before the war, now standing there like an awkward ex at the edge of the room.

After the tour we wandered into Recoleta Cemetery, that bizarrely beautiful city of tombs. I'd been there before, but it still felt surreal. Like walking through a marble neighbourhood where everyone lives forever in family vaults and dramatic architecture. And then, right near the exit, we found a falafel food truck that sold the best falafel pita I've had in my life for the price of basically nothing.

We debated what to do next. Memorial Park or Puerto Madero. Puerto Madero won on logistics. We walked, again, because walking is my favourite way to feel like you've earned a city. It felt more like "real Buenos Aires" to me. People moving with purpose, doing errands, shopping, walking home from work. There were tango show sellers, sure, but there were even more men calling out "*Cambiooooo! Cambiooooo!*" offering dollars for pesos like it was a normal street soundtrack.

The economic crisis wasn't theoretical here. It was on the sidewalk. People were trying to convert their money into something stable as quickly as possible, because the peso was dropping like it was in a race to the bottom. Apparently, the government had tried to cap how much people could exchange into foreign currency, which only made the whole thing feel more desperate. It explained why ATMs were often useless. Empty or broken.

Puerto Madero also hit me with memory in this weird, crystal-clear way. I remembered crossing the Puente de la Mujer in 2016. I remembered my friend telling me it was a classic photo spot for girls turning sixteen. I remembered my first ever *empanada*, cheese and corn, and the mortifying moment I walked into the men's toilet because I didn't know Spanish and made a wildly confident guess that "M" must mean male. Spoiler: it means *mujeres*. I can still feel the heat of that embarrassment in my bones.

That evening we met up with that friend's cousin. Someone I'd stayed with two years earlier. Seeing him again felt like stepping into an old version of myself and realising she'd grown up without fully noticing. We talked careers, politics, and what the hell was happening in Argentina, and he confirmed the energy I'd been sensing all along. That crisis is almost... familiar here. Not enjoyable, obviously, but woven into the national psyche in this resigned, gallows-humour kind of way. Bad financial management. Dumb politicians. Been here before. Probably will again.

And yet, he was warm, thoughtful, present. The dinner was simple, but it left me buzzing. There's something about meeting someone in their own environment in a foreign country, being invited into their daily reality, that makes travel feel like the most honest kind of education. It's not just sightseeing. It's intimacy. It's the quiet privilege of being allowed to understand a place through a person.

The following day we saved for La Boca, because you can't come to Buenos Aires and not. We packed ourselves into the subway. Horrifically hot, disgustingly humid. We transferred onto a *collectivo* and finally arrived in this working-class neighbourhood that looked like someone had painted an architectural rainbow with a heavy hand.

The buildings weren't soft, dreamy pastels like Chiloé. They were bold and defiant. Royal blues, emerald greens, colours that practically shouted. Cobblestones underfoot. Zinc walls. The main tourist strip, Caminito, was full of Italian restaurants and tango dancers performing in the street like this is just what you do when you pop out for a loaf of bread.

Sales people were noticeably more intense here. In the rest of the city, I'd been pleasantly surprised by how few people hassled us. In La Boca, it was a different energy. Staff hovering at exits in souvenir shops like you had to buy something to earn your freedom.

We did buy one thing. A Christmas tree ornament painted with tango dancers. I've started a tradition where I buy one ornament from every country. My future Christmas tree is going to look like a confused museum exhibit. A knitted llama from Peru, a wooden turtle from Samoa, a little bottle of salt from Uyuni, a koala from Australia. Now, tango dancers from Buenos Aires. It made me ridiculously happy.

At one point we crossed train tracks to look at a shop and thought nothing of it. Later, standing outside the iconic Havana on the corner of Caminito, we got approached by a middle-aged man with a clipboard. My body braced automatically. Here comes the pitch, here comes the performance, here comes the "special deal."

Instead, he said, very calmly "don't go more than one block that way; at the end is a train track; don't cross it. And no more than four blocks that way. *Peligroso.*" Then he wished us a good day and walked off.

No sale. No scam. Just a warning.

Those train tracks were the exact ones we'd crossed getting here. By about two metres. Whoops.

We retreated back toward the centre, and on the way we made a holy pilgrimage to Guerrín, a pizzeria that's been open since 1932 and deserves every ounce of its reputation. We bought a gigantic, single slice for the price for pennies. It carried us through a long walk back—six kilometres—toward dinner at El Club de la Milanesa near our Airbnb.

We arrived ridiculously early by Argentine standards, which meant the restaurant was empty and we could enjoy our food in peace. There was a sign offering a discount if you paid in US dollars. Another little, quiet punch of reality. The peso was sliding so fastest that even restaurants were basically saying, please, for the love of god, give us something stable.

And still, somehow, the city felt alive. Not naïvely cheerful, but resilient. People still singing "*Cambiooooo*!" like it's just another Tuesday. Tango dancers still posing for photos while history sits heavy in the plazas. Families and workers and tourists moving through it all, together, as if the city has collectively agreed *we will keep going.*

I realized that Buenos Aires felt like a reunion. One with the city, but also with myself. Returning here after months on the road didn't just refresh old memories; it rewrote them. The places that once felt exotic now felt legible. The stories I'd once skimmed over now had weight. And underneath the landmarks and neighbourhoods and pizza slices, what stayed with me most was this strange mix Buenos Aires holds so effortlessly. Beauty and grit, warmth and wariness, celebration and sorrow. It reminded me that travel isn't only about discovering new places. It's also about coming back to the familiar and realising you're not the same person who left.

Following Dad's Footsteps

- MAR DEL PLATA, ARGENTINA -

The bus arrived an hour late. And when it finally groaned into view, it wasn't just tired. It was alive.

Alive with cockroaches. Everywhere.

They ran up and down the armrests, their legs appearing from seams in the upholstery like the bus itself was moulting. I sat rigid, hyper-aware of every itch and brush of fabric, trying to exist without inviting a single one of them to explore my face. Carlos was too deep in his gravol induced coma to notice, but I couldn't keep my eyes off the wiggling antennas running around me. The bus company Condor Estrellas immediately went onto my internal blacklist.

Argentina, I was discovering, also loved a toll road. There were so many bridges and booths it felt like the country charged admission for its own geography. Still, there was something hypnotic about watching Buenos Aires thin out behind us. City blocks loosening into improvised shacks, then unspooling into endless greenery so lush it looked newly painted. Not jungle, just grasslands. Vast and calm and quietly insistent. The walking tour guides hadn't been exaggerating. Argentina really was a country built on fields.

We crossed rivers the colour of coffee gone wrong. So brown they looked like liquid mud until you caught the shimmer of a ripple and remembered they were water. It tugged at an old memory. A river near San Nicolás de los Arroyos where I'd once been thrown off a jet ski and come up laughing, coated in that same earthy brown. I found myself wondering if this was the Amazon's influence reaching out in offshoots and sediments, or if it was something else entirely. Clay, silt, the whole continent steeping in itself. The coastline had that same strange brown tint too, like the sea had been stained. It didn't look remotely inviting in the "tropical beach" way I'd once assumed Argentina might offer. But it was beautiful in a different way. Not postcard-pretty. More like honest. Strange. New.

By the time the bus finally wheezed into Mar del Plata's terminal, I was ready to vault off it like it was on fire. We grabbed our bags and did a quick toilet break. There was no chance I was using the bathroom on the bus after what I'd seen crawling around its seats. Then we went to the tourist information office for the basics… How to get to our hostel, how much it should cost, which option would get us there without drama.

A taxi seemed simplest. There were no Ubers here. We were tired. And the day had already been gross.

Then we saw the taxi queue.

The first driver looked… wrong. Not "rough around the edges," but genuinely sketchy, like he'd wandered in from a different storyline. We tried to avoid him and approached the second driver instead, asking the price. He quoted something reasonable. About five bucks in New Zealand money. Then shrugged and told us we had to go with the first guy because it was "his turn."

It was almost enough to make me choose the four-kilometre walk out of pure stubbornness.

Carlos went to negotiate with the sketchy one anyway. The man acted vague and evasive, like he didn't know where our hostel was, which was ridiculous because the other driver had known instantly. It felt like a performance. I *don't know, I'm confused, but hop in and we'll see…* The kind of confusion that always ends with you paying triple.

Then it got weirder. A friend of his dragged over a young woman and insisted she take the ride. The driver's attention snapped away from Carlos like we'd never existed.

Strange, yes. But also perfect. We slipped back to driver number two and climbed in before anyone could change their mind.

He laughed as we pulled away. Of course, the guy knew where our hostel was. He was "playing dumb," our driver said, because Carlos had asked the price directly and that made it harder to rip us off. He could've looked it up on his phone, he added. It was 2018, after all. We sat there, relieved, and then immediately I felt a pang for the woman we'd left behind, hoping she'd be fine, hoping she'd also know how to ask the price upfront. Hoping the only danger posed to her was that she might get ripped off.

We barely explored Mar del Plata that first day. We were too late, too wrung out, too aware that a cockroach bus had drained something from us. Instead, we tried to do the responsible thing. Get cash.

And that's when Argentina's wider crisis reached right into our pockets.

We were down to about three New Zealand dollars' worth. The ATMs, one after another, were empty. Not "declined," not "try again," but out of cash completely. It felt absurd, standing there with two bank cards and no usable money, watching machines that were meant to be reliable just… shrug.

The next morning, Mar del Plata revealed itself properly. A seaside city with beach resorts strung along the coast like pearls, boutique shops in the centre, and beaches still half-asleep because tourist season hadn't fully arrived. A few people patrolled the sand selling sunglasses and bracelets and the usual beach things. Commerce always finds a way.

But we were still chasing the same thing—cash. Desperately.

Every bank had a line. Every ATM refused. We moved from bank to bank like we were trying to unlock a level in a game, each time expecting the next one to work, each time watching another "no" appear in some cold, bureaucratic form. Even when staff tried to help, they couldn't fix it. The system felt flimsy. The rules invisible. Our panic, quiet but real, grew.

Eventually, three banks later, we found one that worked. It spat out the equivalent of sixteen dollars, and charged us seven dollars to do it.

I wanted to laugh and cry at the same time. It was barely anything, but it was enough to keep us afloat. Enough to eat. Enough to move.

Then the city offered another clue about what was happening: signs everywhere advertising a 40% discount if you paid with MasterCard. Supermarkets. Cafés. Random shops. I couldn't figure out if it was marketing or desperation or both. But it felt like the whole place was leaning on incentives like crutches, trying to keep money moving, trying to coax people into spending when everyone was bracing for the next drop.

Once we'd solved our own tiny economic emergency, we went to the waterfront. And the climate shift hit immediately. Mar del Plata was colder than Buenos Aires by about ten degrees and missing the humidity entirely. The wind came in sharp. I put my fleece on for the first time in weeks and felt oddly grateful for the bite of it. It was refreshing, like the air was washing something off me.

This was also my first time seeing the South Atlantic Ocean.

Not the river mouth. Not the muddy-brown edge of the world. The actual ocean. From here it was a shifting rainbow of greens and greys. Honestly, it still didn't look inviting. It looked like it would swallow you and hand you back salt-stung and shivering. But it was powerful. A different kind of sea. A different kind of beauty.

Later, in the main square, we noticed a commotion and drifted toward it like we always did when a city hinted at a story. There were placards. Words like "movement" and "liberty," and fires being used to cook food that was handed out for free. Simple plates like rice, tomato sauce. People sat on curbs and roads to eat. Flags waved. Roads were blocked further down by men holding protest banners like barriers. The crisis was no longer something you heard about from a guide. It was there in the street, warm in the smoke, visible in the need.

The next day the sun returned, and the beach was suddenly dotted with old, overweight men walking around topless, as if that was the official dress code, and the occasional horse and cart clopping past like time had folded in on itself. There was something surreal about seeing that in 2018. Like modernity was optional here, like the present and past could coexist without explaining themselves.

We wanted to check out the aquarium, so we rented bikes from the hostel. Cheap, old, awkward, seats too high, brakes that barely worked, and somehow, they carried us into one of those days that becomes a whole chapter in your memory.

We rode.

Forty kilometres.

The coastal path was incredible. Endless sand, skyscrapers towering behind it, bodies everywhere soaking up sun as if the warmth might be rationed tomorrow.

Cycling through the crowd was like steering through a living obstacle course, but we didn't care. We kept ooh-ing and aah-ing like tourists with no shame.

After five kilometres, the beautiful path spat us onto a highway. Sharing the edge of a road with buses and trucks didn't feel like an empowering travel experience. It felt like a gamble. So, we cut through the suburbs instead, which turned out to be its own kind of hazard. Dirt tracks, potholes, and aggressive dogs charging our back wheels like they'd been waiting for us.

We made it to the aquarium anyway, sweaty and triumphant. Then got punched in the face by the entrance fee. Six hundred and fifty pesos each. Expensive enough that I had no idea how locals afforded it. But we'd come all this way. We went in.

The place was nearly empty. Friday, so everyone was at work or at school. It felt like we'd rented the aquarium for ourselves.

Penguins. Seals. Flamingos. Dolphins.

Afterwards, we had another destination. The Mar del Plata Polo Club. It was the real reason I'd dragged myself on a five-hour bus down here. My dad had been there forty years earlier when he worked for the British Merchant Navy, and asked for a photo of what it looked like now. A simple request, a sweet little thread connecting my trip to his past.

But the further we cycled, the sketchier it felt. Buildings grew rougher. Roads more broken. People drinking alcohol in the street. Houses sliding into shack territory. The air changed. Even the way we held ourselves changed. More alert, less playful.

We were so close though. Google Maps said five minutes. So, I hid the GoPro, shoved it out of sight, and told myself we'd be fine. We turned off the main road into a suburb, then followed Google's next instruction to turn right, and suddenly we were in a park. Trees, gravel driveway, brick barbecue structures. Pretty, even.

But we both knew instantly… This is not smart.

Through the trees I could see a beautiful brick building that might have been the polo club. So close it made my stomachache. But it wasn't worth it. Not worth being mugged for a photo that would become a story of "remember when we were idiots." We just knew it wasn't a safe place to be, and we had to trust our gut instincts. We turned around and left the club behind, unphotographed, and I felt the sting of disappointment wrapped up inside the relief.

The ride back was a gift. The wind that had fought us earlier now pushed us home, and when we reached the beach near our hostel, we found a kiosk selling calamari and fries. I didn't even hesitate. I ate those fries like I'd earned them with my entire body.

Mar del Plata ended quickly, the way some stops do. Intense, specific, and then over. We had to get to Montevideo by the next day for a Maluma concert, so we checked out early and took a taxi to the bus terminal. On the way, Carlos tried to ask the driver about hurricanes, and the man looked confused. I remembered that down in the southern hemisphere we call them cyclones, and I said it out loud with a Spanish accent—*see-clon-es*—and for once my instinct was right. The driver understood immediately, and I laughed at the small victory of being understood in the exact moment it mattered.

The bus ride back to Buenos Aires was with a different company. Clean. No cockroaches. A miracle. But outside, it rained so hard I couldn't even see the landscape.

We arrived back in Buenos Aires for one night only. Our accommodation was in Recoleta this time. Perfect location, but barely used because we were doing what we always did. Winging it and calling it spontaneity.

We dropped our bags, looked up tango shows, and immediately realised we'd left it dangerously last minute. Saturday. Almost everything sold out. There was precisely one option. We grabbed it without thinking.

Then we had fifteen minutes to become tango-presentable.

We were absurdly efficient. Showered. Dressed. Out the door. It's amazing what you can do when adrenaline is driving and you don't have time to argue.

The Señor Tango show was waiting for us in Puerto Madero like a dream with a price tag. We arrived three minutes late and somehow still won. We were the only ones there, which meant we got first pick of seats. Men in bow ties greeted us with cheesy grins. Our seats were perfect. High enough to see everything, low enough to feel close to the action. Later, people rolled in two hours late and complained about their view and I felt a small, petty satisfaction. You snooze; you lose.

The tickets were expensive. About a hundred New Zealand dollars each. But they included a gourmet three-course Italian meal, a bottle of wine per person, the show, and a ride home.

The show was spectacular in the most theatrical way possible. Horses on stage. A woman flying through the theatre on aerial hoops. Endless tango performances, music, drama, a Spanish rendition of "Don't Cry for Me Argentina" that made the whole place feel like it was humming with its own mythology. I couldn't stop thinking *I'm in Buenos Aires watching a tango show.* It felt like checking a box you didn't even know you needed to check. Like drinking beer in Munich, riding camels in Dubai. This was one of those iconic, cliché experiences that somehow still lands as real.

There were only two slight blemishes. One neighbour at our table kept dropping methane bombs like it was their personal contribution to the evening's atmosphere, and another sat through the entire thing with a face like she was being punished. But otherwise, it was magic.

And then we realised we'd forgotten to get extra cash.

We had cards, of course. This was a huge tourist venue. Surely, they took card.

But this was Argentina, where nothing is ever guaranteed.

We soon learned that card wasn't an option. Cash only. We didn't discover this until after we ordered coffees and they were placed in front of us, steaming and accusatory. We counted our money. 110 pesos. We were 90 pesos short.

Embarrassing. Small. Human.

The waiter smiled anyway and accepted what we had, like he'd seen this exact situation a hundred times and knew that tourists don't always understand the rules of this country until the rules slap them in the face.

Crossing the River

- MONTEVIDEO & LIBERTAD, URUGUAY -

Uruguay arrived like a blank page.

We were up early again, but this time the fatigue tasted different. Less grind, more anticipation. A new chapter. A whole month in a country I barely knew existed in any meaningful way beyond that small shape beside Argentina. Two years earlier I'd almost come here, then detoured deeper into Argentina instead. Now I was back, staying longer, and it felt quietly significant that I wasn't arriving alone. Carlos was half Uruguayan. This wasn't just another stop. This was roots.

The Uber dropped us at the ferry terminal in Buenos Aires, and I did a border crossing by boat for the first time. As we cut across the water the ferry staff blasted celebratory music over the megaphone. We landed in Colonia del Sacramento and slipped onto a bus bound for Montevideo.

The ride was confusing in the best way.

I'd expected something dustier. Poorer. More visibly "developing continent." Instead, Uruguay unrolled outside the window as endless, rolling planes of fluorescent green. The kind of green that looks edited until you realise it's just well-fed land. Green on green on green. Soft horizons. Low foliage. Wind farms turning steadily, like someone had sprinkled modernity across the countryside. Herds of cows clustered in the open like they had nowhere better to be. It reminded me so much of home that my brain kept trying to overlay New Zealand logic onto it.

And that's when the questions started stacking up faster than the scenery could answer.

What does it even mean to be Uruguayan?

What keeps this economy running? What do they export?

What do people eat? How do they live?

Is the *mate*-and-thermos guy in my head a stereotype, or an accurate portrait?

When we arrived in Montevideo, we did what we always do when we're disoriented.. Found a tourist information centre, grabbed a map, and pretended we had a plan. Our bags were light enough to make walking manageable. Thirteen kilos, the kind of weight you forget is there until you stop moving. The streets were strangely empty at first, and then, like the city was saving its punchline, we hit a massive market lining the road where we were staying.

And there it was.

My imagination hadn't been exaggerating. Everyone had *mate*. The famous caffeinated herbal tea that you often see throughout the lower half of the continent.

Mate cup in one hand, thermos in the other, walking with the quiet devotion of people who've turned a drink into a lifestyle. It was so universal it became funny, like I'd stepped onto a themed film set. And when someone didn't have *mate*, they often had a joint. Casual. Ordinary. Like it was no bigger deal than a cigarette.

I learned quickly that recreational cannabis had been legal here since December 2013. The first country in the world to do it. But with rules: only for citizens and residents. Still, the energy was unmistakable. Uruguay felt like a place that had decided to exhale and just *chill*.

The next morning, I woke with that now-familiar confusion. Where am I, what language, what currency, what street noises? And then laughed when it hit me. *Uruguay*. I couldn't even keep track anymore, which was both ridiculous and kind of thrilling. Like my life had become a revolving door of places.

We'd booked a full week in one apartment, which for us felt like signing a mortgage. Montevideo was the exception. Carlos wanted time to connect with his roots, and I needed stable Wi-Fi and a real desk to wrangle life admin back home. The place was perfect. Clean, spacious, a proper kitchen, a balcony for people watching and drinking wine, a shower with actual pressure. And the best detail of all, the *Persianas enrollables.* Steel blinds that rolled down over the bedroom window and erased light completely. The kind of darkness that convinces your body that it's midnight no matter what time of day it actually is.

Our first impressions of the city landed softly and confidently. Montevideo felt cleaner, safer, calmer than the last three and a half months of everywhere else. I half-joked that it was the cannabis and the *mate*. Why wouldn't you be chilled? But honestly, it ran deeper than that. The city moved at a different speed. The air was warm but not humid. On multiple occasions we said, out loud, like idiots who couldn't believe our luck. This is literally the perfect temperature.

We didn't sprint through tourist spots because we had time. We walked. We watched. Colonial buildings and palm trees. Apparently, it was the city's entire aesthetic. We ate cheese and olive *empanadas*, drank fresh orange juice, got approached by strangers offering weed like they were selling gum, and passed pockets of music. Drumming, dancing, small street performances that made the city feel alive without being frantic.

Because I was determined to understand what "Uruguayan" even felt like, we committed fully to the cliché. We bought a *mate* cup and *bombilla* from the street, grabbed *yerba mate* from the supermarket, and sat in a park drinking it while a man played the Amélie theme on a flute. It was so perfectly cinematic.

That night, the trip snapped into a different kind of excitement. It was time for Maluma.

A chain reaction that started months earlier in Bolivia—me losing my mind at a *fiesta* when a band played Felices los 4 live, then a road trip from Uyuni to San Pedro de Atacama with a Uruguayan couple in the car, them casually mentioning Maluma would be playing Montevideo in November, and me immediately filing that away as destiny.

So, we'd bought the tickets back in Santiago. And now it was happening.

The Antel Arena was packed, mostly with women, and the energy was loud and glossy and feral in the way pop concerts are when the performer knows exactly what he's doing. Maluma was a genuinely good live singer, but more than that, he played the "lady's man" card like it was written into his contract. He kissed a woman on stage while she grabbed his butt. He asked who was single and said it didn't matter if they had boyfriends. The crowd basically drooled.

I watched, half amused and half anthropologist, thinking, if this man ever settles down seriously, a chunk of his brand collapses overnight.

But the concert itself? Unreal. One of those moments where you suddenly realise you're living a version of your own fantasy. I was in South America, listening to a South American artist, hearing one of my favourite Spanish songs in a country I'd barely known a week earlier. It felt like a reward for the sheer absurdity of building a life out of movement.

In the days that followed, Uruguay kept confusing me. This tidy little haven in a continent I'd mentally labelled chaotic and dangerous. The internet was the fastest we'd had yet. The Spanish sounded familiar but warped. More "*sh*" and "*ja*," a dialect that made words I already knew feel freshly invented. I went down a history rabbit hole. Spain and Portugal fighting over it, Brazil and Spain tug-of-warring it, the dictatorship of the 1970s leaving scars that hadn't fully healed even if the streets now looked calm.

And still, under the calm, reminders surfaced.

One afternoon at the waterfront, the wind whipped at us like angry ropes. Waves snapped hard. The vibe shifted in that subtle way you learn to read as a traveller. Men with protruding ribs, draggy clothes, the look of being chemically elsewhere. Uruguay wasn't dangerous in the way other places had been, but it wasn't a utopia either. A kid chatted to us. He was polite, alert, oddly adult, and mentioned his friend had been shot two days earlier. Just like that. Dropped into conversation as if violence was both shocking and normal.

It recalibrated me. Again.

Because that's what travel kept doing. Giving me joy and ease, then reminding me that no country is one story. Not even the safe ones. Not even the ones that look like home.

Nevertheless, Montevideo rewarded me in the way I love most... Through people.

We were headed to Los Yuyos, one of those "you have to go" places, when we realised every table had been reserved. So we took two seats at the bar and waited for our friends—the couple we'd met on that four-day Uyuni-to-San-Pedro tour, the kind where strangers become your temporary universe. Now we were in their home city, finally getting the version of Uruguay you can't buy—an ordinary night made extraordinary by locals.

We started with *caña*, which is a clear sugarcane liquor, thick and syrupy, with flavour lists that looked like they'd been written in a language I didn't know existed. Then came Tannat, Uruguay's signature red wine. Smooth, fruity, dangerously drinkable. We talked for hours. Politics, history, immigration, economics. I kept bumping into the edges of my Spanish, wanting to understand everything without a translation buffer. It was satisfying and maddening all at once.

At one point our friend dropped a fact that made my brain tilt. Uruguay, apparently, invented corned beef. He spoke about British influence in Uruguay like it was obvious. The only thing the British did wrong, he said, was leaving. I countered with the aftermath left in India and Fiji. He countered with New Zealand and Canada.

I left buzzing. The way you do after a conversation that makes the world feel larger and more complicated.

The next day, I had a religious experience of my own. A bookshop near Plaza de Independencia that felt designed to trap me forever. Floor-to-ceiling shelves. A marble staircase splitting left and right. A café tucked among the books like a reward for curiosity. We sank into leather couches with frothy coffee and tango music floating through the space. I looped the politics section three times, just to be sure I wasn't missing something that might rearrange my understanding of everything.

I've always loved reading the way I love travelling—as a way of living other lives. Through books I'd crossed oceans, ridden camels through Australia, explored Siberia by horseback, lived inside histories I hadn't survived physically. And yes, I'd travelled a lot by now. Enough that it sometimes blurred—but reading still took me further. It made me want my own story to one day sit on a shelf somewhere.

That evening reminded me travel isn't always gentle. A drunk Colombian man at Mercado del Puerto wouldn't leave me alone, asked me repeatedly for an iPhone charger, talked about women degradingly like I wasn't there. He assumed I didn't understand Spanish. He was wrong. An older Uruguayan man clocked it instantly. *Ella entiende lo que tu dices.* He shut it down quietly. The conversation died.

The next morning the city woke us with drums and barbecue smoke. *Sunday.* Feria de Tristán Narvaja stretched for blocks. Fruit, clothes, beer, street food, joy. Later we moved apartments because Carlos' mum, Rosemarie, was arriving from Canada. The country she'd been living in for the last forty years since she left Uruguay.

When she finally arrived, there were hugs and wine and stories and a shift in the room. Carlos started asking real questions—why she left, how it felt, whether she regretted it. Watching him reach backward like that made me proud in a way I hadn't expected.

Walking the city with Rosemarie slowed everything down, in the best way possible. I noticed more. I hung back. It reminded me how travelling with someone builds a bubble—warm, intimate, but slightly insulating too. You get so wrapped up in your own conversations that you forget to just look around quietly.

That evening we met our Uyuni friends again at Parque Rodó. *Mate* passed around. *Bizcochos* shared. We walked to the *rambla* and watched as the sun slipped into the water, and strangely, people clapped as if this didn't happen every single night.

Later, drums pulled us down side streets as people practised for Carnaval. Music everywhere. The rhythms African-rooted, joyful, alive. Uruguay fed me something I didn't know I needed. Slowness, community, sound that found you instead of being scheduled.

By the time we left Montevideo, it felt like we'd been skating on luck. No thefts. No disasters. Just one near-miss—someone had overheard Carlos give his name at a *lavandería* and later tried to impersonate him and collect our laundry without the receipt. That left us with an itchy awareness of being watched.

Rosemarie insisted we stop at Emporio de los Sandwiches before we headed out for the day. She said they make the best damn sandwiches in all of Montevideo. I was skeptical. And then I bit into one and immediately had to eat my judgement.

They were ridiculously good. So light and buttery they basically dissolved into happiness. I don't know what kind of witchcraft they're doing in that shop, but if someone offered me an Emporio sandwich in exchange for my passport, I'd at least pause to negotiate.

The weather wasn't particularly pleasant. It was windy and spitting with rain, the kind of drizzle that doesn't commit enough to justify going home, but still manages to ruin everything. Except it was also warm. Around 23°C. Since it wasn't particularly beachy weather, I decided to go for a run.

I hadn't run much on this trip, and that disappointment had been quietly sitting in me. Running is one of my favourite ways to be alone without feeling lonely. It's time to myself that doesn't feel like hiding. It's also the best way to see a place without turning it into a checklist. You notice small things on a run. The way streets change block by block, the smells, the sudden pockets of music, the dogs that look like they run the neighbourhood, the people who stare at you like you're doing something deeply suspicious by moving quickly.

I took the long way on purpose. I wound through side streets and quieter blocks to avoid the main roads. Less stares, fewer catcalls. The footpaths were cracked and uneven, so I was hopping over broken concrete, stepping around puddles, choosing my route like a little urban obstacle course. Headphones weren't an option. I needed my ears to keep myself safe.

And wow, it felt good.

My body remembered. My brain unclenched. It was the cleanest kind of relief. Like I'd found a version of myself

I'd been missing. I came back flushed and steadier, already dreaming of this weekend's organized run along the *Rambla* that I desperately wanted to do. A proper organised race in South America had been on my list like a little private dare. The only problem was that I still hadn't figured out how to register.

The next day, the heavens opened properly. The roads started flooding. Rain hammered down with the confidence of a weather system that had found its purpose. Uruguay's weather was the most unpredictable we'd had the entire trip. Sunny one minute, biblical the next. And yet it still wasn't cold. Even drenched, it hovered around 18°C.

We had a full day of social visits planned, which meant I mostly didn't know what was happening, and honestly? I loved that. There's a particular joy in being carried along by someone else's context. Being the tag-along foreigner while life unfolds around you in a way you couldn't manufacture. It felt like another small step toward the version of Uruguay I was craving. Not the postcard one, but the lived-in one.

We drove through the fancy districts of Montevideo, including Pocitos and the sleek coastal stretch. Watching angry waves smash into the beach alongside the *Rambla.* Then we headed inland and the city softened into something else entirely. The quality of the roads deteriorated quickly. The car bounced and skidded on loose dirt. Houses stopped having numbers.

We had to call ahead and ask our host to come outside so we could find the right place, which felt like arriving in a world where directions are still spoken in human language instead of pin-dropped coordinates.

The house was small and homely, paint long past its prime, the kind of place that looked tired in a practical way. Not negatively, just lived in. The garden, though, was alive. Chickens. Cats. Dogs. A whole ecosystem of animals moving like they owned the plot. One of the cats immediately decided my lap was his new residence.

The toddler belonged to our host's family too—her granddaughter—and we learned she'd been born blind. That hit me hard. I thought about how much support it can take to navigate life with a disability even in New Zealand, where we like to believe we have systems and safety nets. And here, in a rural pocket of South America, no matter how "developed" Uruguay felt compared to its neighbours, it would still be harder. Everything takes more effort when resources are thinner.

Then our host mentioned the drugs.

She told us the area had become dangerous at night. It didn't compute at first. This was practically the middle of nowhere. Dirt tracks and open space. But she insisted. And suddenly I felt the weight of our bags and valuables sitting unattended in the car outside.

We didn't stay long, but I tried to absorb everything while I was there. The religious items on walls and windowsills, little shrines of comfort; the oversized goldfish circling endlessly in a too-small tank; the way the tiled floor was clean despite all those paws coming and going.

As we drove away and found real road again, we still saw men using horse and carriage like the country was living in multiple decades at once. Rosemarie started reminiscing—her father selling fish and fruit around the neighbourhood. History riding beside us in the rain.

Our next stop was another family near Ciudad de la Costa, and I fell into their life the way you do when people are warm and you're open enough to let them. We were greeted by a smiling woman in her early thirties standing in the rain like weather was just a minor inconvenience. Hugs. Cheek kisses. Immediate welcome. Two children, including a twelve-year-old girl and a toddler not yet two.

Before I knew it, I was painting the twelve-year-old's nails while Carlos blew raspberries on the toddler's belly and Rosemarie caught up with the mother. *Mate* passed around endlessly, a little social ritual that made hydration feel like communion. I sat there feeling quietly victorious in my growing understanding of Uruguay. One home at a time, one cup at a time, one story at a time.

One of those stories punched through the cosy atmosphere. A woman had been stabbed in the neighbourhood not long ago. I couldn't believe something like that could happen in a place that felt so remote, but it had, and what stayed with me wasn't just the violence. It was the response. Someone had painted graffiti—*never again.* And now, when someone has to get off the bus late or when it's dark, a group will go and walk them home.

Humanity at its best. Tender, practical solidarity. The kind that makes you feel both safer and sadder, because it exists because it has to.

Somewhere in the middle of all this, my little running dream took a hit. I'd wanted that weekend race along the *Rambla* so badly. Something official, something I could point to and say I did that here. Our Montevideo friends had even tried to help me register when I couldn't figure it out. No spots left. Full. I was gutted in that petty private way, like the universe had dangled a finish line and then snatched it back.

The next day we went to Libertad, a small town less than an hour from Montevideo, and it mattered in a way I couldn't fully articulate until we were there. The town surprised me. It had proper roads, a tiny high street, a sense of "town-ness" that felt more structured than the rural pockets we'd visited the day before. Rosemarie commented on how much it had changed since she'd left in 1972—shops, roads—and how she kept recognising faces but couldn't place them. That specific kind of disorientation is its own emotion. Memory reaching for itself and coming up just short.

Navigation in Libertad was gloriously human. To find someone's house, Rosemarie would roll down the window and ask random people on the street if they knew the person and where they lived.

Most of the time, they did.

If they didn't, Rosemarie directed us by memory, because half the streets didn't have signs. It was chaotic and perfect, like the town was operating on an older system of belonging where people are part of the infrastructure.

And the best part was that she hadn't told anyone she was coming.

Every visit was a surprise. Doors opened to confusion, people squinting at her like she was a riddle, and then she'd say her name and the confusion cracked into laughter and bear hugs and that startled joy you can't fake. Watching it felt like being invited into something intimate. Proof that the past isn't gone, it's just waiting behind someone's door until you knock.

It made me ridiculously happy. Especially when you paired it with the smaller moments, like listening to Rosemarie sing along to "Échame La Culpa" in the car.

We met people who made the place come alive. Including a hilarious guy with Syrian heritage who'd lived in Europe most of his life and was now back in Libertad caring for his elderly aunt. He hated it and took every opportunity to swear and rip into Uruguay. I loved him instantly. There's something deeply refreshing about someone refusing to romanticise their own country for your benefit.

That night we arrived at our Airbnb, which was its own reward for surviving the "middle of nowhere" drive to get there. We turned into a long driveway tunnelled by trees, three dogs launching themselves at the tyres like an overly enthusiastic welcome committee, honeysuckle thick in the air, and then a cottage that felt a hundred years old in the best way. Rustic, but clean; old bones with modern comforts; forest behind it like a private world.

And then the fireflies.

Hundreds of them, floating in the dusk and deeper into the trees, flickering like sparks while crickets and toads started their nightly chorus. We stood there watching them the way you watch something that feels like it's been put there on purpose. Like the universe had briefly decided to be gentle.

Life back home, of course, did not get the memo.

I was in the middle of sorting out work, and the emotional whiplash was real. Being wildly free and still tethered. Interviews. Waiting. Rejections that weren't really rejections. Feedback that was almost annoyingly positive. I'd scored high. I'd interviewed well. I'd conquered the fear. But someone else was better qualified. At twenty-six, that shouldn't have surprised me. It still bruised.

Carlos was brilliant through it. steady, grounding, reminding me that timing isn't a verdict, and rejection isn't always personal. He reminded me that you can only connect the dots looking back, and he had his own example ready—being shoved into work he didn't want when he was younger, only for it to become his speciality later, the thing people now wanted him for from all corners of the world.

He was right. I knew he was right. But I still needed a moment to lick my wounds.

The days blurred into more visits. Retirement homes, ranches, surprise reunions that made people cry and laugh at once. Watching Rosemarie do this was both beautiful and uncomfortable. She'd left decades ago, but she'd stayed connected in a way that stunned me, especially when I compared it to myself. I'd been away from my hometown in England for ten years and was basically only in contact with family and one friend. Even that one friend, barely. I couldn't imagine showing up on anyone's doorstep to surprise them. It would be awkward. So awkward.

And yet watching her open-arm reconnection made me think about my own choices. I'd left with total adamance to start a new life and not turn back, and that had helped me assimilate into New Zealand in a way that felt seamless. It's probably a huge part of why I identify as Kiwi more than British now. I don't regret it. But there was no denying that watching her made me wonder what that choice cost me too. What I'd cut off along with the old life. What "roots" even mean when you've moved countries and rebuilt yourself.

In between all the emotional complexity, Uruguay kept feeding us. We were treated to an *asado*. Almost every house had a *parrilla*, an open fire grill like a sacred backyard fixture, because meat isn't just food here; it's identity. I thought about my family back in New Zealand watching half-metre steaks sizzle away with reverence. Meanwhile, I, typical vegetarian, was deeply excited about capsicum with cheese melting on top.

I kept being surprised by how easy it was to stay vegetarian in South America. People had warned me I'd starve. Instead, I'd been offered more meatless options than I'd expected, and people were often more educated about vegetarianism than I gave them credit for. In Libertad a woman even asked if I was vegetarian or vegan, like it was the most normal thing in the world.

By the time we circled back toward Ciudad de la Costa, we'd built up a kind of rhythm. Social calls, *mate*, stories, rain, car rides through soft green plains and small *pueblos* with houses that looked like they'd been patched together through sheer practicality. We chose the same Airbnb as before because we remembered it didn't have mosquitoes.

We were wrong.

That night turned into a full-blown mosquito war. Carlos was leaping out of bed to kill them with his bare hands like a sleep-deprived action hero. At one point the power went out around 1 a.m., so we hunted them with phone torches like it was a low-budget horror film: *The Mosquitoes of Ciudad de la Costa.* I swear we killed at least fifteen in an hour, and then, cruelly, found more in the morning hovering around our heads like they hadn't noticed the massacre.

Still, Uruguay was dreamy.

Even the drive days here had a kind of ease to them. When we went into Montevideo for the *feria*, we did the very South American thing of paying the local homeless guy to "watch" our car. Back home, that would make me furious on principle. Here, it comforted me. It's a relationship. You keep him sweet, he does what he can to protect your stuff. It's informal and imperfect, but there's logic to it. We gave him a bit extra because all our luggage was in the car, and later we bought him a burger to say thanks. I used to hate the messiness of these systems. Now I found them weirdly functional. Human in a way that felt like part of the continent's texture.

The *feria* itself was a mix of pleasant and hectic. Random treasures, bargaining victories, street food, souvenirs, a cheap AUX cord for the road trip. We bumped into our Uruguayan friends, and I did an awkward cheek-bump hello that haunted me immediately. Another entry for my ever-growing "Why Am I Like This" list.

I blame my culture. In England and New Zealand, we either hug or do the awkward wave- "hey" thing from a safe distance. I kind of wish we did cheek kisses. They're warmer. More human. Less like you're greeting someone from across a moat.

That afternoon we visited another family. Kids, dogs, pizza. *Mate* kept circulating. I was hooked. It felt like you couldn't show up to a social event without it, which meant constant caffeine and constant hydration and a slow, steady feeling of being absorbed into the rhythm of a place.

It was frustrating being able to understand more Spanish than I could speak. I could follow enough to feel included, but not enough to be the version of myself I actually am. I had thoughts. Opinions. Funny comments. Whole personality traits trapped behind toddler-level sentence structure. And yet it never felt awkward here.

People were patient. Carlos and Rosemarie bridged the gaps. If anything, I just felt lucky. Exposed to the kind of Uruguay you can't access through tourist sites. *Asados. Mate.* Family stories. That's what I'd wanted. That's why I travel. Not just for beauty, but for proximity to other ways of living.

Coastal Roads and Tarantulas

- PUNTA DEL ESTE, URUGUAY -

Then we hit the road to Punta del Este, and the whole mood shifted into that clean, golden feeling travel sometimes gives you when everything just works.

Coastal roads. A glimpse of hills, which were Uruguay's version of mountains, bless. Christmas music blasting across decades and genres because I'm incapable of letting December pass without turning it into a soundtrack—Michael Bublé, Mariah Carey, The Jackson Five, Shakin' Stevens. I felt that tug of missing New Zealand at Christmas, missing my grandparents being there on a six-week trip, missing the particular warm chaos of home traditions. While also feeling giddy at the absurdity of listening to "Feliz Navidad" while driving through Uruguay. Both things true at once.

Punta del Este appeared in the distance like a brochure. Towering apartment blocks and hotels lining wide sandy beaches, sun out, warm but not humid, and that perfect coastal breeze that makes your body relax without you noticing. The kind of temperature that feels like the world is being kind.

We found a beautiful apartment in a tall building. Modern, speedy internet, glorious view and, most importantly, no mosquitoes. We were close to Los Dedos, the hand sculpture poking out of the sand like a giant trying to escape the beach. The city felt polished and holiday-ready, all bright edges and ocean light, and I felt instantly settled.

So, obviously, I ran.

Six kilometres along the waterfront, a boardwalk that practically begged for it. And as I ran, I felt that familiar truth click into place again. I love the ocean. I'm not even a strong swimmer. It doesn't matter. Being near it soothes me. It steadies me. I've lived close to it most of my life, and my nervous system knows what to do when it smells salt and hears waves.

It reminded me of Wellington runs back in New Zealand. Warm air, cool breeze, other runners doing that little "we're in this together" wave as you pass. Except here there were surfers and roller skaters and, everywhere, *mate* cups and thermoses, like people were born holding them. The ocean smelled mild but salty, the waves either lapping gently or crashing onto sharp rocks, and the whole scene felt like a quieter, shinier version of everything I'd been craving.

When I got back, dinner was on the table. We filled our *mate* cups with *yerba* and drank them on the balcony, watching the last of the sunset bleed out over the water like a slow exhale.

And I thought, again, how Uruguay kept doing this to me. Surprising me quietly. Feeding me in ways I didn't fully understand until after. A country I'd barely known a month earlier, now offering me rain-soaked home visits and fireflies and roadside *ferias* and buttery sandwiches and a coastline that made my body soften.

Maybe that's what makes a place feel like a hidden treasure. It doesn't scream for your attention. It just keeps pleasantly surprising you.

We drove back along the coast for a day trip to Piriápolis. Piriápolis was pretty in that gentle, off-peak way. Nice *rambla*, nice views, the kind of place that probably transforms in peak season into a cheap, cheerful beach town where families return year after year.

But it didn't quite have that spark for us, not compared to what we'd already been soaking up on our doorstep. It was a place to eat lunch, tick off a viewpoint, maybe wander past a castle, and feel quietly pleased you weren't paying summer prices.

The standout moment, absurdly, was wildlife. Not cute wildlife. Not photogenic wildlife. The kind that makes your heart stop.

A tarantula—hand-sized, furry, unapologetic—scuttled across the road right in front of the car.

Carlos swerved gently. We pulled over immediately because you can't *not* pull over. I stared at it with the stunned logic of a tourist who still half-believes animals stay inside documentaries: is this… someone's escaped pet? Do tarantulas just… live out here in the wild?

It was enormous. Bigger than my hand. So furry it looked like it should be wearing tiny boots. It crossed the street and disappeared into the bushes.

Another couple saw it and pulled over too, and one of them was local. She said, very calmly, yes, it was wild. Like it was no big deal.

It felt like Uruguay kept slipping small surprises into the margins of otherwise ordinary days, just to keep me alert.

We drove up to Cerro San Antonio after that, and as we were leaving the tarantula scene behind, we set off an alarm somewhere. We must've been too close to a fence, too close to someone's property line. It was one of those sharp, sudden noises that makes you walk faster without discussing it. We climbed up anyway, because the hill was the whole point, and at the top the view was the reward. Miles of coastline, beaches stretching out like a promise. Souvenir shops clustered near the lookout. A little church sat up there too, simple and quiet, and Carlos and I sat on its steps sipping *mate* while Rosemarie browsed.

Back in Punta del Este that evening, I ran again, because once I'd tasted how good it felt, I couldn't not. The wind had picked up, and the surfers had thinned out, but I finally understood the geography enough to stop accidentally looping into confusion. I followed the *rambla* through the port and kept going until it turned into a wooden boardwalk and the scene changed into something that felt unmistakably Uruguayan. Couples and friend groups sprawled on grass under palm trees, bare feet in sand, thermoses tucked under elbows, *mate* cups held like extensions of their hands.

Punta del Este itself felt like it was holding its breath. We'd arrived in that awkward shoulder season where summer is technically here, but the town hasn't fully woken up yet. A lot of attractions were still closed, waiting for tourist season like a stage waiting for actors. We spent the day half-chasing lighthouses and markets that weren't open, half just enjoying the simple pleasure of wandering the peninsula, grabbing *empanadas*, browsing souvenirs, letting the place be what it was instead of what we'd imagined.

We met a Brazilian guy running a shop so colourful it felt like stepping inside a *piñata*. He greeted us like a long-lost friend and somehow it felt genuine. Not sales-y, not desperate. Just warm. He showed us his weed stash like it was a family photo album, gave us a quick lesson on the differences between his stuff and the pharmacy's, then tried to convince Rosemarie that Brazil was beautiful and worth visiting while she looked at him like he'd suggested we take up base-jumping as a hobby. He raved about Uruguay—its open-mindedness, its legality, its laid-back vibe. And honestly, standing there in Punta del Este with its white sand and eccentric hippies, it was hard to argue.

We tried to be ambitious later. We headed out toward José Ignacio, attempted a lighthouse that was closed, drove to a horse ranch with vague intentions of doing a ride the next day, discovered there was no one available to answer questions, and then saw the price tag: $120 USD for two and a half hours. The enthusiasm drained out of us like a plug had been pulled. We chose to keep our money for other things.

So we finished at Punta Ballena instead, a small peninsula named after whales because it's supposed to be a good spotting point. We skipped Casapueblo because it was wildly overpriced, and opted for the better version of travel luxury. Browsing little souvenir stalls with *mate* in hand while the sky did its sunset thing.

By midday the next day, Rosemarie was exhausted in that particular way only travel can destroy you. Joy fatigue, sun fatigue, constant stimulation, the relentless requirement to be "on." She looked like she could fall asleep mid-sentence. So we gave her our room, shut the curtains, and let her disappear into deep recovery sleep behind South America's favourite invention. *Persianas enrollables.* The external metal blind that makes your bedroom feel like a cave.

It reminded me how easy it is to forget to rest when you're travelling. You start treating exhaustion like a personal flaw, like you're wasting the gift of the trip by needing downtime. That works when you're young and doing a couple of weeks. But months? Or travelling with someone older? Rest stops being optional. It becomes part of the survival kit, right alongside money and clean water and common sense.

We were actually pretty good about it most of the time. Rest days, vegetables whenever we could, vitamins when we felt ourselves slipping into that "why do I feel like a deflated balloon?" zone. Feeling healthy mattered as much as having cash. It's hard to enjoy paradise when your body feels like it's quietly mutinying.

With Rosemarie asleep, Carlos and I wandered down to the port to find somewhere warm to sit because the wind was surprisingly cold. We landed in an Irish-style pub called Moby Dick and promptly ordered enough pizza and fries to undo every wholesome thing I'd just said about vitamins. Two rounds of beer later, we'd made friends with two elderly women at the table beside us. Exactly the kind of travel magic you can't schedule.

They were curious about our trip, and then they started unfolding their own lives like they'd been waiting for someone to ask. The younger one reminisced about living out of a van for six months when she was younger. Perfect timing, because I'd literally been scrolling through Instagram van conversions an hour earlier, fantasising about the same thing. They talked about art and said things that landed with unexpected weight. The older one announced, flatly, that when people talk, they always lie, but paintings are honest. We talked about pets and travel and how loving animals can become its own kind of heartbreak when you know your life doesn't have room for them yet.

It was one of those conversations that shouldn't matter. Pizza isn't even a good talking food. But it did. It reminded me, again, that travel isn't just landscapes. It's these collisions with strangers where you borrow a slice of their life and carry it with you.

When we walked back along the waterfront later, we saw the apartment curtains open in the distance. Rosemarie awake again, back in the world. We collected her and went out for another walk, *mate* in hand, the ocean looking silvery under cloud cover while the sun still managed to feel strong. And even as I loved Punta del Este, I felt that itch for the next place. Tomorrow we were driving to Punta del Diablo.

The point of the devil.

Point of the Devil

- PUNTA DEL DIABLO, URUGUAY & CHUÍ, BRAZIL -

The drive north was easy and gorgeous in that slow-breath kind of way. Coastal roads, sand dunes, then inland, then back to the coast. Smooth highways with the occasional reminder that Uruguay runs on its own timeline—overtaking horse and carriage, swerving around a giant lizard like it was a normal road hazard. Pastures rolled out endlessly like home, except without mountains, and with cacti scattered around the landscape.

We'd expected Punta del Diablo to be another Punta del Este. Fancy resort, yachts, inflated prices.

It was none of that.

It wasn't even a city. It was a village. Shack-like buildings, fishing boats, a beach lined with rustic stalls that looked deliberately shabby, like the town had decided to lean into its own barefoot mythology. There was more Portuguese in the air, more backpackers slouching along with big packs, more dreadlocks and ankle bracelets and sandy feet. The tourism here wasn't champagne and high-rises. It was surfboards and cheap beer and "I live in a hammock for the summer" energy.

Even the town centre was small. Just a cluster of bright single-storey buildings, part homes, part shops, mostly restaurants, leading down to the beach and then to the rocky section called Punta del Diablo itself.

Our Airbnb sat down a dirt road where quad bikes seemed like normal transportation, and at first, we thought we'd chosen somewhere remote. Then we realised no, that's just the town. Dirt roads are the aesthetic. Rural but intentionally so. Underdeveloped in a way that felt charming. Like the place had resisted being polished into something it wasn't.

I could imagine being young and spending a summer here working hospitality, drinking on the beach after shifts, falling in with a rotating cast of other drifters. The kind of summer you would talk about forever.

Our biggest fear, of course, was mosquitoes. Libertad had destroyed us. We were still healing, still scratching, still covered in bites that had turned into scabs from sheer inability to leave them alone. At this point I understood how people lose their minds with fleas. I also had a mysterious new injury. I'd put on a dress and immediately felt my back burning like I'd been branded. It raised into an angry patch of skin and later left a purple mark, and I never found out what caused it.

But Punta del Diablo had its own comforts. Our Airbnb had a *parrilla*. An actual proper Uruguayan barbecue, and Carlos was delighted. He got to cook *asado* in the yard, smoke and fire and roots and ritual.

The next day was what twenty-four-year-old me would have assumed South America was. A beach, a hot sun, a perfect summer day. Only now, twenty-six-year-old me knew that this continent is everything at once. Mountains and rainforests and deserts and altiplano and yes, beaches too.

Today was the beach chapter, and Punta del Diablo did it properly. High twenties, dry coastal heat, weekend crowds arriving, beach umbrellas sprouting like mushrooms. More surfers. More stalls open. The sand felt good underfoot until it became so hot it was painful, and we kept switching between flip-flops and barefoot like idiots. And overhead, spiders were flying.

Not metaphorically. Literally.

They were ballooning. Kiting on strands of web. So we kept waving our arms in front of our faces, pulling invisible cobwebs off our skin as we walked. Uruguay's animal kingdom continued to humble me.

We found Rosemarie posted up happily at a food stall, munching *buñuelos de algas*, little seaweed fritter balls, served with an aggressively strong Brazilian garlic sauce that made my whole body feel like it was waking up. It was so good we later bought the same brand at the Brazilian border like it was contraband.

We crossed the dirt road for lemonade. Lime, mint, fresh. We sat there watching dogs sprint into the ocean, people hauling in a fishing boat, and a group of friends carrying their wheelchair-bound friend into the water so he could be part of it too. Everyone was smiling. Staff danced to Portuguese music overhead like the day was carrying them too.

And in the middle of all that softness, I noticed a pleasant surprise. The bill deducted 18% again because we were paying by foreign credit card. GST returned like a quiet reward for being from somewhere else. Just like in Argentina.

That night I stayed up late reading Wild by Cheryl Strayed, the kind of book that makes you feel both vulnerable and invincible, while somewhere behind the Airbnb, hippie drumming thudded into the dark.

We chased the border today, not because we needed to, but because we wanted the symbol of it. A stamp. A line on a map. The childish thrill of saying, "Yep. Brazil too."

It was only a thirty-minute drive from Punta del Diablo to Chuy, pronounced like "Tui" with a CH. This strange twin-town split personality where Uruguay spells it

Chuy and Brazil spells it Chuí, and they share the same main avenue like they couldn't be bothered building a proper border. One street. Two countries.

The drive there was all sun and farmland. Low-thirties heat, cows grazing like it was their job (it is), horses galloping in a way that made everything feel cinematic. Like we'd accidentally driven into the opening scene of a *gaucho* film.

Chuy itself surprised me. Punta del Diablo had felt tiny, like a village dressed like a lifestyle. I'd assumed Chuy would be even smaller. Border towns, in my head, were always dusty and forgettable. But Chuy had proper buildings. Nothing taller than a couple of storeys, but solid structures. Real. And it was absolutely drenched in duty-free commerce. There were a hundred duty-free shops. At least.

They all sold the same categories. Electronics, cosmetics, booze, mountains of chocolate. And it was instantly obvious this city lived and breathed off the border's loopholes. Even the currency was a little identity crisis. Prices in US dollars at the duty-free stores, supermarket labels in both Brazilian and Uruguayan prices, produce labelled in Portuguese. Being in Chuy felt more like being in Brazil than Uruguay, even before we'd done anything official.

And Portuguese, wow, it sounded exotic to me. Written down, it teased familiarity, like Spanish with a secret. But spoken fast in a group? It might as well have been a spell. I suddenly realised how little exposure I'd actually had to it, despite years of Brazilian exchange students at my Dunedin high school. My brain had filed it away as "language I know exists" and never revisited.

Nevertheless, we did what border towns are built for. We shopped.

Carlos bought a ridiculous amount of alcohol. I kept it tame. Just my favourite mascara, and a bottle of wine intended for my friend in Chile.

Then we decided to actually cross the border.

We drove and drove and suddenly absolutely everything was in Portuguese, and I laughed out loud because for a split second it felt like we'd done it accidentally. Did that make us illegal migrants? Would I have to go home with the story "So anyway, I accidentally illegally entered Brazil"?

But no, we were in this oddly lively no-man's-land between the two countries, which was what made the whole border feel so bizarre.

Getting our passport stamps took effort, because our reason for crossing was embarrassingly pure. We simply wanted to walk through the border so we could say we'd entered Brazil, and then walk back out. No paperwork for the car. No time. No grand itinerary. Just a token step into another world. It took a while, but eventually the border officers understood, even if they clearly thought we were strange.

It was a fleeting moment of entry, but that tiny switch, Uruguay to Brazil, fired up my sense of adventure. Brazil felt fun and loud and new. Different language, dance music blasting, sun, the sense that it was its own continent masquerading as a country. I knew instantly I didn't want to "do Brazil" in a couple of days. I wanted to come back and commit. It would be a future trip, for sure. I'd come back for a long duration and make sure I had the time to really explore it. To stay on coffee farms and cacao plantations and go to festivals and eat delicious food. *One day.*

The Farm That Fought Back

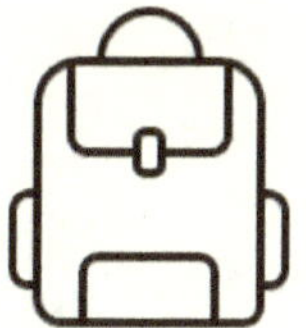

- TACUAREMBÓ, URUGUAY -

The next day was one of those drives that becomes a highlight, even if, on paper, it's just… a drive.

We were leaving Punta del Diablo behind, stopping in Chuy again, then heading all the way up toward the north of Uruguay for a two-night farm stay. It was already roasting by 10 a.m. as we packed the car. The neighbours' dogs, the little unofficial security team we'd grown attached to, came to say goodbye. An old black dog, a younger black lab-looking one, and a golden retriever type. They'd hovered outside our windows like bouncers all week, and we fed them as a thank you. It felt like the same informal contract we'd made with homeless guys watching our car. Protection in exchange for kindness. A weird little travel economy of trust.

And then we drove.

Hotter and hotter, creeping from high twenties into mid-to-late thirties, the kind of heat that makes the air feel thick even when it's dry. The stretch between Punta del Diablo and Chuy was packed with hitchhikers. More than I'd seen anywhere else, even more than summer New Zealand. They all had that same beach-hippy look we'd seen earlier. Sunburnt, loose clothes, "I live off rice and vibes" energy. I had no idea if they were Uruguayan, Brazilian, or from somewhere else entirely. They just existed like part of the landscape.

Then the scenery shifted into something surreal. Miles and miles of palm trees, not dense like a forest, but dotted across the horizon like someone had scattered them by hand. We drove with the windows down at 100km/h, wind blasting through like a hairdryer on full heat, and I sang loudly with my hand out the window like I was starring in my own music video.

I was genuinely, stupidly happy.

It was rural almost the whole way. Few settlements, and the ones we passed looked agriculture-based. Meat and dairy, small-scale versions of home. The dark side of that rural life was roadside death. Not just the usual small animals—but dogs. It made my stomach sink. And birds kept clustering on the road, so we hit a few despite trying not to, one exploding across the windscreen in the most disgusting, tragic slapstick moment imaginable.

Eventually it became too hot even with the windows down. We surrendered and blasted the air conditioning, but the sun still burned through the windscreen onto my legs like a slow grill. I'd never driven in heat like that. Still, the view kept giving. We saw endless farms, palms, rolling hills, and horses, majestic, everywhere, often ridden by actual *gauchos.* Not costumes. Real men on horses, working the land. I wanted to climb onto one immediately, like the desire lived somewhere primitive in my bones.

The road turned bumpy for a stretch, full of potholes and heat mirages that made the surface ahead shimmer like water. It messed with depth perception. You'd see "water," then realise it was a deceptive wave of heat, then hit a crater anyway. But we survived it without disaster, and after six and a half hours we reached Tacuarembó, a small northern city, and I felt that end-of-drive relief in my whole body.

Except I'd apparently selected the farm stay without double checking that it was actually in Tacuarembó. Google Maps told us it was another hour and a half north.

I was... not popular.

I apologised profusely to Carlos and Rosemarie, mortified by my misjudgment. But then, miracle, when we checked the Airbnb app directly it clarified actually, it was only twelve kilometres outside town. Google Maps had been dramatic. I wasn't completely off with directions.

We grabbed burgers and fries in a plaza and nearly died eating in the heat, then drove into the countryside and down a long, sheltered driveway lined with every kind of tree imaginable. The second we opened the car doors, the air hit us. Rosemary and lemongrass, thick and clean, like the land itself was preparing a home cooked meal.

And there it was. A thatched cottage on a farm, rustic and warm and quiet. Dim golden lights. Wooden everything. Old furniture that felt well-loved rather than shabby. A little cabinet displaying homemade jams you could buy. Bedrooms up a steep ladder-staircase with low ceilings and the thatch roof exposed, like we'd stepped into some storybook version of rural life.

That night the host cooked us dinner with ingredients from the farm. Vegetarian, fresh, absurdly good. Even dessert was poached fruit from the land. Afterwards we went outside and the sky made me stop. The stars had been pretty at the coast, but here they were New Zealand-level sharp and dense, the kind that makes you feel small in a comforting way.

Tacuarembó was already paying off.

But then came the next day. The comedy of errors.

It began with mosquitoes exploiting a tiny hole in the window screen. I woke up bitten to hell, arms swelling like I had broken a bone. Then I went downstairs and saw the bookshelf moving. Thousands of ants, including flying ones, swarming like the cottage had turned into a horror film. They were on the floor. Near Rosemarie's bed. Everywhere.

I messaged Carlos: *We have a problem. Come and look at the bookshelf.*

To their credit, the hosts reacted fast. Breakfast arrived—fresh bread, homemade jams—while they dealt with the nest. Rosemarie took insect spray and started sweeping bodies like a warrior queen. The whole thing was so intense we were genuinely close to packing up and fleeing.

But we stayed, because we were supposed to go horse riding.

The horses were saddled and waiting. We got a short little farm wander, and then couldn't go any further because roadworks on this remote country road were kicking up dust storms and blocking the route. Later, driving confirmed we had made the right decision. Riding horses in that would've been like volunteering to swallow sandpaper.

So, no riding.

Then the weather turned apocalyptic.

Not drizzle. Not a cute storm. Black clouds rolling in like *The Day After Tomorrow*. Because Uruguay is so flat and we were out in open countryside, we could see the whole system approach for miles. Watch it come, hear it arrive, feel the wind rip through the trees before the rain even hit. The rain hammered the thatch roof, and I stared upward like prayer could reinforce roofing.

And then, because the day wasn't ridiculous enough, a sparrow somehow got into our upstairs bedroom and spent hours panicking, trying to fly through the light toward freedom, not understanding the screen was permanent. Windows didn't open. The bird was beyond reach. We now had mosquitoes, ants, a cockroach cameo, cancelled horse riding, a violent storm, and a trapped bird with the power to shit on us in our sleep.

At some point we accepted our fate and leaned into the comedy of it all.

The thunder wasn't normal thunder. It felt like earthquakes. Pure bass that made the windows vibrate and the room shake. We taught Rosemarie how to play Uno, played until the power died. Lights out, fan stopped, everything silent except the storm—then waited. Hours. No internet. No reading, because my books were digital. No cards, because we couldn't see. Just sitting there in storm-time, remembering that in South America, power outages don't owe you a timeline.

Eventually enough light returned to keep playing Uno. Then something dropped somewhere, and Rosemarie shouted "WHAT THE F* WAS THAT" in English and we almost wet ourselves laughing, and right then, as if on cue, the power returned. Lights on, fan blasting, the cottage revived.

The storm didn't fully quit. It changed direction repeatedly like it couldn't decide who to threaten. South, then east, then west. We stepped outside briefly to watch, and it genuinely felt unsettling how clearly we could see it reorient above us.

Still, dinner saved the day again. Homemade vegetarian lasagne, caprese salad, chips, more vegetables, and *flan*. Farm-to-table comfort food, the kind I'd choose at home, only better because it was fresh and grown right there.

By then I realised something about myself I maybe didn't want to admit. I like a little drama in travel. Not danger. Not trauma. Just chaos. The kind that becomes a story instead of a scar. Too smooth and you don't learn much. Too rough and it breaks you. This was the perfect middle. Enough trouble to laugh about forever, and enough safety to soften it.

Because even in Tacuarembó, in the middle of our little nightmare, people were good. The bakery in town gave us free pastries. Everyone felt like they were quietly helping each other, and that, more than the ants and the thunder, was what stayed with me about the place.

The next morning the sparrow was still flapping frantically above my head at 7 a.m. and I simply refused to deal with it. Covers overhead. Not today, bird.

We left with bags full of food. Bread, jam, leftover pasta, fruit. And paid for two massive bags of organic farm vegetables and herbs for about 300 pesos, feeling absurdly smug about it. Farewell, Nangapiré farm, you were beautiful *and* you were a pain in the arse.

The drive to Salto was mostly grass plains and broccoli-shaped tree clusters, cloudy enough that we could open the windows without being roasted alive. Then a hornet-sized wasp—one of those gigantic Uruguayan ones that prey on tarantulas—landed on Carlos' lap while he drove at 110km/h on bending country roads.

I didn't tell him why. I just ordered, loudly: *PULL OVER NOW. PULL OVER.*

He anxiously searched for a safe spot, glanced down while we were still moving, and immediately started panicking, car swerving, while the wasp relocated to my footwell and I folded my legs onto the seat like a startled cat.

We pulled over. Hazards on. Poor Rosemarie screamed and swatted, and of course the wasp stung her.

We treated it with hand sanitiser and something cold and laughed after, because what else could you do?

Then came roadkill that felt like an unwanted nature documentary. Armadillo, skunk. And yes, skunks really do stink. Even dead.

We arrived in Salto around 3 p.m., public thermometer reading 35°C, and hid inside our air-conditioned accommodation. The town looked more run down than the Uruguay we'd been falling for, closer in vibe to Argentina, which made sense, because the river border was right there, close enough to feel the bleed-through.

And then it hit me. We'd entered the final month of the trip.

That weird mix arrived. Time feeling both huge and suddenly short. The fear that I'd go home, and it would feel like no time had passed at all, like the trip would compress into a highlight reel. And the longing for home comforts I hadn't realised I missed. Family hugs, English language, bowls of WeetBix, Marmite on toast, Whittaker's chocolate. The joy of travel isn't just what you gain. It's what you learn to appreciate again when you return.

Salto's main claim to fame was its thermal baths, and because travel turns you into the kind of person who will do something purely for the sentence it creates later, we went.

It was a five-minute drive, 150 pesos each, about seven dollars, and they slapped wristbands on us so we could come and go all day, as if we were about to settle in for a long, spiritual soak. But outside was already well over thirty degrees, and we weren't here for healing or transcendence. We were here so we could say "we went to thermal baths in Uruguay."

The place wasn't really a spa anyway. It was more like a waterpark pretending to be therapeutic. Still, I had to admit I was impressed. For the cheapest option, it delivered. Eight pools or more, different temperatures, and one glorious cold pool. At times I genuinely couldn't tell what was hotter, the water or the air. I learned the pools here are the hottest in Uruguay, reaching forty-six degrees Celsius, and the water is full of iodine, iron, calcium, magnesium, fluorine. Proper mineral credentials. So yes, it was legitimate. And yes, it was also hilarious doing hot pools in peak heat with the sun trying to kill you.

Afterwards we decided to check out the local zoo, and that was a mistake. It was free, which should've been the first red flag, but the real warning arrived as soon as we pulled into the carpark. Something felt wrong. The kind of wrong you can feel in your gut before you've even seen anything. Inside, the people wandering around looked sketchy and bored in a way that made me uneasy, and we saw two young guys poking sticks into cages just to piss the animals off.

The exhibits were heartbreaking. The monkey cages were concrete floors with a single branch, as if someone had designed them to erase any last shred of dignity. At one point the stench became so overwhelming we were convinced there had to be a dead animal somewhere. We lasted less than ten minutes before leaving, furious and sick to our stomachs, wishing we could've paid an entrance fee if it meant the animals weren't living in what felt like punishment.

The only bright spot were the cats, hundreds of them, lounging everywhere like they owned the place. But even that couldn't soften the fact that the zoo felt unsafe, neglected, and cruel. We walked out, immediately ashamed that it was "free" when the cost was clearly being paid by the animals.

Salto, overall, was brief. A nice, clean Airbnb with air conditioning, a novelty-soak in mineral pools, and then a clear sense that one day was enough. I still didn't understand how there were hot pools here. There were no volcanoes, no dramatic geothermal landscape. But I accepted, as I did so often on this trip, that South America didn't owe me explanations.

That night, Uruguay reminded me again what it loved doing best. Thunderstorms. I woke at 5 a.m. to what genuinely sounded like the world ending. Our Airbnb was basically a little box tucked behind someone's main house, and the trees around it were four times its height. They thrashed and scraped the roof like claws. Bins were being thrown around. Rain dumped in sheets. Lightning struck every second, so constant it felt like the sky had turned into a strobe light. I lay there in the dark worrying about the car, worrying about us, realising it was the first time a storm had actually scared me. There was nothing to do but stay in bed and wait for the sky to calm down.

By the time we were ready to get up properly, the worst had passed. The rain was still heavy, but the wind had dropped, and we did that frantic wet-weather dance where you pull the car right up to the door, pack quickly, and pretend you're not slightly traumatised. Then we drove to the next dot on the map. Paysandú.

The Dog Attack

- PAYSANDÚ & COLONIA DEL SACRAMENTO, URUGUAY -

The drive to Paysandú was drama-free in the way only travel-drama can be. Lightning still blasting around us, but at least no flooding. The real challenge came when we got close. Our accommodation was out in the countryside north of the city, and the property was enormous, with several houses on it that all looked identical. The same colour, the same shape, the same "this might be it?" energy. We found the turn-off, drove all the way down a long driveway, then realised we had no idea which door to aim at.

So, Carlos decided to get out and knock on a few doors to ask. Every property had dogs. Guard dogs. One of them, a huge asshole of a dog, launched itself at our car and started biting the tyres.

Carlos, optimistic as ever, reported back "They're trying to bite the tyres, but I don't think their teeth can go through."

Spoiler: their teeth definitely could.

We eventually found our place. It turned out everyone on this giant property was related, which somehow felt very Uruguay. After dumping our things, we went back into the city to do groceries. Near the mall, two different cars honked at us to signal something was wrong. We pulled over, and there it was. One of our tyres was completely flat.

I wasn't going to pretend I knew how to change a tyre, so I stood back and let Carlos handle it. What struck me, though, even in a city that looked run down and smelled like actual sewage, was how kind people were. Strangers pulled over and offered to help. Carlos initially refused. Too proud, too stubborn. But one guy just calmly walked over and insisted. He helped confidently, quickly, like it was nothing. When we tried to give him cash, he refused.

We dropped off cake, Coke, and chips later anyway, as he mentioned he lived in the house just over the road. Some part of us can't accept genuine kindness without wanting to return it.

With the spare tyre providing us with temporary relief, we discovered a garage around the corner and went there next. They said it would take half an hour, so we did groceries while we waited. It was Friday. The timing mattered. Weekends in South America have their own rules, and one of them is: if you don't fix it before closing, you might be living with it until Monday.

They "fixed" two tyres. They didn't charge us anything. We drove away relieved, although the warning light stayed on. We assumed the car was just adjusting, like it needed a moment to emotionally process being repaired.

Nope.

By the time we got home twenty minutes later, the first tyre sounded weird. We got out. It was flat again. The garage hadn't fixed it properly.

It was nearly 5 p.m. We had one hour to put the spare on again and race back before they closed at six, because if we got stranded here over the weekend, I would've been gutted. We'd only planned one day in Paysandú, and I felt like I'd already smelled enough poop to last a lifetime.

Carlos changed the tyre again, and we flew back to the garage. They were ready for us, laughing and smiling like this was all part of the afternoon entertainment. I waited in the car at first, until I heard the soft, unmistakable sound of another tyre deflating.

Of course.

It was one of those perfectly-timed disasters that is both a pain in the arse and a blessing. Because if they'd fixed the first tyre properly the first time, the third one—already weakened by dog bites, hanging by a thread—would've gone the next day, when we were back on the road and the garage was closed for the weekend. So yes, humiliating. But also, lucky.

Carlos had to ask them to change another tyre, which made them laugh harder. This time they actually inspected all of them properly. The conclusion was both ridiculous and informative. Yes, dogs can bite through tyres. And yes, this apparently happens all the time in South America. We decided it would be the last time we worried about running dogs over when they attacked our car. A dark little travel lesson I hadn't expected to learn.

But like I said before, I don't mind things going a bit wrong. I never want catastrophe. No broken bones, no serious illness, no violence. But these small misadventures are the ones that teach you. Patience. Flexibility. The ability to laugh while your plans unravel. And somehow, we always seemed to land on our feet.

The next morning everything was calm. The tyres held. The sun was out. Our Airbnb sat right on the river, and the Uruguay River looked silver under cloudless skies, even though the water itself was undeniably brown. There were small islands dotted with lush green foliage, and we even spotted a Juan Grande, which is a large, pelican-like bird that's apparently rare. It felt like the river was giving us a soft goodbye after the chaos of the day before.

We drove to Mercedes, the roads horrific in places, the kind that make you clench your jaw and pray your brakes remember their job. At one point the brakes didn't work, and we went flying over a bridge and then, like nothing had happened, they seemed fine again.

Mercedes, at least, was pretty. Cobbled streets. White-painted buildings. We parked outside a fancy *empanada* store and bought twelve. Then, naturally, we discovered our Airbnb wasn't actually in Mercedes at all. It was forty-five minutes away through the countryside, in a tiny village called Villa Soriano, which I'd never heard of and later learned was the first town established in Uruguay.

It didn't feel historic. It felt abandoned. A ghost town. Even the Plaza de Armas was empty on a Saturday. We wandered to its main attraction, which was a wooden jetty opening onto the river, and heard distant swimmers somewhere far off. That was basically it.

But the lodge we were staying in… that was something else.

It looked like an old French lodge, rustic but spotless, decorated with care. The owner was a character. Straw-like bleached hair, probably late sixties, skin weathered like she'd lived under sun and salt and pure stubbornness. She moved dramatically, dressed eccentrically, spoke like someone who'd seen too much of the world to care what anyone thought. I assumed she was just a bit whacko.

Then I noticed a photo of her on a book cover on the shelf.

And then another.

And another.

She was the author. Of multiple books. She'd lived on a boat for twenty-three years. She'd sailed the North and South Atlantic solo. The woman I'd quietly labelled "crazy" was actually legendary. Not crazy in the unstable way. Crazy in the brave way. The kind of crazy I secretly admired.

She became my hero in about ten seconds.

We hugged her goodbye the next day, took photos, packed up the car like seasoned Tetris champions, and drove with the windows down. The countryside smelled like summer. Bright yellow chamomile fields that smelled like baby lotion, plus lemongrass and eucalyptus drifting in on the wind. Cows everywhere. And wild ostriches, which felt like a glitch in the landscape.

As we drove, the end of the trip pressed in around the edges. I'd loved life on the road and I'd disliked it, and I knew the real impact wouldn't hit until I'd been home long enough to stop moving. But still, there were moments—warm wind through the car, the same flat horizon stretching forever—where I felt choked up by how quickly it was all slipping away.

Then we reached Colonia del Sacramento, the place everyone "does" in Uruguay. The one-hour speedboat day-trip fantasy from Buenos Aires. It was instantly more touristy, filled with baseball caps and tote bags, but still mostly Spanish-speaking tourists, which I loved. It felt busy without feeling like it had been handed over completely.

Colonia was genuinely beautiful. Cobbled streets, preserved and UNESCO protected, shaded by trees that offered mercy from the sun. It reminded me a little of Mendoza. That same calm charm, that same sense of being built for strolling slowly. There were souvenir stores everywhere, and we found the perfect *artisan feria* for Rosemarie. She went off like a kid in a candy shop, buying keychains and coin purses and whatever else delighted her. I was so happy to see her in her element. After everything—ant infestations, wasp stings, couch beds, steep stairs, and a road trip that probably wasn't always her idea of fun—she deserved a place that felt easy and enjoyable.

That's when I noticed something else. Uruguay (and Argentina) might be the only places in the world that sell *materas*—bags designed specifically to carry *mate*. A whole accessory category for a drink.

We accidentally booked another place with two flights of stairs (sorry, Rosemarie), but it had air conditioning in nearly every room and, most importantly, no bugs. No mosquitoes whining at our ears. No ants trying to colonise our belongings. We slept like blessed people.

And that evening we went to the waterfront for the sunset, because our wild sailor-author host had told us it was the best in the world.

She wasn't wrong.

The sky burned red-orange, so intense it looked unreal. I joked it was probably pollution drifting from Buenos Aires, the silhouette of which we could see faintly in the distance, but even that couldn't ruin it. People gathered to watch, and when it ended, some of them clapped, just like in Montevideo, like gratitude had become a habit in this country.

Later the wind rose again. Back at the apartment, the lightning returned, zapping across the Río de la Plata and striking toward Argentina. I could actually see the difference between the Argentina side and the Uruguay side. When it hit the river near us, it was crisp white; when it hit Argentina, it glowed orange.

That night the storm battered Colonia relentlessly. I fell asleep around 1 a.m. and woke again at 5 to rain so loud it felt like it was inside the room. Carlos wasn't beside me. I found him asleep in the living room with the lights blazing, headphones still plugged in, mid-escape via movie. It was his way of coping. If you can't silence the storm, drown it out.

The next day was grey and low and threatening, the kind where you're always waiting for rain to hit. We did a bit more souvenir shopping for Rosemarie, and I managed to break a fridge magnet. Carlos would definitely tell his seven-year-old Chilean cousin about it later. Especially since I'd already broken that kid's Minecraft sign and a new toy in Chile. I was building a legacy.

We wandered through Colonia's historic quarter. Pastel buildings, old churches, the gate and wooden drawbridge, cobblestones and gawping tourists. But the rain eventually came, and "cold" arrived too. Not truly cold, just nineteen degrees, which felt chilly only because we'd become acclimatised to Uruguay's heat.

We ducked into a café for lunch and made our classic mistake. We forgot to check payment options. My debit card still wasn't working, Carlos' hadn't resurfaced, and our cash was nearly gone. We'd spent the last two months trying to navigate South America's chaotic "cash only / card only / discount if you pay like this" roulette. This place was cash only, naturally, so we dumped most of our remaining notes on lunch like idiots and then sat there silently recalculating our budget for the rest of our week.

With wind and rain fully committed, we retreated home with supermarket *pan dulces*—those chocolate breads everyone eats at Christmas—and did something we hadn't done in a while. Stayed in. Just listening to weather, eating sweet bread, and trying not to stare too hard at the countdown.

Twenty-seven days left.

We did a quick budget check, dividing what I had left by the days remaining like a ritual, and realised we'd averaged about fifty dollars a day in Uruguay. Shockingly low for such an "expensive" country. Partly because storms had trapped us inside, partly because the horse riding we kept trying to do never happened. Every *estancia* replied with some variation of: Forecasted to rain today and tomorrow, sorry.

It felt like Uruguay had decided our trip would not include horses.

Only thunderstorms.

The Best & The Worst

- LIBERTAD & MONTEVIDEO, URUGUAY -

"What was the best part about Uruguay, and what was the worst part?"

It was such a simple question, asked over lunch in Libertad, in the middle of another of Rosemarie's social calls—another living room, another table that somehow held more food than physics should allow, another slice of the real Uruguay I'd been craving since we crossed the river.

We'd woken early and driven out from Colonia while the day was still soft. It wasn't a long drive, but it felt like shifting back into a different Uruguay. Away from the polished tourist version and back into the warm, lived-in one. Now we were mid-*asado* again, treated like family, plates refilled before we could protest.

Best and worst?

"The storms were the best," I said, in English to Rosemarie, because I had no idea what the Spanish word for storm was and I didn't trust myself not to accidentally announce something obscene. Rosemarie translated for me, and everyone nodded like that made perfect sense. Because it did. Uruguay's storms weren't just weather. They were theatre performances. They came in like a personality. They rattled the windows and lit up the sky and made the whole country feel alive.

And the worst?

"The mosquitoes."

That one didn't need translating. The evidence was on all of us. Rosemarie in particular looked like she'd contracted some tropical disease. Red blotches everywhere.

This lunch was my favourite social call so far, mostly because the woman across from me was unexpectedly worldly. Not in the performative way, but in the calm way of someone who has lived a full life and actually pays attention. She answered questions I didn't even realise I'd been carrying.

Those endless palm trees we'd driven through in Rocha? Not random. Planted deliberately like that by natives, she said. Landscape as decision, not accident. Most people here had some kind of Indigenous DNA, she told me matter-of-factly, like it wasn't a political statement, just truth. And in Uruguay they study British English, not American English.

Then she dropped the kind of information that makes your skin crawl.

Apparently when Paraguay floods, spiders and snakes can latch onto floating chunks of tree and debris and drift down the Río de la Plata, until they end up squirming onto Uruguayan territory.

I stared at her, halfway between fascinated and horrified. This whole country is basically a beautiful, calm place where the sky explodes, and the wildlife arrives by river raft.

Her lounge was full of travel souvenirs—little pieces of the world on shelves—from trips she and her husband had taken, and from their son who now lived overseas. It made me want to give her something back that felt like it actually meant something. We handed over one of our kiwi bird souvenirs—the small stash we'd brought from New Zealand as "only for the people who truly stand out" gifts. We were down to two now out of the original ten, and suddenly I wished we'd packed double. There were more people than I expected who deserved one, but we'd been rationing them like they were rare currency.

And then we ate.

Lentil burgers. Eggplant *milanesas*. Salads. *Asado* meat. So much food that by the end I genuinely couldn't imagine fitting anything else inside my body without cracking a rib.

It was time to go, so we did the goodbye chaos. Cheek kisses, thank you's, promises we'd never be able to keep because who knows when we'll ever be back in this exact living room again. We drove a few blocks to visit another friend, and as we pulled into the driveway, we saw the husband from lunch racing toward us on his bike, plastic bag of leftovers in one hand, waving it like a flag.

We'd forgotten the food they wanted to send with us.

Of course he was bringing it. That is Uruguayan hospitality in its purest form… Unless he'd been riding a horse, which would've been the only way to make it more Uruguayan.

If we thought we were full before, the next visit pushed us straight past full and into dangerously over-loved. Another set of friends. Another round of food offered like it was non-negotiable. Homemade cake. Pizza. Smiles that didn't accept refusal. It was the thing I kept being in awe of. Every household seemed to have something ready in the fridge or freezer just in case someone turned up. And we were turning up unannounced constantly, and still, we never left hungry or thirsty. Not once. The opposite. We left loaded.

The only thing that ever bothered me during one of the conversations was a quiet comment made by an older gentleman. It was meant casually: how lucky I was, because being with Carlos meant I got to see all of South America.

I smiled, but it stayed with me. That familiar assumption that I was here because of a man's sense of adventure, rather than because I'd always planned to go. The truth was the opposite. I would've travelled anyway. This trip was already in motion. I don't speak the language, but I would've figured it out, just as I had when I explored other parts of the world alone.

It wasn't something to correct. If anything, it was a moment of reassurance. I wasn't lucky to be following someone. I was lucky to be living a life *I'd* chosen.

Nevertheless, Libertad, by the end, felt like the emotional centre of our Uruguay chapter. We'd been welcomed into so many homes that it stopped feeling like "meeting locals" and started feeling like being folded into a web of people who had known each other forever. It wasn't just food and conversation. It was grief and history and identity moving quietly beneath the surface.

There were moments that cracked open without warning. Rosemarie crying at the cemetery where her father's ashes were. Someone bursting into tears when she surprised them, overwhelmed by being remembered. And the everyday lessons threaded between those heavier moments. How to make an *asado* properly, what Uruguay used to be, what it is now, what it cost people to leave, what it meant to return.

It was also, for me, a deeper look at Carlos. Not the version of him who was just my travel partner, but the version connected to a place and a family history that pre-dated us.

Libertad held all of it at once. The laughter, the feeding, the generosity, the tears, the pride, the stories, the small irritations, the big meaning.

A place that didn't just show me Uruguay.

A place that showed me people.

By the time we rolled back into Montevideo, it felt less like arriving somewhere new and more like returning home. That feeling was rare on this trip. We usually moved on just as a place started to feel familiar, but Montevideo had been different. We'd stayed long enough to develop routines, favourite streets, preferred supermarkets. Coming back after our road trip through the country felt oddly comforting, like slipping back into a jacket you'd forgotten you loved.

We spent the day doing very normal things. Shopping along Avenida 18 de Julio, printing documents because some bus companies were still living in a paper-only universe, popping into TaTa for groceries. Standing in the aisles, loading up our basket, it hit me how quickly Uruguay had become normal. *Zapallitos*, *panettone*, cheese *empanadas*, *Malta*—these were no longer exotic finds but staples. That's always the sneaky thing about travel. One day you're wide-eyed over unfamiliar labels, the next you're irritated that your favourite *empanadas* are out of stock. I already knew that when I eventually went home, an endless supply of *empanadas* would be one of the things I missed most about South America.

Rosemarie absolutely insisted that we go to La Cigale for ice cream, claiming it was the best in Montevideo. She wasn't wrong. We ordered flavours like *bombón roche, dulce de leche,* and tiramisu, and then walked out with an enormous tub "for later." That night we made pizza topped with *zapallito* and vegetables, drank *Malta*, and watched Love Actually. It's a movie I watch every December without fail, and sitting there in Uruguay, ice cream melting faster than we could eat it, I realised I was quietly blending traditions. Home and away, old rituals and new landscapes.

It was Rosemarie's final night, and I felt a surprising ache about it. Travelling with your partner's mum sounds, on paper, like it could be challenging. In reality, it had been pure joy. She brought laughter into every day, mostly through her elaborate system of buying treats "for herself" because she had diabetes, and then immediately handing them to us. She somehow always knew when I was craving chocolate, turning up with *Bombón* bars or *alfajores* at precisely the right moment. More than that, she gave me access to a Uruguay I never could have found on my own—introducing me to friends and family, revisiting places from her past, filling in the emotional gaps between history books and lived experience. Because of her, this country felt layered, personal, and deeply human.

Our last full day in Uruguay arrived too quickly. We all overslept—victims of pizza, ice cream, and one too many movies the night before—and suddenly had a mad dash between waking up and heading out for lunch. We met up with our friend again, who took us to what he confidently declared were the best *chivitos* in Montevideo. El Tinkal sat right along the *Rambla*, sea stretching out behind it, and he was absolutely right. My vegetarian version was stacked with eggplant *milanesa*, fried egg, vegetables, and cheese, and despite having cake for breakfast, I demolished it in record time.

After lunch and one last flurry of photos by the Montevideo sign, reality hit hard. We had minutes to grab Rosemarie's bags and get to the airport. When I tried to lift her suitcase, I genuinely thought something had gone wrong. It took both Carlos and I, one end each, to manoeuvre it down the stairs. At the airport, the damage became clear. Eleven kilos overweight. The bag was essentially a shrine to Uruguay. *Yerba mate,* bottles of *caña* and Tannat wine, plus various items people had asked her to deliver across borders. After a brief debate about unpacking her entire life in the terminal, the decision was made to pay the extra fee and send it on its way. Uruguay, quite literally, was coming with her.

Once she was through departures, hugged goodbye, and waving from behind security, the finality of it settled in. But there was no time to linger. We had one last evening to savour. We met up with our Uruguayan friends again and returned to Yuyos, our favourite spot in the city. Plates of *gramajo* arrived with endless fries tangled with eggs, washed down with *grappa.* We talked, laughed, translated, and laughed some more. Even with the language barrier, this couple had become such a meaningful part of our time here. They'd guided us to hidden viewpoints, local markets, spontaneous nights fuelled by *caña,* and a deeper understanding of how people actually live here. I hoped, genuinely, that one day they'd make it to New Zealand so we could return the favour.

We were wildly underprepared that morning. One of those classic travel blunders that happens when you're in a pair and each of you quietly assumes the other has thought it through. We had apartment keys to return, a rental car to drop off, and a bus to catch, all before most of Montevideo had even opened its eyes. It took us an embarrassing amount of time to realise we couldn't wake the neighbours to hand over the keys, that the car rental place didn't open until the exact moment we were supposed to already be at the bus station, and that we weren't even entirely sure where the bus station was. The address on the ticket made no sense, Google offered conflicting answers, and panic started creeping in.

With minutes to spare, we surrendered control and trusted the guy behind the rental counter, who confidently told us to get an Uber to Tres Cruces. So, we did. We sprinted through the terminal with our overstuffed backpacks, ran to the very end to grab our tickets, mourned the *empanadas* we didn't have time to buy, and collapsed onto the bus just in time. Breathless, sweaty, victorious. We promised each other, again, that we'd be more organised from here on out. Christmas chaos was only just beginning.

And just like that, Uruguay was over. Country number five. As the bus pulled away along roads that had become strangely familiar, it hit me that I wouldn't be seeing anywhere new for the rest of the trip. Everything ahead was somewhere I'd already been. It felt oddly fitting. A gentle deceleration after months of intensity.

At the border near Mercedes, we crossed the bridge over the Uruguay River into Argentina. The passport check was quick and painless. I glanced at the passenger list and noticed that Carlos and I were the only ones without Argentine or Uruguayan passports. It made me smile. For once, we were the exotic ones.

So what would I remember Uruguay by?

A country where everyone walks around with a *mate* cup in one hand and a *thermos* wedged into the crook of their arm, often with a joint not far behind. A place where Spanish sounds softer and stranger, full of "*sh*" noises that still confuse my ears. Where dinner revolves around an *asado* cooked slowly on a *parrilla*, dessert might be peaches in syrup or *pan dulce* if it's Christmas, and everything is washed down with *caña* or *grappa*. A country that hugs the coast with sandy beaches and long sunsets. But rewards you deeply if you venture inland, where the land barely rises, stretching out in endless green plains dotted with cows, wild ostriches, and *gauchos* galloping past in black berets. Sometimes even stopping your car to let a tarantula cross the road feels completely normal.

Christmas Elsewhere

- ROSARIO, ARGENTINA -

Argentina rolled by outside the window in familiar shades. Fields of corn, wide paddocks of grazing cattle. I thought about something I'd recently read on the carbon footprint of food, about how South American beef topped the charts thanks to deforestation and methane emissions. It was a strange contradiction. Environmentally costly, yet the cows here looked undeniably content. Happy cows, complicated ethics.

The bus ride was long. We left in the morning and didn't arrive in Rosario until evening. As the sun dipped lower, the landscape shifted and water began to appear. Lakes and wetlands near the Río Paraná, shimmering under a cloudless sky. I remembered this river instantly. Two years before, I'd spent a hot summer day out there on a boat and jet skis, repeatedly failing at wakeboarding and loving every second anyway. The memory rose easily, warmly.

I sipped the overly sweet tea our bus host handed me. So sweet it instantly transported me somewhere else entirely. Auckland in 2015. My elderly Afghan neighbour. Cups of tea with four heaped teaspoons of sugar and a single cardamom pod. She used to tell me stories of an Afghanistan I would never know—open, progressive, curious—before war and extremism closed its doors to the world. And it struck me then how fragile accessibility really is. How Chile and Argentina, places I'd just wandered through with ease, were once known globally for dictatorships and disappearances.

It felt like a quiet reminder of why travel matters. Places change. Borders harden and soften. Opportunities open and close. You never really know where you'll be able to go in the future, or when somewhere you love might become unreachable.

By the time we rolled into Rosario, the dragonflies were already out in force. Hundreds of them, darting through the air like tiny helicopters. I'd forgotten about that. The last time I'd been here, I'd noticed the exact same thing on the drive from Buenos Aires to San Nicolás de los Arroyos. Apparently, it meant rain was coming.

Despite the heat already being offensive by mid-morning, we decided to try our luck with a free walking tour. The website looked like it hadn't been touched since 2011, which somehow made it feel more legitimate. Miraculously, we'd landed in the city on the one day of the week the tour supposedly ran. At 9:30 a.m., sweat was already sliding down my back and gluing my T-shirt to my skin, but after weeks of being confined to a car, I was desperate to walk.

When we arrived, the only person there was the guide, standing alone in a bright orange T-shirt that boldly announced, "Rosario Free Walking Tour." We did that awkward tourist thing… Walked past, pretended we weren't interested, then turned around and sheepishly came back. We didn't want to be the only ones, but eventually a Brazilian couple joined and made it feel slightly less like a private lecture.

The tour itself was simple, but meaningful. Rosario isn't flashy, but it's quietly important. I learned that both Che Guevara and Messi were born here. Two wildly different exports from the same city. We walked along the Río Paraná, learned more about Argentina's 2001 economic crisis, and how, alarmingly, the country seemed to be edging back toward something similar. Even in the short month since we'd last been in Argentina, the exchange rate had shifted dramatically. It was unsettling to witness history repeating itself in real time.

We ended at the National Flag Memorial, a place that felt oddly comforting. I had such clear memories of standing there back in 2016, thinking, I'll come back to Argentina one day. And here I was. Follow-through felt good.

We kept exploring on foot for hours afterward, shovelling down leftover pizza that had long since turned warm, wandering along the river, hunting for *ferias*. One led us past the Alto Shopping Mall—a polished, modern space I remembered well—only to reveal, just one block away, a settlement of rusting shacks. Behind them rose luxury high-rise apartments with river views. The contrast was brutal. I wanted to take a photo, but my instincts told me not to. Some images are better carried quietly.

Later, we stumbled across a better *feria* tucked closer to the city centre. Colourful, creative, full of life.

After weeks of questionable nutrition, my body was screaming for vegetables, so I found a vegetarian spot for dinner that had glowing reviews. It was unreal. Falafel burgers on buns that felt more like seeds than bread. I felt my soul thanking me.

Naturally, the healthy intentions didn't last. Back at the hostel, beers appeared, cookies were shared, and suddenly we were part of a courtyard Christmas party with strangers from all over the world. German girls who looked barely old enough to order drinks, Argentine guys teasing each other endlessly, mosquitoes feasting on every inch of exposed skin. It was hot, chaotic, loud, and perfect. What was meant to be one drink turned into many. By the time I stumbled back to bed, I knew my liver was furious, but my heart was full. This was why we stayed in hostels sometimes.

The hangover the next day was ruthless. Splitting headache, dehydration, mosquito bites everywhere. Still, we dragged ourselves out, craving fresh juice and greens like our lives depended on it. We returned to the vegetarian restaurant, stocked up on gifts at the *feria*, and made a critical stop at Havanna for *alfajores* and a *pan dulce* to take to San Nicolás. Christmas fuel.

Our Uber never came, so we threw our packs on and walked three-and-a-half kilometres to the bus station in the heat. It hurt, but it helped shake off the cobwebs. The bus ride was short, and we slept through most of it, jolting awake every so often in panic that we'd miss our stop. We didn't.

Miguel, a dear family friend and a local from San Nicolás, was there waiting, just as he had been years earlier. I'd first met him when he travelled to New Zealand for the Rugby World Cup in 2011. By chance, he'd ended up sitting next to one of my dad's friends on the flight between Auckland and Dunedin. They struck up a conversation, as you do. When they arrived, my dad's friend asked if Dad could give Miguel a ride to his hotel. Dad's response was immediate: *Why stay in a hotel? Come and stay with us.*

And just like that, Miguel became part of our lives and, very quickly, a great friend.

His parents' house felt instantly familiar. Full of people, laughter, food, a pool shimmering in the heat. It felt like coming home to a life I'd briefly lived before. Since the last time I'd stood in that house, I'd been to thirteen more countries. Russia. Bolivia. Mongolia. Samoa. Tahiti. Ukraine.

China. Uruguay. Just to name a few. The world had stretched out in every direction, and somehow brought me back here.

Christmas came early, literally. In Argentina, Christmas is celebrated on the 24th, and we woke into a long, indulgent day of food, swimming, and preparation. Six hours in the kitchen, Spanish Christmas music blasting, movies playing in the background, cinnamon whiskey flowing. I was happy. And a little sad. I missed my family deeply. But I also knew this was exactly what I'd wanted. To experience something new, properly, from the inside.

Dinner didn't start until 11 p.m., when the heat finally eased. The table overflowed with food. Wine poured freely. Mosquitoes and a spider the size of my hand roamed unapologetically. At midnight, fireworks exploded into the sky. More than any New Year's celebration I'd ever seen. We spilled into the street, watching colour and noise fill the night, kids lighting fireworks from empty wine bottles, neighbours releasing lanterns. Christmas and New Year fused into one wild, joyful moment.

Then, magically, the presents appeared. Children tore into them with pure, unfiltered joy. I hadn't expected anything at all, but was handed a beautifully embroidered sarong. Perfect for pool days. Carlos received the perfect gift. A traditional leather *asado* toolkit. An item he'd admired days earlier, now given by people who had known him barely more than a day. He was glowing.

We finished the night with champagne blended with lemon sorbet—*LimCham*—and stayed up washing dishes until 4 a.m., wanting to earn our place in this borrowed celebration. When we finally walked home (Miguel let us use his entire apartment), the sky was already blue with morning.

What a night.

Christmas Day arrived for me in a slightly warped way. Technically Christmas, emotionally Boxing Day, spiritually… whatever day comes after you've been up until 6 a.m. eating, drinking, and watching fireworks. The upside was that having "Christmas" the day before meant I'd celebrated at the same time as everyone back in New Zealand, which felt oddly grounding. Like I'd managed to be far away and still in sync.

I woke around 11 a.m. feeling groggy. Carlos had given me my present when we got home only a few hours earlier, and I'd been too excited (and too wired on sugar and adrenaline) to go to sleep. We hadn't bought any groceries yet, so we kept ourselves alive on coffee until it was time to head back to Miguel's parents' place for what I was quickly learning was the true Argentine Christmas tradition—feed everyone constantly until they're too full to speak.

When we arrived, everyone was still in *siesta* mode, so we did what any reasonable people do in 36-degree-Celsius heat. We jumped straight in the pool, then started snacking on leftovers like it was our job. Eventually the parents woke up, deck chairs were dragged into the shade, and we settled into what felt like a postcard version of Argentina—*mate* being passed around, *alfajores* and *pan dulce* from Havanna making the rounds, the air thick with heat and contentment.

And then I committed the cultural crime of the day. I said thank you too much.

Apparently, in *mate* culture, "thank you" doesn't mean "I'm grateful." It means, "No thanks, I'm done." So, every time someone handed me the *mate* and I chirped "*gracias*," I was accidentally announcing, I would like to exit this experience now. Yet that was definitely not my intention. I wanted infinite *mate*. I wanted to be absorbed into this family's orbit forever. I tried to stop myself, truly—I did. But not saying thank you felt like my tongue had been glued to the roof of my mouth. Miguel's mum gently told me that once was enough. She believed I was thankful. I didn't need to say it every time I was given food.

I couldn't get over how generous they were. We weren't blood relatives. We'd arrived through a weird chain of travel connections, like stray cats who'd wandered into their yard. And yet they fed us again and again, let us use their pool whenever we wanted, treated us like we belonged. I kept turning it over in my mind—how effortless their hospitality seemed. I wanted to be like that. The kind of person who could welcome strangers of any background into my home and make them feel safe and celebrated. I kept thinking of ways to thank them, and everything felt too small. A bottle of wine. The best *pan dulce* we could find. It wasn't enough. I already knew that when we got back to New Zealand, I'd be posting them *Kiwiana* magnets and anything else I could find that screamed thank you for giving us a home in the middle of our trip.

Heat and Homesickness

- SAN NICOLÁS DE LOS ARROYOS, ARGENTINA -

The next day, though, my mood dipped. I couldn't quite pin it on one thing. Maybe it was the holidays and the ache of not being with my family. Maybe guilt for not being there with them, especially because my grandparents were visiting New Zealand from England for the first time in years. Maybe the fact that the end of this trip was suddenly so close it felt like someone had hit fast-forward. I was excited to see my family again, but I also knew, because I've done this dance before, that once I got home, a weird reverse homesickness would creep in. I'd crave the motion. The unknown. The constant novelty of waking up and needing five seconds to remember what country I was in. The grass-is-greener problem.

We tried to go for a walk and immediately regretted being so ambitious. The heat was suffocating, like walking through an invisible wall of exhaustion. Everything was closed anyway. *Siestas* were alive and thriving here, the way they are in other parts of Argentina, because honestly, during the hottest hours, functioning is just a ridiculous idea. We ended up back inside, sitting basically naked in front of a fan, sweating in silence, and learning a new respect for air conditioning. I've been to hot places before, but this was different. In Australia you can escape into cool buildings. In Samoa you can dive into the ocean. Here, I just… existed. In sweat. For hours.

The night itself was equally uncomfortable—still stifling, even after dark. We lay naked on top of the sheets with the fan pressed against the bed like it could physically push the heat away.

And then the next morning, an explosion.

I went from horizontal to upright in a fraction of a second, heart racing, because the sound was so loud the windows vibrated. A storm had rolled in. One of those violent, theatrical South American storms that doesn't arrive politely.

The upside was that the temperature dropped substantially. Instantly I felt more human.

With the air finally bearable, we explored San Nicolás properly. It was still raining on and off, but it felt like relief. We found Havanna (critical for my *alfajor* addiction), loaded up on fruit and vegetables, and I felt my mood lift just from being able to move without feeling like I was going to melt into the footpath. Being in San Nicolás for longer than a couple of days also reminded me of one of travel's less glamorous joys. The fact that it was cheap. We were living way below our NZ$75-a-day budget without even trying. Future me—returning to New Zealand in a few weeks, rebuilding life, stepping straight into work—was going to be grateful for every extra dollar.

At sunset, the town transformed. We went down to the river with Miguel's mum and sister, and it was like stepping into a different version of the place I remembered from 2016. Back then, I'd thought it felt quiet, even a bit run down. This time it was pumping. People running, cycling, rollerblading, fishing, picnicking with *mate* in hand. The sky turned soft pink and orange, and I learned that on Sundays, fitness instructors come down to run free workouts for the community.

That night we ate with Miguel's parents. There was a whole pig roasting on the *parrilla*, which wasn't for me, but Carlos was in his element. He'd been too creeped out to try it as a kid, and now he was a grown-up in the right setting, praising the parents like a food critic. I got special treatment too. Homemade eggplant lasagne. I honestly don't know how they kept producing meals like this. The dad's red wine supply seemed endless. Miguel's whiskey collection wasn't exactly dwindling either. My liver was begging for early retirement.

Then, mid-dinner, I got a comment that cut me deep. Miguel's mum said that when I visited two years ago, I communicated better than I did now.

Ouch.

Two years ago, I knew no Spanish beyond "*Hola*." But I did have French. Years of it, classroom learning, movies, podcasts, tenses, vocab. It was familiar. Because his mum was born in Morocco, we'd been able to hold a solid conversation in French.

This time around, after months in South America, I'd been trying to learn Spanish… except I'd also become dependent on Carlos. I let him translate. I leaned on him. I defaulted to him. And suddenly I realised I'd somehow managed to downgrade myself. Native English, shaky Spanish, and now… shaky French too. My brain just couldn't compute French now that Spanish words had infiltrated my brain.

Whoops.

But once the initial sting wore off, I did what I always do when I'm embarrassed. I got stubborn. That night I made myself contribute in Spanish without outsourcing my brain to Carlos. And when we got home—tipsy, late, buzzing—I went straight into Duolingo. If I was going to feel dumb, I was at least going to do something about it.

The next day was even hotter. My weather app said, "feels like 39°C," and for once, I didn't think it was being dramatic. We didn't attempt anything. I stayed in my nightdress, glued to the fan, peeking through the curtains at the blue sky like it was an enemy. Carlos tried to do a quick water run; everything was still closed. *Siesta* wasn't a cute cultural quirk anymore. It was survival logic. Between noon and five, you simply do not exist outdoors.

In a strange way, though, it was perfect. After months of moving every two or three days, after a full six months of trying to absorb an entire continent, we were being forced to stop. To hibernate. To recover. We were so close to going home, where everything would speed up instantly. Family visits, flights, Wellington, work, reality. Here, in this ridiculous heat, in this sleepy town, time stretched. It made space for the feelings I'd been postponing.

When the sky finally began to bruise into dark clouds and the first breeze arrived, I opened the window and inhaled that thick humidity like it was medicine. I caught myself craving "bad weather," which felt like the most ironic thing I'd ever become. And it hit me, I was already starting to miss this life even while I was still living it. The cracked footpaths. The disintegrating buildings. The smell of rain on hot ground. The inconvenience. The intensity. The fact that every day required a little bit of improvisation.

I knew exactly how this would go. I'd get home, settle into routine, and within weeks I'd be daydreaming about a time when my biggest problem was finding a fan and not accidentally "thank you"ing my way out of another round of *mate*.

The one time we did go out for dinner, I learned two things. First, that Argentines have a wildly different definition of "dress up," and second, that I am absolutely capable of being shamed out of wearing flip fops.

Miguel told us he'd pick us up at 9:30 p.m. and made what I thought was a joke about needing to dress nicely. I put on a dress, but both Carlos and I were still planning to rock up in flip flops because it was still 30 degrees, and I wasn't trying to sweat through my soul. When Miguel arrived, I asked if what we were wearing was okay.

His answer was an instant, deeply unimpressed "no."

So, we did a frantic footwear swap like teenagers about to meet strict parents, and then we were off. Except the restaurant wasn't even in San Nicolás. We drove and drove, out into the dark, which made me nervous because holiday season + roads + people = lots of drunk drivers. On the way we passed the oil refinery, which is ugly in daylight but at night looked grand and surreal. Glowing structures, bright lights, and a huge flame whipping in the wind like a dramatic candle.

The restaurant was in a town called Ramalla, and walking into it felt like teleporting back to a fancy place at home. Strong mahogany chairs. Thick leather menus. Calligraphy on chalkboards. It was comfortingly familiar in that "oh wow, I remember what civilization looks like" way.

Miguel had been panicking about vegetarian options, bless him, but he was wrong. There were heaps. I've learned that non-vegetarians often genuinely think vegetarians survive on lettuce and seeds. They don't notice the veggie options because they're not looking for them. Meanwhile I was living my best life on a *tapas* explosion—cheese *milanesas*, bruschetta with sun-dried tomatoes and basil, fancy mushrooms, fries drowning in cheddar. I was eating so fast

I had to keep stopping to breathe. Wine. Beer. Bite. Sip. Bite. Sip. Joy.

And the craziest part? How cheap it was. Carlos and I quietly paid for the whole thing as a thank you—for everything Miguel and his family had done, for the Christmas chaos, for the pool refuge, for the feeling of having a home base. The bill came to about NZ$90 total for five people, including heaps of *tapas*, multiple rounds of drinks, desserts, at a genuinely high-class restaurant. I felt like I was getting away with something. Argentina had been brutal in so many ways, but it was also weirdly generous. You could live comfortably on very little, if you knew how.

We made it home, and as soon as we arrived, the sky started putting on yet another show. Lightning flashed in every direction. Wind whipped through the courtyard, flinging loose bits around like they were in a tumble dryer. I'd become so used to these storms that I honestly loved them. Still, we learned later that this one had been unusual for San Nicolás, and people were bracing themselves for what damage the morning would reveal.

The next day, the rain had moved on, but the wind lingered, and it felt like mercy. The temperature dropped to a comfortable 27 degrees Celsius with a cool breeze. Funny, because back home my heat threshold was about 20 degrees Celsius. Travel really does recalibrate you. When I looked out the window, the courtyard looked like it had been shaken upside down. Miguel told us the storm had wreaked havoc on properties all over town. We saw fallen trees and, heartbreakingly, baby birds that hadn't survived being flung from their nests. They never stood a chance.

Now that we could walk without turning into puddles, we wandered through town and even stopped to help an elderly woman pull a massive cluster of branches off the road. Then we went to Miguel's parents' place to say goodbye to him. He and his kids were heading north for New Year's, while we were staying behind with his parents. We hugged, did the *beso*, thanked him properly, and it felt unmistakably like "see you later" rather than "goodbye." I just didn't know where or when "later" would be. That's the thing with travel friendships... They rarely end, they just scatter.

After that, we went down to the river armed with a picnic blanket and industrial-strength insect repellent. Carlos had mastered *mate* prep by now, and he made it with the thicker, chunkier *yerba* that Argentina seemed to favour. More rugged, less polite than the Uruguayan stuff we'd been drinking. As he poured boiling water from the *thermos*, my brain finally connected a warning Miguel's mum had given me earlier.

She'd told me, in Spanish, not to use the tap water.

Not even for boiling.

I warned Carlos. He shrugged. It was boiled. Surely she was being overly cautious. I didn't want to test fate, but after sitting in the sun for a while, my thirst won.

Just one cup of *mate*. Surely that won't hurt.

Twenty minutes later my stomach gurgled. I had to interrupt Carlos mid-sentence to announce that we needed to go home immediately. Lesson learned. When a local tells you not to do something, *especially* after a storm, don't argue. Just do as your told.

Regardless, I didn't mind being stuck at home. I was reading another travel memoir, and reading in that sleepy little town felt like the perfect in-between. Physically still, mentally still roaming. It was also around then that my excitement about going home became impossible to ignore. I knew it was ridiculous. I was still in Argentina, still inside the dream I'd worked so hard to create. But I kept checking the calendar like a kid counting sleeps until Christmas.

Maybe that's what the end of long-term travel does. It doesn't cancel the wonder; it just layers it with longing. The trip had been everything. Eye-opening, uncomfortable, exhilarating, lazy, scary, comforting, hot, cold. It had stretched me and softened me and exhausted me.

And now, instead of daydreaming about the next hostel or the next bus or the next border, I was daydreaming about future adventure ideas that would be in smaller, sharper doses. Maybe six weeks sailing from California to Tahiti, a month walking the *Camino de Santiago*, salsa school in Cuba, a desert trek somewhere that would terrify and thrill me. I was learning what kind of traveller I was, and what kind of traveller I wanted to be next.

New Year's Eve arrived like the quiet final page of a very loud book. When I looked back over 2018, it felt almost impossible that it had all fit into one year. A road trip around Samoa, salsa classes, Arabic lessons, helping a former refugee pass her driving test, landing a permanent role in a government department I loved, devouring fifty travel books like they were fuel. And then, the cherry on the top. Six months backpacking South America.

I felt proud in a way that wasn't smug, but solid. I knew luck played a role. Pure privilege, the accident of where I was born, the safety net of having a passport that opened doors. But I also knew I'd done the other part. I'd wanted something, and I'd gone after it. I'd asked for a version of life that most people only talk about, and somehow, I'd made it real. *I had made the time.*

We welcomed 2019 quietly at Miguel's parents' place, which somehow felt perfect. We ate at 10 p.m., which felt absurdly late but was just another reminder of where in the world we were. I learned that wearing white is traditional for New Year here, and of course I had nothing to wear because white is the stupidest colour to travel with, unless you enjoy looking permanently stained. I wore a black-and-white floral dress and hoped they accepted the effort.

Dinner came in waves. Seafood salad with white wine, then one of my new favourite oddities—melon sprinkled with salt and pepper, served with cheese. Weird, but perfect. Carlos happily demolished pork and potatoes. And then came our favourite drink again, the one that felt like somebody's genius fever dream. Lemon sorbet blended with champagne. *LimCham.*

Midnight arrived quickly. Fireworks popped somewhere beyond the high walls that all the properties have here, muted compared to the Christmas insanity, and a few lanterns floated into the starry sky. The real celebration wasn't the spectacle, it was the quiet conversation and the quiet thinking. Carlos and Miguel's dad talked about romantic parts of life, and I sat there letting my brain sift through the year.

I thought about how lucky I was to have met Carlos. Someone willing to take six months out to live. While also admitting to myself that I hadn't exactly been easy to travel with. I'd entered the relationship fiercely protective of my independence, convinced that anyone who truly loved me would simply cope with whatever I chose. On this trip, I'd learned that independence is beautiful, but so is compromise. I'd caught glimpses of myself that weren't flattering. Selfish. Stubborn. Certain I was right. The kind of stuff you can ignore at home, but you can't outrun when you're living out of a backpack together for half a year.

And yet, here we were. Safe, full, a little tipsy, surrounded by a family who wasn't ours but treated us like we belonged. I wasn't in front of Big Ben or on a mountaintop or doing anything cinematic. I was in Argentina, in a town that held memories, with a glass of champagne-sorbet happiness in my hand, thinking about how much I still had to learn.

That was the emotional shape of this stretch. Not big landmarks, but quiet self-reflection. Rest after intensity. Gratitude mixed with pride. A sense that I'd lived a hundred little lives in one year. And that as 2019 arrived, the adventure wasn't ending so much as changing form. Soon I'd be back in New Zealand, back in routine, back in the "real world," but I could already feel it. The itch would return.

New Year's morning arrived far too early. I woke up feeling vaguely poisoned. Hangover? lack of sleep? The lingering emotional whiplash of midnight reflections and *LimCham*? Who knows. The only mercy was that we'd packed the night before, which meant there was no frantic "where is my passport?" spiral. We showered, shouldered our bags, and stepped into the first adventure of 2019 with the confidence of people who definitely had not thought this through.

The plan, if you can call it that, was a seven-kilometre trek. A quick dropping of keys at Miguel's parents, then another six kilometres to the bus station. We'd been told taxis would be impossible at 7:30 a.m. on New Year's Day, so we walked. In the early hours of the morning, it wasn't stifling yet. Mid-twenties, tolerable. But then we cut through suburbs that looked like they'd been assembled from whatever was lying around. Tin roofs pinned down with a single brick. Shack homes. Streets that made my gut tighten.

Miguel had warned us that people would still be out and drunk at this hour, and suddenly my earlier stubborn confidence felt reckless. Sure, we'd navigated our way safely through a good chunk of South America, but there's something about being the only obvious outsiders in a town with zero tourists that turns your senses up to full volume. We avoided groups. We walked fast. We scanned everything like we were in a low-budget thriller where the backpackers do something stupid in the first ten minutes.

Also, who else is wandering around at 7:30 a.m. on New Year's Day with backpacks on both the front and back like a deranged sherpa? No one. We stood out like a sore thumb holding a neon sign that said rob me.

Adrenaline did a great job of masking the blisters bubbling under my toes. It also did a great job of providing the cheerful reminder that if we went missing, no one would realise for a while. We weren't due to be in Arauco for two days. No one was waiting for a "made it!" message. Travel logic is weird like that. Some days you feel invincible, and other days you realise you're basically a tiny dot in a massive system and you could disappear between bus stations.

So when we walked into the bus station intact, with every single one of our precious possessions still attached to us—phones, iPads, laptop, GoPro, multiple passports—we high-fived like we'd just completed an extreme sport. Because honestly, we were absolute gold mines with all that equipment and important documents. Someone had been watching over us that morning. And maybe that's why, when a strung-out couple approached us asking not for money but for food, we handed over bananas and walnuts without hesitation. A small way to rebalance the universe after we'd just waltzed through the slums carrying our entire net worth.

It took a while for my body to calm down. My t-shirt was drenched. I couldn't tell if my hair was still wet from the shower or if I'd just sweated through my scalp. Either way, not ideal when you're about to begin a 48-hour relay of buses and terminals.

Buenos Aires was the first leg. Three hours where I half-napped, half-stared, and then three more hours in the station playing sudoku because it was a holiday and most kiosks were closed. We hovered around fifty different platforms trying to work out which one was ours, and then discovered we had a fresh drama waiting for us as a little treat.

We'd skim-read the ticket and celebrated the part where it said we didn't need to print it. Electronic was fine. What we'd missed, of course, was the part that this only applied to domestic trips, not international ones. We didn't find that out until the kiosk finally opened twenty minutes before departure.

Now, printing things in Argentina is rarely straightforward. We needed credit to top up the phone, needed to send the ticket via Wi-Fi, needed the ticket to actually load, and it refused to cooperate even when they let us use their connection.

Then, miraculously, they informed us that if we could pay them, they could "make it happen." Cash only. No cards. A bit suss. We had no Argentine money left because Carlos had been giving it all to people who needed it more than we did. Luckily, I remembered I had a few American dollars tucked away for emergency bribes. They accepted it, produced the printed ticket like magic, and we sprinted through the terminal with minutes to spare.

Back Through the Andes

- ARAUCO, CHILE -

We splurged on the bus to Santiago. The "treat yourself" option with extra-cosy leather seats right at the front. Prime real estate. Legroom, easy bathroom access, and the comforting illusion that this was going to be anything other than a long day sealed inside a moving tube of air conditioning, snacks, and hours of Netflix.

Argentine and Uruguayan bus companies are weirdly generous with food. Snack packs, sandwiches, a steady parade of little offerings that made you feel mildly parented. At one point, the staff even came through pouring red wine, as if this were all perfectly normal behaviour. Somewhere in the middle of the night, Gravol did what Gravol always does. That tiny Canadian motion-sickness pill is essentially a tranquilliser in disguise. Within half an hour, I was fully unconscious.

I woke just before the driver blasted the lights on, jolting everyone upright as breakfast packs were handed out—fruit cookies, crackers. As we rolled into Mendoza, I pulled back the curtain and there they were… The Andes, glowing red and caramel in the early light, quietly showing off. The sun rose later out here, and my brain did that familiar travel recalibration. Time zones, light angles, trying to work out where exactly I was in the blur of weeks and borders. October? November? I couldn't remember when we'd last crossed this line.

The border crossing itself was smooth, but Chile always feels like the one country on the continent that genuinely cares what you bring in. Their customs officers have a very *try me* energy when it comes to agriculture. I declared everything like I was confessing sins. Yes, powdered seeds inside a Christmas ornament, I was telling the stern man in the crisp uniform. It all passed without incident, but I prefer my travel stories free of fines and shame.

Then came the part I love most. The looping mountain road, the endless switchbacks where the bus seems to fold back on itself again and again. For a moment I thought I'd slept through it and felt genuinely heartbroken, only to realise it was still ahead. Carlos would have happily missed it. I sat there gawping, as if I hadn't spent the last six months chasing scenery. The mountains still got me. They always do.

By the time we reached Santiago, I was operating on pure backpacker level hygiene—deodorant, cold water on the face, teeth brushed in a public bathroom. Good enough. We stored our bags at a *custodia* for the price of a coffee back home and did what any exhausted backpackers with nine hours to kill would do. We went to the movies to watch Aquaman, dubbed in Spanish. I followed the plot the same way I'd been following conversations the past six months. Context, facial expressions, the occasional word I recognised.

Santiago felt familiar. This was our sixth time passing through, and each visit came with small markers of competence—knowing Chile has the best avocados on earth; that walnuts translate to butterfly nuts *(nuez mariposa);* that sea lions are sea wolves *(lobo marino).* I'd missed the crispness of Chile, the contrast to the sticky heat we'd just left behind in Argentina and Uruguay.

And yet, on the way back to the terminal—fuelled by what might genuinely have been the best *empanada* of my life from a dodgy spot near the buses—I felt an uncomfortable clarity settle in. Long trips give you too much time to think. Somewhere between borders and cinemas and too many books, I realised I probably wouldn't do six months backpacking like this again. Not because I didn't love it. I did. But because the magic thins when you don't have roots anywhere. You're always arriving, always adjusting, always leaving. Opening chapters without ever quite finishing them. No time to fully process what is happening.

The bus to Arauco, using the same company we'd used several times to get there previously, made us realize our bus standards had evolved. Narrow seats, no blankets, air conditioning cranked to punishment levels. We shivered through the night, freezing in mid-summer. We arrived stiff and aching to an Arauco morning that smelled like woodfire and home. Maribel picked us up, even though we'd stupidly insisted we'd walk to her house from the bus depot, and when we stepped into warmth—tea, cake, familiar faces—my body relaxed like it had been holding its breath for days.

Even in summer, the evenings carried a smoky softness, as if the town was gently insisting you slow down. We napped, then woke to garlic and the kind of food that makes you feel safe. Señora Erica, Maribel's paid help, was there, producing quiet miracles. Salads of unfamiliar things, silver beet fritters that disappeared alarmingly fast. Guests arrived with *sopaipilla* dough, which we fried and drowned in *pebre*. I ate like I'd never see food again and promised myself I'd resume running the moment I landed back home.

Rosemarie was in Arauco too. She'd flown there from Montevideo a few weeks before. Spending time with her niece before eventually flying from Santiago back to Toronto. She'd be taking the bus north with us.

We slept in the garage on an inflatable bed under a plastic roof, bundled in blankets, cats padding across above us. Absurd, cosy, perfect. The kind of setup you'd complain about anywhere else, but here it felt like being invited into the real texture of someone's life.

Days slipped into a gentle rhythm. Dune trips filled with chaos and children's laughter, picnics that appeared as if by magic, cars stuck in sand and freed by strangers who materialised out of nowhere. Being by the ocean grounded me in ways I didn't fully understand until travelling—how much salt air and open horizons soothe my nervous system, how deeply being raised near water had wired me.

Weekdays meant Señora Erica cooking before we woke up and became human, effortlessly producing vibrant vegetarian meals that made my body feel quietly grateful. Weekends meant Concepción daytrips, mall wanderings, emergency *empanadas*, and the strange ache of knowing time was ticking. I was desperate to go home and already grieving this life. I longed for fluency, ease, understanding, but I also knew I'd miss the friction the moment it disappeared.

There were visits to Maribel's friends' homes that reminded me you can't judge anything by its exterior. Shack-like buildings opening into warmth, generosity, endless *sopaipillas*. Laughter that didn't require full comprehension. Language slips that dissolved tables into tears. It didn't matter that I only caught half the story. The energy carried me.

As the end crept closer, everything sharpened. Farewell barbecues. *Merkén*-dusted capsicum. Corn rolled in butter. Wine clinked in the cooling air. That surreal moment of realising, again, that this life was actually happening. That foreignness still had the power to catch me off-guard.

When we packed our belongings, we realized that we'd somehow accumulated twenty-two extra kilos, mostly in wine. Bottles given, bought, accepted because generosity is hard to refuse.

Arauco, once small and confronting, now felt like refuge—warmth, functioning showers, stocked kitchens. Luxury, after months of unreliable everything.

We ate *completos* one last time. Hugged everyone long and tight. Especially Maribel's seven-year-old son, who'd claimed our hearts without effort. It didn't feel like goodbye so much as see you later, even though I didn't know when later would be. I just knew I'd return.

The overnight bus to our final stop and city we'd be flying home from, Santiago, worked its usual trick—Gravol coma, sudden arrival. Rosemarie looked wrecked. She doesn't sleep in transport. I wished I'd known. Night buses save time but steal rest unless you've mastered pharmaceutical surrender.

And that was that. Another chapter closed. One that wasn't about scenery or highlights, but about the patchwork of people. The ones who fed us, teased us, drove us when we were cold, laughed until they couldn't breathe, and made a foreign continent feel, again and again, like somewhere we belonged, right up to the final chapter.

The Before and After

- SANTIAGO, CHILE -

We pulled into Santiago around 6 a.m., which is a deeply rude time to arrive anywhere if you can't check in until 2 p.m. Nothing is open. You can't do much. You're just a tired human with nowhere to go. We checked our bags into a *custodia* at the bus station, so we weren't hauling our entire lives on our backs, and then we found a café that opened at 7 a.m. and took refuge. Coffee, bathrooms, the comfort of sitting down somewhere that didn't require us to be charming or functional.

Then we wandered slowly toward the Santa Lucía *feria artesanal,* taking our time because the sun wasn't fully up yet and because it was strangely nice to walk through Santiago with the day still stretching ahead.

Rosemarie came alive at the *feria.* Completely at home. She flew from stand to stand like a woman on a mission. T-shirts, wallets, little gifts for people back in Canada. An actual year-long Santa Claus with incredible stamina. Watching her made me smile. I picked up a few final things too. The last little pieces I wanted to carry home as proof that this all happened.

By the time we finished, it was almost check-in time, so we wandered over to the Airbnb. Rosemarie looked genuinely relieved at the thought of a bed. But we entered, and immediately saw the place hadn't been cleaned at all. Not even vaguely. And sure, we were half an hour early, but it wasn't "half an hour early" messy; it was "no one knows we're coming at all" messy.

It got to 2 p.m. and then we heard the door unlock. In walked the owner, who looked absolutely shocked to see us standing there in her apartment.

It turned out that she owned two apartments in the building, and we were meant to be in the one two floors below. The clean one. Down we went, dragging ourselves and our patience.

We didn't get to relax for long anyway. Carlos and I had to walk five kilometres back to the bus station to collect our bags, then Uber back again. I didn't even mind the walk. I absolutely loved Santiago. It was one of our anchor cities.

Our sixth time passing through, and still it kept giving me little sparks.

That evening we met up with my friend Alex, the one I knew from studying in Poland. He sent us the restaurant name and address. Carlos ordered an Uber, and we arrived somewhere that was definitely a restaurant, but not where Alex was. We messaged him on Wi-Fi, and he replied that he was there too. We asked if he was upstairs.

He responded, "It seems that we are not in the same place."

At that point, I turned to Carlos with the slow dread of someone who knows exactly what happened. He hadn't used the address. He'd used the restaurant name. Which, fun fact, was not unique in a city the size of Santiago.

So, we sprinted twenty minutes through Providencia, through leafy streets and polished buildings, laughing and mildly panicking. We arrived breathless but triumphant, armed with a bottle of Tannat as a thank you, because Alex had been holding some of our stuff for us like an absolute angel.

Dinner was the kind of comforting, delicious chaos I love. Sandwiches, thick-cut fries sprinkled with *merkén*, wine, gossip, and that electric "before and after" feeling of catching up after six months away. We talked about everything that had happened, and everything that might happen next, and I felt this quiet gratitude for friendships that can disappear for years and then pick up like you've just been busy, not absent.

The next day, our absolute last on the continent, we went to lunch with the same man who had picked us up when we first landed in Santiago months earlier. This truly felt like the clearest "before and after" moment possible. I remembered that first day on the continent six months before, when he'd picked us up from the airport. The broken communication, the cultural clunkiness, and me sitting there with the Spanish vocabulary of *hola* and a few animals and colours.

Now, he commented on how much our language capacity had improved.

And I felt this warm, private pride. Because he was right. I could understand so much more. I'd catch conversations between Carlos and taxi drivers without translating word by word. Sometimes whole sentences would land in my mind almost as easily as English. Even later, on the plane, when the hostess rattled off meal options in Spanish, it was crystal clear in my head. I almost turned to translate for a girl next to me before the hostess did it in English anyway.

It was such a small thing, but it mattered. Especially because I'd spent so much of this trip feeling like an intelligent person trapped inside the vocabulary of a toddler. We'd both made so, so much progress.

To commemorate, lunch consisted of final Chilean greatest hits. Cheese *empanadas* smothered with *pebre*, *ensalada chilena* on the side, and a glass of Carménère.

Then came the goodbyes. First to him. Then to Rosemarie. Then to the apartment. Then to the last slow hours of wandering around with that aching awareness that everything you're seeing is the last time, for now.

Packing took hours. The alcohol situation made me anxious. I once arrived home from Brisbane to Auckland with a bottle of Midori in my bag. It was wrapped, marked fragile, all the careful things. And still, I opened my suitcase to a wave of melon stench and shards of glass tangled through my belongings like a crime scene. So this time I wrapped bottles like I was preparing them for battle and prayed to whatever travel deity had been keeping us intact so far.

On the drive to the airport, Santiago slid past the windows in a haze of pollution, and behind it the Andes—the massive, intimidating, now-familiar spine of the continent—slowly disappeared from view. I turned in my seat to watch them fade until I couldn't see them anymore. Our driver, who was also our Airbnb host, bantered with us the whole way and even walked us inside to the check-in counter to make sure we had no issues. It was 10/10 service, and it felt like the perfect final reminder of how people here had been so good to us. Again, and again. South America has its horror stories, sure. But our experience was overwhelmingly one of being helped, welcomed, fed, guided, protected.

And then… that was it.

Sitting at the boarding gate, I felt two truths at the same time, equally loud. I was thrilled to go home… To comfort, to fluent conversation, to familiar food, to clean tap water and flat white coffees. To my family (especially with relatives visiting from England), to my friends, to my job, to income, to routines and stability, to wearing office attire, and not having to think about whether toilet paper goes in the garbage.

But I was also so sad.

Because South America had been everything. Beautiful and ugly, easy and hard, boring and wild, frustrating and hilarious. I hadn't had some dramatic movie-style revelation where I decided to become a travel journalist and abandon my life. If anything, the trip reinforced how much I love what I do and how much more empathy I now have for people trying to navigate a system that isn't theirs, because I'd felt it myself, in a hundred little ways. The simple things that become complicated when you don't know the rules. When you don't have the language. When you're constantly translating not just words, but norms.

And the irony was cruel and perfect. In the final week, just as I was finally starting to feel confident in my Spanish. I was ordering more confidently, making small conversations without freezing, feeling brave enough to make mistakes... I was leaving.

That's how it goes, isn't it? You spend months learning how to live somewhere, and the moment you start to feel like you belong, you're already halfway out the door.

And so, as we boarded the plane, I realized that what I carried with me wasn't just souvenirs or too many bottles of wine. It was the sound of street vendors calling out "*helaaaado*," the smell of fried *sopaipillas* in old trolleys, Latin music leaking out of every shop, the taste of *pebre* and *merkén*, the warmth of Arauco as a second home, and the deep, steady knowledge that this continent had changed me in ways I wouldn't fully understand until I was standing back in my own life… Missing it, craving it, and already, inevitably, beginning to wonder where I'd go next.

Epilogue

- WELLINGTON, NEW ZEALAND -

Coming home didn't happen all at once.

It happened in pieces. In small, quiet moments that didn't feel particularly cinematic at the time. It happened the first time I stood in a New Zealand supermarket and felt overwhelmed by the sheer amount of choice. The first time I heard someone complain about a minor inconvenience and had to physically stop myself from saying, *you have no idea how easy this is.* It happened when I caught myself instinctively listening for Spanish on the street. When my body still expected *empanadas* to be within arm's reach. When silence felt louder than music ever had.

For six months, life had been movement. Buses, borders, bags repacked and unpacked again. New beds, new bathrooms, new currencies, new ways of asking the same basic questions: Is this safe? How do we get there? Can I eat this? The constant motion had become normal. Stillness, on the other hand, felt heavy.

I had imagined coming home would feel like relief. And in many ways, it did. There was comfort in familiarity, in not needing to explain myself, in understanding jokes without translating them in my head first. There was joy in frothy coffees, having access to in clean tap water, in knowing instinctively which bus to catch and how long it would take. There was deep gratitude in being surrounded by people who knew me, who didn't need context or backstory to understand where I'd been.

But relief isn't the same as ease.

What no one really tells you about long-term travel is that returning isn't a finish line. It's another transition. One that can feel just as destabilising as leaving. When you travel for months, your identity stretches. You adapt constantly, absorb new norms, shed old ones without noticing. And then you come back to a life that expects you to slot neatly back into place, unchanged, as if the world didn't just rearrange your insides.

People ask, *"So what was your favourite place?", "What was the highlight?", "What's next?"*

And you smile, because smiling is easier than trying to answer them properly. That the trip wasn't a highlight reel. It was a slow accumulation of moments that changed how you see everything. That choosing one favourite place feels like choosing a favourite chapter in a book that only makes sense when read as a whole.

South America didn't give me a single, tidy lesson. It gave me many layered ones.

It taught me humility. Mostly through language. There is nothing quite like being reduced to gestures, broken sentences, and apologetic smiles to remind you how much intelligence we attribute to fluency. I learned what it feels like to have complex thoughts trapped behind simple words. To know exactly what you want to say and not have the tools to say it. To sound childish when you're anything but.

That experience stayed with me long after I left. It changed how I listen. How patient I am with people who speak slowly, who choose their words carefully, who hesitate. It made me acutely aware of how much power language carries, and how easily we confuse confidence with competence.

It taught me adaptability in ways I didn't expect. Not the glamorous kind, but the everyday version. Figuring things out when plans fall apart, laughing when things go wrong, trusting that most problems are solvable with enough patience and a willingness to ask for help. I learned that discomfort isn't something to avoid at all costs. It's often the entry point to understanding.

It taught me restraint. That not every frustration needs to be fixed immediately. That sometimes the best response is observation. That you don't always get to impose your logic on a place that has its own rhythms, its own rules, its own reasons for being the way it is.

And perhaps most unexpectedly, it taught me about privilege. Not in an abstract, theoretical way, but in daily, tangible ones. In the ease of movement that comes with the right passport. In the safety nets I carry invisibly. In the fact that my discomfort was always temporary, my exit always guaranteed. That awareness didn't come with guilt so much as responsibility. To notice, to remember, to do better where I can.

The trip also stripped things back.

When your life fits into a backpack, priorities become clearer. You stop accumulating and start choosing. You learn what you actually need, and what you've been carrying out of habit. You learn that happiness doesn't require perfection. Just enough comfort, enough connection, enough curiosity.

Somewhere between overnight buses and shared meals, I stopped needing constant stimulation. I became better at sitting with myself. At being present. At finding joy in small, ordinary things. A good conversation, a familiar song, a meal that tastes like care.

That shift didn't disappear when I came home. It followed me into my routines, into my work, into my relationships. It softened some edges and sharpened others. It made me more certain about what I value, and more honest about what I don't.

I didn't come back wanting to escape my life. Quite the opposite. If anything, South America made me more invested in the one I have. It reinforced how much I care about meaningful work, about fairness, about systems that shape people's lives. It deepened my empathy. Not because

I'd seen everything, but because I'd seen enough to know how partial any single perspective is.

It also reminded me that belonging isn't about permanence.

For a while, Arauco felt like home. So did a handful of cities, kitchens, backyards, bus routes. Those places didn't lose their meaning just because I left. They live on as reference points. Proof that connection doesn't require ownership, and that familiarity can exist without permanence.

I learned that home isn't a fixed location. It's a network of relationships, memories, and habits that move with you. That you can be rooted and restless at the same time. That wanting to explore doesn't mean you're ungrateful for where you are. It just means curiosity is part of who you are.

Coming home meant learning how to hold both things at once.

There were moments when I missed the chaos. When silence felt too quiet. When the predictability of daily life felt dull compared to the constant novelty of the road. But there were also moments of deep contentment. Of knowing where I was meant to be right now, even if I couldn't articulate why.

And so, South America didn't just give me a new destination. New stamps in my passport. New photos in my camera roll.

It gave me perspective.

And that, I suspect, is the kind of souvenir that lasts the longest.

ABOUT THE AUTHOR

Mai González is the author of **Routes and Roots, Buses and Backpacks**, **Between Stations**, and **UnSettled.** She grew up in Southern England and New Zealand, but currently lives in British Columbia, Canada with her husband and children. She has a passion for global travel and has international experience working extensively for governments and non-profit organizations.

MORE FROM MAI GONZALEZ (Travel Memoirs)

MORE FROM MAI GONZALEZ (Children's Books)

www.ingramcontent.com/pod-product-compliance
Lightning Source LLC
La Vergne TN
LVHW041057080826
845145LV00007B/1613

* 9 7 8 1 0 6 9 6 8 2 1 4 7 *